$15

LANDLORDING

DEDICATION

This book is dedicated to the scrupulous landlady in my life. Ivy, that's you.

LANDLORDING

A Handymanual for Scrupulous Landlords and Landladies Who Do It Themselves

WRITTEN BY
LEIGH ROBINSON

ILLUSTRATED BY
DAVID PATTON

PUBLISHED BY

P.O. BOX 1373, RICHMOND, CA. 94802

FIRST EDITION	SEPTEMBER, 1975
SECOND EDITION	MAY, 1976
REVISED	FEBRUARY, 1977
REVISED	JUNE, 1977
REVISED	MARCH, 1978
REPRINTED	SEPTEMBER, 1978
REPRINTED	NOVEMBER, 1978
REVISED	JUNE, 1979
THIRD EDITION	MARCH, 1980

TYPESETTING BY ELLEN ROBERTS AND GWEN TUNZINI OF E & J, SANTA ROSA

TYPING BY MARGARET MIGLIA

PASTEUP BY IVY ROBINSON

LIBRARY OF CONGRESS CATALOG CARD NUMBER: 79-57253

INTERNATIONAL STANDARD BOOK NUMBER: 0-932956-01-7

PRINTED IN THE U.S.A.

PREFACE & ACKNOWLEDGEMENTS

PREFACE TO THE FIRST EDITION (1975)

After I bought my first rental property, I soon learned how little practical information there was to help the landlord and landlady through the many tribulations they face day after day after day. So, I took "Landlording" at Hard Knocks College. The tuition was dear, but I learned what I needed to survive.

This book was written to be the text for the course at good old HKC. If you study it carefully, you should be able to make a good grade.

As a landlord who does in fact teach school and who also does all of the bookkeeping chores, some of the maintenance, some of the repairs, and some of the managing of thirty-five rental units, I have indeed spent many years at HKC, but I have had little uninterrupted time to write. These pages bear the marks of many interruptions to fix cold heaters, broken windows, leaky faucets, leaky roofs, dead electrical outlets, wet-bottom water heaters, and so on and so on. Sympathize, if you will, dear Landlord or Landlady. No one else will.

PREFACE TO THE THIRD EDITION (1980)

Since *Landlording* first appeared in 1975, I have learned much more about the residential income property management business from my tenants, my students at dozens of University of California Extension seminars, and from readers of the first two editions who have kindly taken the time to write.

This new edition incorporates those suggestions made so generously, as well as some new ideas which have occurred to me spontaneously over the past four years. In addition, that information in the earlier editions which was specific to California has been deleted, so that barring certain local laws and regulations, this edition may be used anywhere in the U.S. or Canada.

The old evictions chapter has been replaced by a new one on getting rid of problem tenants, both because the old one contained information useful only in California and because there are other good ways to "evict" which you should know about and which you should try as your first resort, good ways landlords and landladies can use anywhere. That old evictions chapter, by the way, is still available, but in a new guise. It has been expanded and now appears separately under the title, *The Eviction Book For California.*

There are other changes in this edition which are equally important. Some, such as the discussion of whether or not you should do a task yourself, have resulted from an increase in the size of my own landlording business. Those 35 rental units my wife and I used to have in 1975 have become 244. With that many tenants to look after, there's no way we can handle everything ourselves. We have had, therefore, to learn more about hiring people to work for us — managers, painters, bookkeepers, gardeners, maintenance helpers, and others. In the process, we learned, surprisingly enough, that some work in this business, no matter how few or how many units you may have, is not worth doing yourself. In fact, doing it yourself may be costing you money rather than saving you money.

Other changes in this edition, such as the much expanded chapter on getting good tenants and the new chapter on keeping good tenants, have resulted from a continuing search for methods which work successfully for many people under varying conditions.

One change suggested by a female reader, retitling the book *Landladying,* I have politely rejected. Someone else will have to write that book.

Incidentally, you will notice that various product brand names and suppliers' addresses appear in this book, and you may wonder whether these companies pay for the plugs. The answer is no.

Having had first-hand experience with each of these products and companies and having been thoroughly satisfied, I am pleased to recommend them to you along with their names and addresses so you won't have to waste the time hunting for them that I did. If you choose to use any product or company mentioned here and you are dissatisfied for any reason, please write me in care of ExPress stating the nature of your complaint, and I will investigate. Likewise, if you know of any outstanding company or product related to this business which would be of use to landlords and landladies throughout North America, please let me know, and I will consider including it in a later edition.

I hope you find this new edition of *Landlording* useful.

ACKNOWLEDGEMENTS

The author would like to acknowledge the following good people for their help in one way or another: Robert Armentrout, Bob Bochemuehl, Maynard Briggs, Wallace Darling, Bud Ekstrom, Ron English, Robert France, Herb Frank, Ruth Furey, Dave Glubetich, Al Good, Vernon Graves, David Halbrook, Scotty Herd, Larry Hughes, Tom Javorina, Robert Jones, John Koczan, Carl Lindh, Robin Maydeck, Oliver McClory, Margaret Miglia, Connie Nakano, David Patton, Richard Randolph, Daniel Robinson, Dario Robinson, Ira Serkes, Jo Stender, Suzanne Wehausen, Jay Wilson, Jim Woollen, and the hundreds of landlords and landladies who've endured the author's landlording classes with many suggestions and few complaints.

Without their help, this book wouldn't be in the shape it's in.

TABLE OF CONTENTS

INTRODUCTION

Of all the people in the world, who's more detested than the landlord? After all, he puffs big cigars, sneers, wears a black cape, drives a Cadillac car, dallies with divorcees, runs down little kids, drives unfortunates from their homes, ignores all tenant complaints, keeps at least one family of roaches in every unit, loves the fresh air which broken windows provide, and welcomes rodents of all kinds to make their homes in his rentals.

And if that landlord happens to be a landlady — well, then, everybody knows what she's like! She's got a nose longer than Pinocchio's, larger than Durante's. Her ears rival Dumbo's. She's got Big Brother's omniscience, and she blabs every bit of it. She's devised ways to pinch her pennies that Jack Benny never dreamed of, and while there may not be snakes growing in her hair, big pink rollers sure do.

You're a landlord or landlady, aren't you? Don't these descriptions sound just like you? They don't?

Aha! Then you must be a scrupulous landlord or landlady and, lucky you, this book was written with you in mind!

You have probably wondered anyway, scrupulous landlord or landlady, how landlords and landladies ever got such bad reputations in the first place and why they get so little sympathy from everybody else, no matter what the situation, no matter who's at fault.

They got such bad reputations deservedly years ago because they were largely unfettered by laws (what laws there were, were of their own making) and could easily take advantage of their tenants, and so some did, arbitrarily controlling their tenants' lives like petty dictators. They were feared for the power they wielded and naturally they were hated, becoming folklore villains who were always portrayed as insensitive, cruel, thoughtless, heartless, and greedy to an extreme.

Although they have been stripped of most of their power, landlords and landladies are hardly liked even today because they provide an essential service (who likes the telephone company or the utility companies?), and they continue in ill repute (tarts are in ill repute, too, of course, but at least they're frequently portrayed as having hearts of gold) because they make such good news stories when they try creative remedies to extricate themselves from seemingly impossible situations. What kind of a story do you think the news media made of the landlord who chopped down the outside stairway to his nonpaying tenant's second-story duplex apartment or the landlady who poisoned her tenant's mongrel pooch which she and the tenant had been feuding over for months? It makes no difference whether the landlord and landlady were really good people at heart who had been driven temporarily crazy when they committed these foolish acts. They committed the acts and thus they unwittingly succeeded in perpetuating the old folklore-villain stereotypes.

Landlord and landlady villains are unsympathetic characters, and they are hissed and booed by almost every adult who at one time or another has experienced the problems of tenanting. Most people can easily sympathize with any poor tenant who's being harassed by an unscrupulous landlord or landlady, for they have worn a tenant's moccasins.

Landlords and landladies get so little sympathy because most people have not experienced the problems and frustrations of landlording. Never have they been cursed or threatened or cheated or robbed by an unscrupulous tenant. They cannot know the mental anguish and anxiety of waiting out an eviction week after week while a devil-may-care tenant who's being evicted for nonpayment of rent uses legal aid to contest the eviction, hammers holes in the walls, puts out cigarettes on the carpets, burns the linoleum, plays music late and loud, and hurls insults at all the neighbors. Most people cannot possibly know what it's like to deal with that unscrupulous tenant and to feel so helpless, so wronged.

If only these unscrupulous tenants would get together with the unscrupulous landlords and landladies of the world to do business with each other, rent to each other and rent from each other! That would solve most of the problems the rest of us poor creatures have in this business. Unfortunately, since that's about as likely to happen as our ever again being able to buy gasoline for 30 cents a gallon or gold for 35 dollars an ounce, we have little choice but to seek help.

To help the scrupulous tenant deal with unscrupulous landlords and landladies, there are pamphlets, books, hot lines, tenant action groups, legal aid, and even publicly funded housing organizations. The scrupulous tenant is hardly alone, while the scrupulous landlord and landlady seem to be so totally alone as they deal with an unscrupulous tenant. Nothing is free to them. They are expected to have unlimited funds available for legal counsel, management, repairs, and services. They shouldn't need any other help.

Well, they do. You know it and I know it. This book is intended for all those scrupulous landlords and landladies who want to do well by themselves and by their tenants but need some help to do so.

DO-IT-YOURSELF LANDLORDING

"$82,000? Holy buckets! That's $8,000 less than I paid for the place seven years ago!"

"It may be, but you've had some pretty rough tenants in here, and there's so much deferred maintenance now that you just can't get any more for it."

Sound familiar? I hope not. "Deferred maintenance" is a euphemism for gross neglect in real estate jargon. Those dilatory property owners who ignore their tenants, neglect maintenance, and do slipshod repairs on their property suffer more losses than they know. They can't get good tenants, they can't get good rents, and they can't get a good price when they sell. Their buildings are depreciating not only on paper at tax time. They're depreciating daily.

THE BUSINESS

Landlording is a funny business. It requires one to know at least the rudiments of the skills of an accountant, appliance repairer, attorney, banker, bill collector, bookkeeper, buyer, carpenter, custodian, diplomat, electrician, financial analyst, garbage collector, gardener, glazier, insurance agent, locksmith, painter, pest controller, plumber, psychologist, real estate agent, roofer, salesperson, secretary, and trucker. In addition, the landlord and landlady must have business sense, common sense, and equanimity.

Breathes there such a person with all these skills and all these attributes? Hardly! The only people I know who have every bit as much equanimity as landlording requires have body temperatures considerably below 98.6°F. (37° C.), and equanimity is their only landlording attribute. They have none of the others nor any of the skills.

No wonder so many people neglect their rental properties and fail at landlording! It is not simply an investment as it is often regarded, one you sink your money into and forget all about. It is a business, a tough business. You have to work at it. You have to know so much. You have to be so self-sufficient, and you have to understand people so well, too.

You even have to understand yourself a little more than the average person does. You have to understand that you are an imperfect landlord or landlady dealing with imperfect tenants and that you will make mistakes, mistakes which hopefully will not sour you on the business forever. "We should be careful to get out of an experience only the wisdom that is in it and stop there lest we be like the cat that sits down on a hot stove lid. It will never sit down on a hot stove lid again, and that is well. But it will never sit down on a cold one either," wrote Mark Twain. You will sit on more than one hot seat in this business. Don't abandon the business altogether because of them.

All of us fail at landlording a little bit in one way or another. We can't help it, and we shouldn't let it worry us so long as we learn from these failures and keep them small. After we have failed, we just have to remind ourselves again that landlording is a business and. must be operated like any other business and then doggedly continue, resolving not to make the same mistake again.

Do-it-yourself landlording is surely more mistake-ridden than the ordinary homeowner variety of do-it-yourselfing, and it differs also because the landlord and landlady must repair and maintain their properties promptly and professionally. They have contracted with their tenants to provide habitable accommodations. That's what the business is all about. They cannot leave messy, unfinished, or neglected jobs if they wish to continue landlording successfully. That might work all right at home, but tenants won't stand for it, nor should they. After all, if they are paying full value for habitable shelter, they have every right to expect full services for their money.

On the other hand, being businesslike when you are handling the maintenance and repairs on your property yourself requires that you do the work as quickly and as well as you can and then leave. Tenants have a knack for finding just one more little job for you to do if you linger around, and you can waste precious time fixing the little things they should be fixing themselves. If you don't have any business there, stay away. Otherwise you tend to develop personal relationships that will hinder your making wise business decisions. Being there too much and getting involved with your tenants is almost as bad for your business as neglecting the place altogether.

Being businesslike doesn't mean you should be austere and avaricious all the time either. Use your common sense. Be flexible when a situation calls for flexibility. If a tenant gives you a six-day notice that he's moving after having been there only two months, and he asks you whether he can get any of his deposit back in spite of his agreement to give thirty days' notice, tell him "sure" so long as he leaves the place clean. Agree to give him back a generous portion of his deposits, even though you may be legally entitled to keep them, and if he does leave the place clean, pay up. Otherwise, what incentive does he have to leave the place in good shape? That's being businesslike and using common sense.

Yes, it is a funny business, but you can make it into a good business for you.

ASSOCIATIONS

It's good business to ally yourself with other landlords and landladies through membership in a rental property owners' association. Such groups offer a wide range of services and benefits to the small-timer as well as the big-timer. Besides distributing a monthly publication, holding periodic meetings, sponsoring seminars, supplying readily available and current landlording information over the phone, and providing access to credit bureau information on rental applicants, these associations advise their members of pending legislation and support lobbying efforts so that not every landlord-tenant law will favor the tenant. And if all this doesn't seem to you to be worth the basic membership fee of around $30 (the fee varies according to the number of units you have), then consider the advantage of meeting people who can keep you current on rents and vacancy factors in your area, people who will listen sympathetically to your woeful tales of landlording despair because the same thing happened to them only last week, and people who know what choice rental properties are coming on the market even before they're listed. Thirty dollars is a small price to pay for all that.

If you can't locate a rental property owners' association in your area, call or write the National Apartment Association, 1825 "K" Street, N.W., Suite 604, Washington, D.C. 20006, (202) 785-5111. They will gladly provide you with the information you need to contact a nearby association.

Do not assume that because you own only one rental house or one fourplex you'd be out of place in such an association. You won't be.

DISCOUNTS

In landlording, you use more supplies than the homeowner do-it-yourselfer does, and suppliers know it.

Your local hardware store may give you charge privileges and a ten percent discount to boot. Ask. Even if you can't qualify for a volume-buyer's discount yet, open a charge account anyway, because it will simplify your bookkeeping to pay only once a month and make only one bookkeeping entry for most of your hardware needs. Many hardware store owners will special-order for you those items which they don't stock regularly, items such as glass-fronted fire extinguisher boxes, apartment house mailboxes, and locksmithing supplies. (My local hardware store owner even found me a portable hand-cranked Keil key-cutting machine which has proven to be a big timesaver.)

Other firms are anxious to do business with you, too, if you let them know who you are and what your requirements are. Sears has a contract sales department in many stores which offers rental property owners special discounts on certain merchandise, like coin-operated laundry machines and tools. Wards offers trade discounts in some of its retail departments if you first obtain a trade discount card at their customer service department.

Check the advertisements in your rental property owners' associations' publications for those firms which are specifically soliciting business from landlords and landladies. They should understand the nature of your business and give you the service and discounts you deserve.

BUSINESS CONTACTS

There are certain business people in your community who are in a position to help you run a successful landlording business, and you should strive to establish personal contacts with them whenever you can. You may have to shop around awhile before you find trustworthy people in these relevant business pursuits, people who suit you and who know their businesses well, but once you find good contacts and you come to know each of them personally, you will find that they will go out of their way to assist you with service, advice, equipment, and supplies. Remember that your relationship should be mutually beneficial, that you are in a position to help your contacts by recommending their services to the other landlords and landladies you know.

At one level, you should seek out and nurture business contacts with an accountant, an attorney, a banker, an insurance agent, and a real estate agent, each of whom has expertise directly related to your making or losing large sums of money in landlording. These people can help you with specific and knowledgeable answers to your many questions in their fields.

At another level, you should seek out an appliance repairer, a carpet layer, a hardware store owner, a painter, a plumber, and a roofer. While these contacts may save you sums of money with their advice, they benefit you chiefly by coming to your aid with their labor and supplies as solutions to your pressing problems.

In addition, and surely as important as any, is that contact you should make with another landlord or landlady who owns as least as much rental property as you do and is willing to compare notes. You are in a position to help each other psychologically and physically more than you may imagine at first.

How well should you know these people? You should know them at least well enough so that you could reach them on the telephone and be greeted familiarly, and then you could pose a simple question about their field of expertise, expecting them to give you a direct answer, perhaps free of charge, perhaps not.

If you elect to expand your business at all, you will come to rely on these people more and more, and they will become a kind of cabinet for you, absolutely essential to your success.

BANKING

It's good business to have a separate checking account for your landlording. Some landlords and landladies even open a separate account for each building they own (if their rentals are single-family dwellings, they have one account for all) and then use that account as their only "bookkeeping system," channeling all of the building's income and expenses through the account, a simplistic but workable approach. Whatever you do, open at least one checking account for your rental properties, and itemize your deposits and checks carefully so your bookkeeping chores will be easier later.

Before you visit the bank, though, select the name you want to use for your property account. This name has nothing to do with how you hold title to your property, who is authorized to write checks, or what street the building is on. It is only the name which your tenants will use as the payee for their checks and money orders.

Presumably to prevent someone else in the area from using the same name you have selected, banks require that everyone opening an account under a business name which does not include the owner's real name has to file a fictitious name statement, a process involving a filing fee and legal advertising.

Whereas your business name would be a valuable asset to you if you were operating the Playtime Tavern or the Capri Motel, it's hardly important in the rental property business, except for large, heavily advertised complexes. Even then, no one else would want to confuse people in the area with a second Sun Garden Apartments if you were using that name already, and it would not likely be used except through an oversight.

You can circumvent the folderol of filing a fictitious name statement by opening your account under your own name and imprinting your checks in bold letters with your surname followed by the word "PROPERTIES." If your name were Lester Landlord, for example, then your tenants could make their checks and money orders payable to "LANDLORD PROPERTIES," and you could distinguish between accounts for different buildings, if you wanted to, by simply calling them "LANDLORD PROPERTIES ONE," "LANDLORD PROPERTIES TWO," and so on sequentially.

If you want to open an account under a fictitious name like "Sun Garden Apartments," expect to encounter a banker who will insist that you file a fictitious name statement. If you do not wish to go to all the trouble of filing, however, and you want to use the name "Sun Garden Apartments" as payee, merely open the account under the name "Lester Landlord's (use your own name here, of course) Sun Garden Apartments", and you may accept checks made out simply to "Sun Garden Apartments." That's really all you care about anyway, simply getting the rent checks deposited to an account that you can write checks on, an account which is easily distinguishable from your personal account and carries a name easy enough for your tenants to remember.

In addition to keeping at least one separate checking account for your landlording funds to flow through, you should open one savings account for refundable deposits only. These monies are not taxable when you receive them and should be distinguished as separate from other landlording income, all of which is taxable. These deposits still belong to your tenants, not to you, and separating them will make them readily available when you need them to use or return. Separating them will also help to remind you to pay interest periodically if you are compelled to do so by law in your area or if you are inclined to do so as a good faith gesture.

Sums designated as last month's rent belong to you, not to your tenants. They are taxable when you receive them, and they should not be kept in the savings account for refundable deposits. All rents paid in advance, whether they are first or last or in between, are designated as rent and nothing else and should be deposited into your property checking account for operations use.

BUSINESS CARDS

After you have opened those bank accounts for your rental property, order yourself some business cards.

"Business cards for landlords and landladies you say? Ridiculous! What a waste of money!"

Although you might scoff at the idea initially, consider some of the many uses for business cards in your do-it-yourself landlording business before you reject the idea completely.

• Use them as your "open sesame" for access to many "Wholesale Only" suppliers of appliance parts, plumbing supplies, and the like who refuse to sell to the public.

• Pass cards out to your tenants for handy reference when they need to contact you (designating yourself as owner, manager, or partner on your business cards lends credibility to your adopted landlording role; see Decisions chapter, "Should You Own Up to Being the Owner?").

• At rental property owners' association meetings, give your cards to other owners who might be thinking about selling their buildings and might consider a direct sale.

• And when those good business contacts you're cultivating hand your their business cards, hand them each one of yours in return. Then they'll understand that you do know one of the first things about running a business.

Besides being useful, business cards are one of the least expensive purchases you will ever make in your landlording business. Local printers will print up a lifetime supply for less than $20, and mail-order firms will print up a sufficient supply for a pittance. Among its many gadgets and gewgaws, the current Walter Drake catalog lists 200 deluxe personalized business cards for $2.98. Can you beat that? Write Walter Drake, Colorado Springs, CO 80940, for a catalog.

While you're ordering cards for yourself, have some printed for your managers, too, if you have managers. Personalized business cards show managers that you have confidence in their professionalism and their permanence and are always much appreciated.

```
123 Neat Street
Littletown, CA 91111

(415) 123-4567


           LANDLORD PROPERTIES



                            LESTER LANDLORD
                               Partner
```

```
             DANDY PROPERTIES

                  LESLIE LANDLADY
                       Manager

453 Sweet Street
Littletown, CA 91111              (415) 123-6789
```

THE TELEPHONE

Much of your landlording business involves communicating with people either face to face, by letter, or by telephone. Of course, there are times when you ought to make a personal visit to talk with someone, and there are times when you ought to write a letter, but there are also many times when you really ought to use the telephone. In most cases, it's cheaper all around. Business letters, excluding postage, now cost companies an estimated $5.59 apiece. Each trip you make to your property as an absentee owner costs you something, no matter how close it is to your home or work. You cannot afford to go traipsing all over the country looking for hard-to-find parts, wayward tenants, special services, best buys, and so on. For many of these tasks, you can communicate just as effectively by telephone, using considerably less time and less money, but you do need to learn to use the telephone efficiently. Here are some hints:

• Keep all your tenants' telephone numbers handy. Make up a little directory of your own or, better still, use the Tenant Record form in the Forms section of this book to keep track of tenant telephone numbers and other relevant tenant information. Because many tenants nowadays have unlisted numbers which no operator or directory could supply, those numbers will save you from having to make a visit to inform tenants of minor, but necessary, matters such as an anticipated utility shutdown the next day.

- Keep a categorized list of telephone numbers for all your landlording business contacts.
- Use the Yellow Pages to shop locally for product availability and prices. Make appropriate notes right in the book next to the listings of those firms you call so you'll have some clues to follow next time.
- If your rental property is located in an area served by another telephone directory, secure a free copy of that directory from the telephone company so you can shop at home from the Yellow Pages for that area.
- Buy a directory of toll-free 800 numbers from your bookseller and check to see whether the firm you wish to call has an 800 number available.
- When you want to contact people or businesses outside your area-code region and you don't have their numbers, find them quickly by using the telephone company's long-distance information number, 555-1212, preceded by the area code of the region you wish to call. Call (800) 555-1212 for information on toll-free 800 numbers.
- Take advantage of the cheapest rates available by scheduling the calls you make to other time zones for checking tenant references or making business inquiries. Place calls to time zones east of you before eight in the morning, your time, and place calls to time zones west of you after five in the afternoon, your time.

Whenever you have any landlording task which involves communication, ask yourself first whether Ma Bell can help before you crank up the Volkswagen or get out the Smith-Corona.

ORGANIZATION

There are many sources of discouragement in this do-it-yourself landlording business, so many of which you can do absolutely nothing about, but there is one source you can do something about — disorganization. Disorganized landlords and landladies make the job much more difficult than it already is, and consequently they become needlessly discouraged time and time again because they cannot find what they need in the chaos of their stacks and piles.

There are tenant records to keep organized, as well as receipts, insurance policies, building records, keys, supplies, tools, and spare parts, and you cannot have a memory sufficient to locate them all when you need them. You have to get them organized or you will fail miserably in this business.

You will find a number of hints and forms in this book to help you get organized. Use them, adapt them to fit your needs, and you will succeed in making your job easier and surely far less discouraging.

CONTINUING EDUCATION

If you own no rental property at all right now, you are wise ("Wise people learn by other's mistakes, fools, by their own." —Old Proverb), not because you own no rental property, but because you are taking the time to educate yourself about landlording before you actually become involved. Few first-time landlords and landladies ever have the training necessary to cope with the multitude of problems they will encounter in this business. Some cope well and thrive. Some give up and sell. Some capitulate and commit hari-kari. But most just manage to muddle through.

There's no reason for you to repeat all the same mistakes that others have made so many times and to pay a high price for making those mistakes again because now there's an abundance of good information available in books, on tapes, in periodicals, in classes, and in seminars, some of which are mentioned elsewhere in this book.

Learn all you can from these sources, but especially take the time to attend classes and seminars. Hard Knocks College no longer has a monopoly on property management courses. Adult schools, community colleges, university extensions, property owners' associations, educational exchanges, and proprietary educational companies all offer sessions for those landlords and landladies who want to know more about this business.

If such sessions are unavailable where you live, ask for them. The people who schedule these sessions try to accommodate local demands, but sometimes they overlook the need for such courses entirely.

New owners obviously profit from attending these sessions, but experienced owners profit from continuing their education, too. Whether you are experienced or inexperienced, you are dealing with large sums of money in this business and you cannot afford to be complacent or uninformed. Times change and laws change and you need to reassess your business operations all the time, picking up one good idea here and another here, and you can do that best by continuing your landlording education both formally and informally. Additional education offers you the opportunity to spend a little and save a lot.

TIME

Remember that all your landlording expenses are tax deductible as business expenses and that there will be times when you'll have to pay extra for something you need in a hurry, or times when you'll have to call for professional help because you can't do a job, because you're fed up and shouldn't do it, or because you don't have time to do it. Call for the help and think of the bill as a business expense. That's what it is. Don't get frustrated because you couldn't do it yourself and save the money. Sometimes it pays you to do it yourself and sometimes it pays you not to. (See Decisions chapter, "Should You Do It Yourself") You're not the ordinary do-it-yourselfer, remember, and you don't have that kind of time to case creation for what you want at the price you want to pay. Let ordinary do-it-yourselfers boast about how they spent long hours scrounging for something and then got it for little or nothing. You have no time for that. You have a business to tend to, a business in which time translates into money.

All this may be tough to do. No landlord or landlady ever said landlording was easy, but if you practice sound business methods, use your common sense, keep a level head, learn enough skills to do some things yourself, and know enough to call for help when you need it, you won't find your property losing in value. It will actually make money for you. Indeed it will!

TAKING OVER & KEEPING GOOD TENANTS

Tenants are important to this business, but maybe you have never stopped to consider just how important they really are. Let me explain.

You probably already know from your reading about real estate that there are four ways to make money in the residential income property business: 1 – appreciation, also known as capital gains (as a result of forced or natural inflation, your building should be worth more when you sell it than when you bought it); 2 – equity buildup (your loan principal decreases each time you make an amortized loan payment); 3 – tax shelter, sometimes called depreciation (at tax time you deduct a portion of your property improvements and consider them paper losses to offset income); and 4 – cash flow (this is the money left over from rental income after you have paid all the bills). Although one or several of these four ways might be more significant than others for a certain property, all of them are important to the overall business we are in.

Of these four ways, however, only one of them will keep working for you regardless of how you treat your tenants. Only one of them will work for you if you neglect tenant matters to the point where tenants stop paying you their rent and even begin tearing the building apart. That one way is tax shelter.

Sometime after you first buy your residential income property, you or your accountant will set up a depreciation schedule for that building, and each year you will depreciate the building for tax purposes according to the schedule originally adopted. You continue depreciating the building on paper regardless of whether the building is shipshape or dilapidated. It makes no difference. As far as tax shelter is concerned, tenants are unimportant.

But in order for appreciation to work for you, you and your tenants together have to keep their places livable, even attractive. In order for you to pay off your loan every month and take advantage of equity buildup, they have to pay you their rent. And if you are ever to have some cash flow, it will have to come from your tenants. They pay you the money that pays the bills and accumulates in your bank account.

Can you afford to cut yourself off from three of the four ways to make money in residential income property? Then don't neglect tenants. You cannot succeed in this business if you do unless, perhaps, you decide to invest in that one kind of residential income property where tenant problems are minimized — cemeteries. Those tenants you could neglect. No matter what you did, you'd have them for keeps, and you could concentrate most of your energies on keeping the property itself in perfect condition.

Come to think of it, there is another way to avoid tenant problems entirely and keep your rental property in perfect condition. Don't rent it out at all. You can get along perfectly well without tenants, can't you? Let your building age and weather gracefully without subjecting it to all that tenant abuse and yourself to all those tenant problems. Sound interesting? It is, except that without tenants you'd lose out on two of the four ways to make money in this business. You wouldn't have any equity buildup, except for what you contributed yourself from your own pocket, and you wouldn't have any cash flow. You would get the old standby, tax shelter, of course, and you would get some appreciation, but not as much as you would get if you had good tenants occupying your rentals. All things considered, renting to good tenants is surely the best way to run a landlording business.

Good tenants even help determine the value of a building. Prospective buyers will always pay more for a place which already has good long-term tenants living there, tenants who pay their rent on time, respect the property of others, and respect other people as well. Such tenants are prime assets. You cannot get along without them, so treat them well.

KEEPING GOOD TENANTS

Recognizing that good tenants are important to you and that losing them will cost you at least several hundred dollars, if not thousands, you are wise to consider various ways to keep those tenants living right where they are as long as you possibly can (on an average, almost half of those renting unfurnished dwellings will move during any given year). You can increase your chances of keeping your good tenants by being friendly with all of them, though friends with none, by being reasonable at all times, and by making an extra effort to please them at certain times. Actually, there are quite a few things you can do.

• Memorize all of your tenants' names, even the pets' and kids', and try to remember a few specific things about each tenant which you might use later in conversation. Everyone responds better to the personal touch, and what's more personal than a name?

• Provide them with useful written information for coping with emergencies and doing things around their home. Include your own name, address, and telephone number on a form along with other important telephone numbers, so all those numbers are readily accessible in one place. Indicate where the utility shutoffs are and how to shut them off, and offer some suggestions for coping with such problems as plugged toilets and ice-jammed refrigerators. Many times you will assume that your tenants understand how to use a garbage disposer or a fire extinguisher when, in truth, they don't understand at all because no one has ever taken the time to explain how to use one before and they themselves are too embarrassed to ask.

For Your Information:

Important Numbers:

Police _555-1212_   Telephone Co. _555-1010_

Fire _555-1896_   Gas Co. _555-1660_

Ambulance _555-6742_   Electric Co. _555-1765_

Doctor _555-2321_   Water Co. _555-1213_

Manager _LESLIE LANDLADY, APT 6, 555-3210_

Helpful Hints:

1) A fire extinguisher is located _UNDER THE KITCHEN SINK_.
Use short bursts aimed at the base of the fire. On grease fires, never use
water; either use the extinguisher provided or throw baking soda on the fire.

2) The electrical shutoff for your dwelling is located _JUST OUTSIDE BACK DOOR_.
Check there to see whether a fuse has blown (have an extra on hand) or a circuit
breaker has tripped. Restore service by replacing any fuse which appears to be
blown (use one with the same number on it) or by flipping the circuit breaker
switch back and forth.

3) The gas shutoff for your dwelling is located _N.E. CORNER OF BLDG_,
but there may be an individual valve on the line supplying each appliance as well.
Shut off the gas by turning the valve 90°, so it crosses (is perpendicular to)
the direction of the supply line.

4) The water shutoff for your dwelling is located _JUST OUTSIDE BACK DOOR_,
but you may be able to shut off the water to an individual faucet by turning off
the supply valve below your sink or toilet (not your tub or shower). If hot
water is leaking anywhere, shut off the valve on top of the hot water heater.

5) Whenever you defrost the refrigerator, turn it off or set the control knob to
defrost. Place a pan to catch the water and empty it when necessary. Do not
force the ice with any instrument; let it melt on its own or hurry it up by
placing a pot of hot water in the freezing compartment. Dry the floor throughly
when you have finished.

6) Whenever you use the garbage disposer, feed garbage in gradually along with lots
of cold water, and let the water run for half a minute after you turn off the
switch. Use the disposer only for those things which are edible; put everything
else in the trash. Keep metal objects out of the sink while using the disposer
and turn off the switch immediately if you hear any loud metallic noises. Do not
put your hand into the disposer (use tongs to retrieve objects) and do not use
any chemical drain openers.

7) Whenever water rises in the toilet bowl, do not try flushing again. The bowl
can hold just one tank of water. More water from the tank will only cause the
bowl to flow over. Use a plunger first, and then try flushing again.

8) Whenever you have showered or bathed, please take a moment to mop up the excess
water on the bathroom floor. A dry floor is a safe floor.

9) Whenever you want to hang anything from or stick anything to, the walls or
ceilings in your dwelling, please ask the manager to explain how to do it
acceptably.

10) Whenever you want to remove the screens from your windows, please ask the manager
how to do it properly. Some screens have to be removed from the inside and some
from the outside. The manager will show you how.

• When tenants first move in, change all the door locks right before their very eyes (see Insurance & Security chapter). Good tenants feel a greater sense of security when they see you change the locks and you inform them just who does have access to their home. Continue to provide them with that same sense of security during their tenancy by changing their locks again whenever they request a change, after a roommate moves out or they lose their keys or their home is burglarized. (Because you are responsible to each tenant who has signed your rental agreement, you may not change the locks to exclude any of them singly. If you do, you will have to provide access to that person later anyway so long as his or her name appears on the agreement. Before you go to the trouble of changing the locks, therefore, advise the remaining tenant of this responsibility you have. Of course, if the excluded tenant has not signed the agreement, you have no responsibility to him or her whatsoever.)

• Whenever possible, hire tenants to work for you, doing such things as cleaning, yardwork, and painting when those jobs are your responsibility. Tenants appreciate the opportunity to pick up some extra money without having to travel any distance from home, and they take more pride in the place where they live if they contribute some of their own labor to make it look more attractive. My best groundskeepers have always been tenants who live on the premises.

• Become familiar with the various kinds of rental housing assistance available through public agencies and other charitable organizations. Help your tenants who might qualify for this assistance to apply for it and run the bureaucratic maze to get it. Many tenants who should be getting assistance are unaware that it exists or are too timid or too proud to apply, and also there may be some you'll encounter who cannot read well enough to fill out the necessary forms. Your help could make the difference between their remaining as your good tenants and their moving to less expensive and less desirable quarters.

• Sometime during the holiday season, send your tenants holiday greetings, express your gratitude for their having been your good tenants for whatever length of time they have lived there, and enclose a check which equals the bank interest earned during the year by their security/cleaning deposits. A few states, notably New Jersey, New York, and Illinois, have laws on the books requiring owners to pay interest on tenants' deposits, so there your payment is no more than compliance with the law rather than a good-will gesture. When the payment is made voluntarily, however, you will find that it makes a pleasing, long-lasting impression on the recipients. Remember, too, that the interest on a $500 deposit at 6% is only $30, and that $30 will pay you a bigger dividend when paid back to your tenants than it would if it were to remain in your own bank account.

• Remember your tenants' special days with greeting cards. People in service businesses have known for years the public relations value of sending personal greetings on special occasions, and you'll find that tenants like to be remembered by their landlords and landladies as well.

• Include your good tenants in your efforts to secure other good tenants. Enlist them in your word-of-mouth advertising campaign (see Advertising chapter), for they have as much of an interest in who their new neighbors will be as you do.

• Recognize as certainties that heaters in rentals will malfunction only on the coldest Sunday of the year and that air conditioners will malfunction only on the hottest holiday. Naturally there are neither parts nor repairers available to repair the heating or cooling equipment right away, and your tenants may tend to believe you are somehow to blame. Keep cool. Anticipate that such problems will occur regardless of how good your preventive maintenance is, and prepare for them. Buy a good portable electric heater which the building's electric circuitry can reasonably accommodate and lend it to those freezing tenants until their broken heater has been repaired. Likewise, buy a large-bladed fan and lend it to your tenants until their air conditioner is back in service. Such thoughtfulness will convince your tenants that you care about whether they are freezing or sweating and that you are attempting seriously to remedy the problem.

• Offer to redecorate their dwelling if it hasn't been done in three or more years and the place is beginning to look shabby. All too frequently good tenants feel compelled to move because their landlord or landlady expects them to tolerate living in a dwelling which needs new linoleum in the bathroom, paint in the living room, drapes in the bedroom, and carpeting in the hallway. When they decide not to tolerate such conditions any longer and they move away to a dwelling which has been completely redecorated by a new landlord or landlady, their former landlord or landlady is forced not only to redecorate but to lose rent while the place is vacant and then to bear the expense and suffer through the process of finding new tenants who will be as good as the old ones. That former landlord or landlady would actually have saved money by redecorating to keep the good old tenants instead of redecorating to attract new ones. You cannot afford to be oblivious to the condition of your occupied rentals any more than you can afford to be oblivious to the condition of your vacant rentals.

You may be a greedy misanthropic landlord or landlady if you want to be, one who pooh-poohs any act of kindheartedness, but your tenants will move out and move in more frequently than will those of benevolent landlords and landladies who value their good tenants and cater to them whenever possible, while still being formidable enough, when need be, not to allow any tenant to kick sand in their faces.

TAKING OVER AS THE NEW OWNER

You have just purchased some residential income property and you are anxious to get started. You have already joined your local rental property owners' association and have bombarded them with questions. You have secured a copy of the local housing maintenance code from city hall and have familiarized yourself with the basic services and amenities which you must provide by law. You have notified the appropriate utility companies about the change of ownership. You have thought about the building itself and what needs to be done there, having made an inspection before you ever bought the place, but because the former owner kept such abominable records, you have no information whatsoever about the tenants you have inherited, and they have none about you. They're now wondering what to do with their rent, whom to call about their roaches, when the rent's going up, and how soon they're going to get the new carpets which were promised them last Christmas.

Tenant Information:

Your Name **Jeremy Youngster**

Your Address **432 Chestnut, Apt. 6**

Your Home Phone Number **555·0012**   Your Work Phone **555-2332**

Who lives with you? (Include ages of the children, please) **Nobody**

_____

What pet(s) do you have? **No**

Do you have a waterbed? **No**

What car(s) do you have? Make(s) **Buick**   License(s) **442-701**

Where do you work? Company name **NA**

Where does your co-tenant work? Company name **NA**

When did you move in? **March, 1979**

What is your current rent per month? $ **345—**

What date is your rent paid up to right now? **April 10**

When is your rent due each month? **10th**

What refundable deposits have you paid? Keys $ **Ø**   Security $ **210—**

   Cleaning $ **Ø**   Other $ **Ø**

When you moved in, you paid your first month's rent. Did you also then pay

   your last month's rent? **NO**   If so, how much was it? $ _____

Which of the following furnishings belong to the owners of the building?
   (Please give room locations if appropriate)

   Carpets **✔**_____   Drapes _____

   Shades **✔**_____   Blinds _____

   Stove **✔**_____   Refrigerator **✔**_____

   Other appliances? (Please list) **None**

   Other furniture? (Please list) **None**

Do you have a rental agreement or lease in writing? **Yes**

   If so, what is the date of the latest one? **March 10, 1984**

In case of an emergency, what friend or relative of yours should we contact?

   Name **Mrs. Amy Youngster**   Telephone Number **333-0210**

Date **9/18/84**   Your Signature **Jeremy Youngster**

September 16, 1984

Dear Mr. & Mrs. Renter,

You probably know already that the building where you live has changed hands. Because tenants usually feel some apprehension every time such a changeover occurs, we would like to take this opportunity to clear the air by letting you know just what you can expect in the future about a few things.

DEPOSITS...One special concern you must have is your deposits. We are concerned, too, and we want to make absolutely certain that all of your deposits are credited to you. To avoid any misunderstandings about your deposits and other matters related to your living here, we would like you to answer the questions on the sheet attached. They are questions which you should be able to answer quickly from memory or by referring to information readily available to you. Please do so as soon as possible and return your answers to us in the envelope provided.

PAYMENT BY CHECK OR MONEY ORDER...Since it is unwise for anyone to keep or carry cash around in quantities, we request that you pay your rent by check or money order (made payable to us exactly as underlined below). You will be protected and so will we.

PROMPT PAYMENT...You are expected to pay your rent within three days after the due date. For example, rent due on the first must be paid by the fourth at the very latest. If you anticipate being late beyond that for any reason whatsoever, please let us know beforehand. If you don't, we will assume that you are deliberately avoiding payment, and we will immediately serve you with the notice which starts eviction proceedings.

MAINTENANCE...We expect you to pay your rent promptly, and you can expect us to respond promptly to maintenance problems. Sometime within the next week, we will visit you to inspect for any building maintenance work that should be taken care of. You can help by starting now to make a list of such work which you notice around the house.

RENTAL AGREEMENT...We will also stop by soon to explain to you the standard rental agreement we use, and we will leave you with a copy of your own.

We are reasonable people and we will try anything within reason to make living here enjoyable for you, but naturally we need your cooperation. If we have it, we will get along well together and we can all take pride in this place that you call home.

Sincerely,

Leslie Landlady (123-6789)
DANDY PROPERTIES
453 Sweet St.

The very next thing you should do is communicate with them. Send them a letter or, better still for establishing rapport more quickly, take a letter around to each of them. Advise them in the letter that the building has indeed been sold and that you are (pick one) the owner, one of the owners, or the manager (determine now whether you intend to stop the buck or pass it — see Decisions chapter). Allay their fears about their deposits, inform them about your rent collection procedure, tell them you do want to hear about their maintenance problems, and mention that you expect to come calling soon with a rental agreement.

Along with your letter, provide a tenant information sheet (see page 24) and include a stamped, self-addressed envelope for its return. This information is intended to supplant most of what you should have in your files on all those tenants you have selected yourself, information contained in the rental application and the condition and inventory checksheet. Neither of those forms is really appropriate to use when you have inherited tenants, however, and you are trying merely to establish some basic facts about them and their tenancy. Because some tenants might prove to be stubborn and secretive, try to be as delicate and inoffensive as possible when securing this information, stressing that their best interests are being served by divulging it. Emphasize especially the concern you have for determining precise sums and dates, both of which you need to establish in order to prevent misunderstandings later.

Unless you want to precipitate a revolt among your tenants, don't even consider raising their inadequate deposits at this time or at any later time, don't make any harsh pronouncements which would radically change the status quo, and don't raise the rent immediately upon assuming possession. You have enough else to do. Wait a month until you have begun to establish yourself and have become better acquainted with the situation you have acquired, and then raise the rents if you believe you should.

Make the transition of ownership as smooth as possible by giving every indication that you are businesslike and reasonable and that you want to improve the operation of the property.

ADVERTISING

You don't know them yet and they don't know you yet, but out there somewhere are some very nice people searching for a suitable place to live and a nice landlord or landlady like you. They may have placed an ad in the "Rentals Wanted" column of your local newspaper (look there), they may have posted notices in public places (look around), they may be pumping their friends for information (keep your ears open), or they may even be out pounding on doors (open up).

Of course, they may not be doing any of these things, either, because they may not be so enterprising and because they may be able to find vacancies aplenty without taking such initiative. Since you can't count on every good prospective tenant to find you so easily, you'll usually have to take the initiative yourself when you have a rental available or coming available. Spread the word out to reach those nice people you want as your new tenants — advertise.

You might let the word out to your tenants and anyone else you know that you have a place available for rent, or you might let people know with a card on a community bulletin board, a handbill in local circulation, a sign on the premises, an ad in a newspaper, or a listing in a rental guide, or you might list your rental with a housing office or with a real estate agent.

You might try any one or any combination of these methods, but first, whatever you do, pay close attention to your building's exterior appearance, for no matter how skillful or how comprehensive is your advertising approach, you will never get your place rented to those desirable tenants who are out there looking for you if they are repelled by the exterior. Any rental dwelling's foremost "advertisement" is a well-kept, neatly painted exterior which looks so inviting to good prospective tenants that they will take the time to inspect the inside.

Once, shortly after my wife and I purchased a sixplex with two vacancies, we prepared one of the apartments for rent, advertised it in the local paper, and found that we couldn't get a single good prospect to stop and inspect the apartment itself. This one apartment had been beautifully redecorated and we were already working on the second, but because the exterior of the building looked so dilapidated, and everyone who responded to our newspaper ad saw that exterior first, no one except the undiscriminating would venture further. We hadn't planned to paint the exterior quite so soon, but we did, and all of a sudden the quality of our prospects improved dramatically.

People do judge a rental by its exterior. And why not? They intend to live there and invite their friends to visit them there, and they want themselves to be identified with a building which projects the kind of image they have of themselves.

Although absolutely essential, a well-kept exterior by itself conveys no message to prospective tenants about vacancies. It has to be combined with more direct advertising methods to spread the word and attract those desirable tenants who are looking for you.

Here are the eight advertising methods most commonly used by do-it-yourself landlords and landladies, together with some advantages and disadvantages of each, and a listing of the various factors affecting any decision to choose one method over another, all of which may assist you first in selecting the best advertising methods for your rental property and then in making them work well for you.

ADVERTISING METHODS

• Word of Mouth — Existing tenants in your multiple-family dwellings have as much of an interest in whom you select to be their new neighbors as you do, perhaps more. That rental building of yours may be your business, but, after all, it's their home twenty-four hours a day, and you can't blame them for wanting to have compatible neighbors.

No matter who they are, what they do for a living, or where they live, above all, they want to feel safe and secure where they live, and they hope that you will select new neighbors for them who will assure their safety and security, not jeopardize it. They might even hope that their new neighbors would be pleasant, accommodating people with a cup of milk or a bottle of brew handy when they run out, if it's not too much to ask.

Because of this common interest in securing good new tenants that you and your existing tenants have (neighbors around a rented single-family dwelling have this same common interest and should be included in any word-of-mouth advertising you do, too), you are wise to advise them of any impending vacancy as soon as you know about it, and, if warranted, even to offer them a finder's fee of, say, twenty dollars for finding the new tenants.

You need not include all your tenants in your word-of-mouth advertising campaign. If you wish, approach only those who, you believe, would be most likely to solicit prospects who would fit in well. Make your offer verbal rather than written so you can direct it to those good tenants more easily and casually shrug off any accusations of favoritism.

If you do elect to offer a finder's fee, forestall any misunderstandings over your obligation to pay by insisting that the finders accompany those whom they have interested in the place on the first visit or, at the very least, that they call you and give you the person's name before the first visit. You don't want a tenant to claim a finder's fee unless that tenant was directly responsible for the prospect.

Besides approaching those who, because of where they live, would be affected by the selection of the new tenants, approach others who, in the course of doing business in the area, meet and talk with the public, people such as Avon ladies, beauticians, barbers, insurance agents, corner grocers, neighborhood pharmacists, service station managers, motel managers, and apartment house managers. These people are certainly in positions to pass the word along.

When you enlist anyone in your word-of-mouth campaign, apprise them of at least these relevant facts about your vacancy — rent, size of building, size of unit, location, and availability and then give them your business card so they'll know how to get in touch with you when they do find someone. There should be no confusion in these matters.

No matter who the referral is, even a relative of someone you know well, reserve judgment on that person to yourself and, by all means, complete the full procedure outlined in "Getting Good Tenants." Sometimes the friends and relatives of finders are not up to your standards, and you may be the only one discriminating enough to understand why you shouldn't rent to them. Make that decision the same way you make it concerning anyone else who applies to rent from you.

Advantages — inexpensive, targeted, usable anywhere for any kind of rental

Disadvantages — uncertain, inclined to be slow, time consuming, awkward for declining unqualified prospects

• Bulletin Boards — Most supermarkets and some other stores provide community bulletin boards as a service to their customers just as general stores used to provide community forums around their pickle and cracker barrels years ago, but the exposure, and hence the efficacy, of bulletin board advertising varies widely. Some boards are prominently located within busy stores, while others are almost hidden from view by stacks of merchandise and rarely ever discovered. Some boards are well organized and well maintained by the management, and others are just a jumble of flyers, business cards, 3 by 5 announcements, posters, and small lost and found items. For best results, select the busiest boards which are within the trading area surrounding your rental.

To make your bulletin board rental ad most effective on any bulletin board, whether it be a community board or a more specialized board such as one where you work, prepare your ad at home on a 3 by 5 card with a large "FOR RENT" at the top, list all the particulars as you would in a newspaper ad, add color or a simple eyecatching design to make it stand out, and date it. Because you are advertising something perishable, a vacancy, the date is important to anyone who is looking for a rental and sees your ad, and therefore, you should try to replace the card every week with one bearing a more current date.

One danger with this kind of advertising is that without your knowing it, your ad card may simply disappear into the hands of someone who is interested in responding but has forgotten to bring paper and pencil. To accommodate these people, you might make numerous cuts into the card at the side and put your telephone number on each removable tab so the entire card won't be removed, just bits of it. Such a card might look like this —

```
★ For Rent ★          123-4567
350 BOONDOCKS LANE    123-4567
Spacious 3 bedroom house,    123-4567
fireplace, carpets, drapes,    123-4567
built-in stove and    123-4567
refrigerator $450    123-4567
3/15    CALL: 123-4567    123-4567
                      123-4567
```

Advantages — inexpensive, localized

Disadvantages — time consuming to prepare and post, limited in exposure

• Handbills — Handbills are a time-honored advertising method for a variety of things, and today with transfer lettering, xerography, and "instant" printing all readily available, you can prepare professional-looking handbills faster and cheaper than ever before, but preparing them isn't everything. You have to distribute them as well. There's the rub. You have to make certain that people see them.

When you do put them before the public, you have to make certain that your handbill distribution doesn't cheapen the image of your rental, either. To keep from cheapening your rental, avoid plastering handbills "everywhere." Avoid stapling them to telephone poles and fences, for example, both of which you should leave to the political messages and lost-dog handbills. And avoid hiring kids to pass them out on street corners. Instead, use handbills primarily to extend and reinforce your word-of-mouth advertising campaign within the community. Give them to the local businesspeople you patronize and ask them to display the handbills by their cash registers or in their store windows. Give them away as reminders to people you know who appear interested either for themselves or others. And post them on those bulletin boards which allow handbills. You'll be reaching the public you want to reach in ways which won't turn them off.

When you distribute any handbills, keep a list of their locations so that when you do rent your dwelling, you will know exactly where to go to retrieve them. If you leave them hanging about for more than a few weeks, people will begin to wonder what's wrong with this rental that won't rent.

Advantages — relatively inexpensive, localized

Disadvantages — time-consuming to prepare, distribute, and retrieve; suitable primarily for less expensive rentals; dependent upon your personality and contacts

• The Sign — You might be surprised by how many people there are who will pick an area where they want to live and then scout that area for vacancies. Believe it or not, almost half of all tenants do it this way, and some of them don't even wait for signs to appear before knocking on doors. When they see any indication that someone is moving, they begin making inquiries about the dwelling's availability. These super-sleuths aren't always around hunting U-Hauls, though. Most people who are looking through a neighborhood for places to rent look for a "For Rent" sign.

The "For Rent" sign you use reveals to the public something about the kind of business you're running and should be consistent with the exterior image of your rental building. A cheap-looking sign indicates a penny-pitching operation run by amateurs, and whereas such a sign will do all the advertising you'll need during periods of high occupancy, when everyone becomes a super-sleuth, it's just not good enough during periods when you're competing with everyone else for good tenants.

There's no reason to skimp on a sign purchase anyway, no matter what the vacancy factor in your area happens to be, because, unlike the classified ad, which costs each time it appears, the sign is a one-time expense, and that one-time expense is actually quite reasonable. One professionally painted sign cost me the same as two newspaper ad insertions and has lasted for years.

Mine is a two-sided 20″ by 30″ sign painted in three colors on 5/8″ plywood, and it is designed to hang at any of my buildings from a yardarm positioned at right angles to the street so that people passing in either direction can see it readily (the hardware used to attach the sign consists of eye bolts, clevis hooks, and harness snaps). The "2" in the "2 BDR" is painted on the board itself because most of my apartments happen to be two bedroom units, but this number may be covered with another one painted on sheet metal which bolts right to the board, and if necessary, a similar provision for changing "unfurnished" to "fur-

nished" could be added. The telephone number painted on the sign is my own, of course, so prospects may call me directly if the manager is unavailable at the site.

Create your own sign design to look as good as your rental units and say whatever you require, and then hire someone to paint it for you. You'll like the image this combination projects and so will your discriminating tenants.

Advantages — inexpensive, orthodox

Disadvantages — dependent on traffic exposure, inviting to troublemakers when used at vacant single-family dwellings

• Classified Ads — For some people, classified ads are their first resort for information when they're looking around for a rental dwelling, and because tenants are so conditioned to consulting the classifieds, no one would begin to question their effectiveness. Many landlords and landladies would question their cost, however, and since they can be expensive, you should make the dollars that you spend on this kind of advertising pay off. Here's how.

Be certain, first of all, that the people you want to reach are among the paper's readers. There's no need to pay for a widely circulated daily newspaper's advertising when a small readership daily will do, that is, assuming you do have a choice. Look also for special-interest newspapers and periodicals which carry classifieds. They're especially useful for advertising vacation rentals.

And don't overlook the local weekly newspapers or those free shoppers which carry classifieds. Because they are so localized, they frequently draw more responses than dailies, and you'll find that their advertising rates are quite reasonable in comparison to mass-circulation dailies. If you do plan to advertise in a weekly, though, be certain you inquire when the deadline for ad copy is, and if you miss it, by all means, don't keep your available rental off the market for a whole week while waiting for the next issue. Advertise somewhere else.

Because many people prefer renting from small-time landlords and landladies, avoid the appearance of a big-time operation in your classified advertising. Restrict each ad to a maximum of two vacancies with different addresses or descriptions. One vacancy per ad is preferable, of course, to emphasize the features of each rental and also to give you greater flexibility for cancelling as each property is rented.

Word your ad succinctly but descriptively and appealingly. Take a look at these two ads.

3 BEDROOM APARTMENT in Boyle Heights. Wall-to-wall carpets, stove, refrigerator, drapes. Close to transportation and shopping. $370 month. Deposit required. Available now. For more information, call 123-4567.

CLOSE-IN 3 BEDROOM. Carpets, stove, refrigerator, drapes. $370. 123-4567.

Just look at all the wasted words in the first ad! The second ad conveys in two lines the same message that the first one does in six.

Because classified ads are arranged under distinct headings, which already tell the readers a few things about the ads appearing there, you do not need to duplicate the same information in words you are paying for. The ads above would be printed in the "Unfurnished Apartments — Boyle Heights" section of a city paper, and they need not specify any of this information again in the body of the ad. Many of the other wasted words in the first ad express ideas that the readers takes for granted anyway. "Deposit required," "Available now," "For more information." Such expressions are completely unnecessary when you're trying to say as much as you can in as few words as possible and still attract attention.

Think of your ad as a billboard which must immediately catch the reader's eye or be missed completely, and you'll understand the importance of your ad's first word or two. Since you can't include a picture of the place in your ad, the descriptive words you use have to conjure up the most appealing picture possible. Words like "sparkling," "just painted," "quiet," "superclean," "cozy," "superbig," and "quaint" all create positive, pleasant pictures in readers' minds. They'll want a closer look. If you have trouble selecting words appropriate for your own rental, scan the ads in several daily newspapers and you'll find enough good words to last for years.

Include in your ad just enough information so you or your manager won't be bothered with lots of calls inquiring where the place is, how much it rents for, and the like. Here are the kinds of things you should include if they apply: number of bedrooms, carpets, drapes, laundry hookups, garage, carport, fireplace, dining room, utilities, stove, refrigerator, child ok, adults, pet ok, yard, storage, and pool. Include the size of the building only if it is favorable, that is, if it is relatively small, below ten units (some people prefer the community feeling of smaller buildings rather than the institutional feeling of large ones). These other items to include are marginal, depending on the rental area: water, garbage, air conditioning, hardwood floors, steam heat. Include price, for sure, along with the exact address and your on-site manager's telephone number, if any, followed by your own. An ad with these ingredients will create a favorable impression and tell readers what they need to know before calling.

Keep your ad readable by using only those abbreviations which are commonly understood. Spell out "bedroom" rather than use "BR"; use "kitchen", not "kit"; "dishwasher," not "D/W." Abbreviations commonly understood are A/C, St., Ave., and OK. Aren't they?

Study the way your newspaper charges for its ads. You might find that an ad running only Saturday and Sunday will bring enough responses all during the week while costing you just half as much as an ad running every day, or you might find that an ad running only one day, no matter what day it is, will do the same. Experiment. Your newspaper's classified rate schedule may be such, however, that your ad could run the whole week for slightly more than the cost of shorter insertions. If so, take advantage of these discounted rates, and cancel the ad when you are certain you have the place rented. Watch also the minimum number of lines, the abbreviations allowed, the size of type, and the number of spaces per line. You can always dictate your ad to the ad taker, ask for a quote on that number of lines, and then add or subtract words to suit yourself and your pocketbook.

Here's an ad for placement in an expensive metropolitan daily that has a one-line minimum and allows any and all abbreviations:

| 3 Rms Riv Vu. 123-4567 |

This kind of ad is all right for a tight rental market and for those readers who are savvy about all the arcane abbreviations used in rental advertising, but just think of all the questions such an ad raises! Why, you could write a play about them!

Here's an attractive ad for placement in a community daily with a four-line minimum and a prohibition against abbreviations:

Quaint two bedroom in fourplex.
Carpets, drapes, stove, carport,
water, garbage. By bus. 858 Sweet
St. $285. 765-4321; 123-4567

Once you have devised a well-worded ad that suits you and yields a good response, make a copy and keep it on file so you can use it over again or at least have a model to follow, and you won't have to waste time making up a new one from scratch each time you advertise.

Advantages — well-exposed, simple, time-saving, orthodox

Disadvantages — relatively expensive

• Rental Guides — Rental guides, if available in your area, provide yet another medium for reaching tenants who are searching for new accommodations. These guides, which are simply mimeographed, Xeroxed, or quick-printed lists of places for rent, tend to flourish mostly in areas with low vacancy factors, where finding that right place to live is such a tiring, time-consuming task that some weary searchers will pay around $20 for the convenient and detailed listings of rentals which may not otherwise be advertised as available.

The guides may be useful to you, landlord and landlady, because they cost you absolutely nothing and because you can be expansive in your praise and specific in your details about your rental, and consequently, you may save time by not having to answer call after call from those who are merely seeking more information. The guides are good for tenants, too, because they are more current and more detailed than newspaper ads tend to be. Before pounding the pavement or telephoning, tenants have a pretty good idea what each listing is like and whether it's still available.

This is the kind of information likely to be included in a rental guide listing —

listing date	drapes	no. children
date available	shades	infant only/OK/negotiable
rental location	blinds	cat only
cross streets	hook-up for washer/dryer	other pets OK/negotiable
no. bedrooms	laundry room	amt. pet deposit
no. baths	den	other restrictions
home	family room	utilities included:
cottage	fireplace	water, garbage,
flat	dining room	gas, electricity,
studio	breakfast area	heat, hot water
apt.	basement	rent per month
size of bldg.	pool	length lease required/
lower/upper unit	sauna	negotiable
furnished	garage	first and last month's rent
unfurnished	carport	required/negotiable
gas stove	off-street parking	security deposit
elec. stove	fenced yard	cleaning deposit
refrigerator	patio	other deposits/fees
garbage disposal	balcony	agent fee
dishwasher	deck	person to contact
carpets	view	phone number
hardwood floors	other features	best time to call

A newspaper ad with all that information would cost half a month's rent!

Remember, though, that rental guide firms earn their only income by selling these listings to tenants. To attract paying customers to their service, they will sometimes place misleading ads in regular classifieds, offering swanky penthouses at basement rents. To find out where these bargains are, tenants have to buy the guide, and when they do, they all too frequently learn that these come-ons have "already been rented." Such flimflam may have alienated those who learn of your available rental through a guide, and they may be chagrined at having been duped, but there is a way you can give them some preferential treatment. Because this advertising is free to you anyway, even over a long period of time, use a rental guide to advertise an upcoming vacancy several weeks before it's actually available, thereby giving the rental guide customer an exclusive, a genuine advantage over everyone else. That way, everyone profits. Then, if you haven't rented your place as the vacancy date approaches, continue using the rental guide, by all means, but begin supplementing that listing with other advertising as well.

To find out whether rental guides exist in your area, contact your rental property owners' association, check the Yellow Pages under "Rental Information — Real Estate," or scan the classified ads in your local daily newspaper, looking for numerous ads that list bargain rentals all without addresses and all with the same telephone number.

Advantages — inexpensive, time-saving, fully descriptive

Disadvantages — limited in exposure to those willing to pay

• Housing Offices — Many college campuses and military installations, as well as large public and private employers, maintain their own housing offices to assist their students and staff in finding local housing. These offices are subsidized as a convenience and hence charge neither the renter nor the landlords and landladies who use the service.

Once you have established which of these local housing offices you wish to use, you may use them repeatedly for only the cost of telephoning, but do remember to call and cancel your listing as soon as you have come to terms with a new tenant, so the housing offices can keep their records up to date.

Advantages — inexpensive, targeted, simple to use

Disadvantages — slow and inefficient at times

• Real Estate Agents — Not every real estate agent will help you find a renter, but those who will, generally list themselves in the Yellow Pages under the same classification as rental guides, "Rental Information — Real Estate." The range of services they provide in this context varies widely from simply advertising your vacancy in their window free of charge to advertising it actively in the newspapers to fully managing the property, including advertising the vacancy, showing it, and screening the prospective tenants.

Seldom do real estate agents make any money by providing these services. Mostly they are just trying to build a dedicated and obligated clientele who will bring them more lucrative business later when old properties are disposed of and new properties are acquired.

Agree in advance upon the exact services your agent will provide, including the kinds of advertising to be used, and agree upon the charges for those services as well. You should have to pay only if your agent secures a renter and only if that renter stays at least six months. Shorter tenancies should qualify you for more services when needed. Get it all down on paper.

Advantages — based on commission (no results, no payment), helpful to owners living out of the area

Disadvantages — obligating, expensive in comparison to other rental advertising

ADVERTISING FACTORS

Now that you know something about the advertising methods commonly used by landlords and landladies and something about the various advantages and disadvantages of each, you might wonder how to select the best methods for advertising your $750-per-month rental house. Should you break with tradition and advertise it with a 30-second TV spot on the six o'clock news? The answer to that question is an obvious "no" because your rental doesn't need that much exposure and because you'd have to sell, or at least mortgage, the property to pay for the ad, but the answer isn't so obvious if you're considering which of the eight methods you should use to advertise your house. All kinds of factors affect that advertising decision. Here are fourteen of them:

• Number of units — Is the rental a house, a fourplex, or a twenty-five unit complex? Use on-site signs at multiple-family dwellings for maximum exposure, but avoid using them at single-family dwellings unless the old tenants are still in possession and agree to cooperate in showing the house to anyone who stops by. As a rental house owner, you do not want people tramping through the roses to get a peek in the windows, and you definitely do not want vandals to suspect that the house may be empty.

• Location — Is it in a high, medium, or low traffic location, Main Street, Middle Road, or Boondocks Lane? Rely upon on-site signs more at high and medium traffic locations. If enough people pass by, a sign might be all the advertising you need.

• Rent — Does it rent for a song or an aria, $95 or $950? Pull out all the stops to advertise the expensive rental because you stand to lose so much more for every lost rent day and because it has a much smaller market than the $95 a month unit.

• Rental's Availability — Is the rental vacant and available now or have your tenants just informed you at Christmas that they're moving by Easter? Before your rental becomes vacant, try the less expensive methods.

• Areawide Vacancy Factor — Are available rentals scarce or in ample supply? The appearance of outward-bound furniture will suffice for advertising during scarcities, while search-lights and sideshows may be insufficient during high vacancy periods. Prepare to spend more on advertising and be more creative when the areawide vacancy factor increases. If a major employer leaves the area and tumbleweeds begin to litter the streets, you may need to change more than your advertising. A changeover to allowing pets and encouraging nudists might save you.

• Distance from Management — Are you managing a rental property seventy miles from where you live or do you live in the building? Find a local contact, perhaps a real estate agent or a next-door neighbor, to take phone calls and show your rental if you live somewhat distant. Few people will dial a number even twenty miles away to inquire about your rental.

• Effort — How much effort do you or your manager wish to devote to your advertising campaign, very little or whatever it takes? Remember that advertising with signs, classified ads, rental guides, real estate agents, and housing offices all take less effort than full-scale word-of-mouth, bulletin-board, and handbill advertising campaigns.

• Time of Year — Is there a seasonal nature to rental accommodations in the area? Vacation and student rentals have obvious seasons but, surprisingly enough, so do other rental properties. The most active periods for permanent rentals precede the beginning and ending of summer as designated by the Memorial Day and Labor Day holidays. People like to be settled in by then. Advertise during those periods with the less expensive kinds of advertising and add the more expensive kinds only in the final week before Memorial Day or Labor Day.

• Targeted Clientele — Are you looking for little old ladies with Kawasakis, students with Moog synthesizers, newlyweds with round waterbeds, municipal bus drivers with tabbies, or Mother Hubbards with umpteen urchins? To appeal to a particular clientele, select certain people as contacts, certain housing offices, bulletin boards, or newspapers. Post-secondary schools have housing offices which should attract students aplenty every September. Some senior centers, businesses, and union halls have bulletin boards and news organs which should appeal to the precise type of renter you seek.

• Exposure — Should your advertising reach 1 or 100,000 people? Naturally each of your rental dwellings can accommodate only one living group at a time and you need to find only that one, but you may have to expose your rental to many people in the general population to find that one, especially if it's an expensive rental. Do not pay for exposure to people obviously too distant to be interested. Renters consult local sources after deciding where they plan to make their homes.

• Advertising Availability — Are rental guides, housing offices, bulletin boards, and real estate agents who list rentals all available in your rental's area? Make some effort to discover all the locally available advertising sources and use those which suit your needs.

• Advertising Cost — How much are you willing to spend, nothing or whatever it takes? Take full advantage of inexpensive advertising — word-of-mouth, bulletin boards, handbills, signs, rental guides, and housing offices, but weigh the cost of eschewing more expensive advertising with the loss of rents you are sustaining so long as your rental remains unoccupied.

• Experience — Have you had previous good experience with a local newspaper shopper, a particular bulletin board, a certain rental guide, or a cooperative real estate agent? Conduct your own advertising survey by asking those who come to look at your rental how they learned about it, and then continue using whatever works for you. When the effectiveness of your old reliable methods diminishes, try others.

• Orthodoxy — Are rental seekers accustomed to using this advertising method? Advertise in ways and places that rental seekers expect you to use so they'll be looking for you there.

Whereas skywriting, TV spots, searchlights, and helium air bags will undoubtedly yield some results, the eight mentioned in this chapter are more orthodox and will yield more results per dollar then unorthodox methods ever will.

Applying these fourteen factors to a specific vacancy you might have would work something like this:

If your available rental is a four-bedroom house located on Boondocks Lane, if it rents for $750 and is one among several similar houses for rent in the area, if you are looking for a professional's family of five or fewer, if you are willing to spend between $50 and $100 on advertising, if it's around the middle of July, if you live next door to your rental house, if the house is now ready for occupancy, if you have little time yourself to spend on advertising, then you would be wise to place a classified ad in your local daily newspaper for one week. If there are no nibbles at all, reconsider very carefully the rent you are charging and reword the ad to expand on the best features of the house, but be prepared to have a vacancy for a few weeks until the market becomes very active again around Labor Day.

Whichever method of advertising you prefer, whichever you use, be sure you keep word about the availability of your rental dwelling before the public, for if nobody knows it's vacant, it might as well be occupied by a nonpaying renter. You're not collecting any rent while those fixed expenses of yours continue unabated. Hustle the place. Lace up your blue suede shoes, slick down your hair, practice your business card tricks, shell out a few bucks, and get the place rented.

GETTING GOOD TENANTS

Vacancy times are times which try landlords and landladies. They're working times, loss-of-revenue times, doubtful times, and if you're a small-time landlord or landlady whose every vacancy represents a high percentage of all your rentals, you are likely to be especially anxious to get that vacant rental filled. Be anxious, but don't be hasty. You want a smooth operation, one which won't continue to be trying when there's no vacancy at all.

The most important key to a smooth operation of rental properties is getting good tenants. If you are adept at this, all your landlording troubles will be little ones, and you can skip the whole of Chapter 7, "Getting Problem Tenants Out," for you practice prevention when you should, and you know enough to "evict" bad applicants in the first place, before they ever have a chance to become your problem tenants.

No matter what procedure you follow to select tenants, if it works, keep at it. No one can argue with success. But if you should have reason to doubt the effectiveness of your tenant selection procedure, consider making modifications until you hit upon a successful combination which works well for you.

Just as anyone can pick a horse to bet on in a race, anyone can pick a tenant, but picking winners ain't easy. It requires prudence, diligence, and lots of patience. Fortunately, though, the odds are somewhat better for picking good tenants than for picking winning horses, and the odds improve geometrically if you follow the ten steps which are arranged here more or less chronologically:

1) Prepare the dwelling for occupancy.
2) Prequalify the prospects.
3) Show the dwelling.
4) Take and scrutinize all applications.
5) Check references.
6) Visit applicants' current home.
7) Review your rules, requirements, and policies.
8) Fill out and sign the Rental Agreement.

9) Request rent or a deposit.

10) Fill out and sign the Condition & Inventory Checksheet.

You may skip all of these steps except the ninth if you're remiss about your business, and you may actually get good tenants. Who knows, you just might be lucky. But you might as well be buying a used car without so much as starting the engine or kicking the tires. Sooner or later you'll get a lemon, and then you'll learn the hard way that getting rid of a lemon tenant is considerably more difficult than getting rid of a lemon automobile. You can always park a car in a tow-away zone or take a sledge hammer to it if you get stuck with one that's a lemon, and after your catharsis, you can forget all about that car's troubles. But you cannot park and forget lemon tenants. You can't even get the cheap satisfaction of pummeling them, much as you'd like to. Once you get bad tenants, you're stuck with them for some time to come, and when you finally do succeed in getting rid of them, they'll likely leave a few remembrances just so you won't forget them.

Cull out the lemons. Follow the ten steps religiously, steps which any landlord or landlady can follow, and you'll never rent to them. Leave the lemons for those unscrupulous landlords and landladies you hear about. They deserve each other.

These ten steps are hardly what one might call difficult, but they do require time and attention, some of them more than others. Take the time and give them the attention they need, for when you consider the dreadful alternatives to getting good tenants, the time and the attention spent on all ten steps are well spent indeed.

After any of the initial seven steps, you might choose to reject the prospective tenants, and you shouldn't be afraid to do so. You are not obligated to rent an available rental dwelling to the first person who expresses an interest in renting it. I repeat, you are not obligated to rent an available rental dwelling to the first person who expresses an interest in renting it. Surprised? Read on. You should wait until you are thoroughly satisfied that you have found an applicant who will be a good tenant for your building and for you, someone with whom you might have a reasonably friendly and enduring relationship.

Be discriminating in your selection, but, by all means, do not be discriminating about race, creed, color, sex, national origin, ancestry, or marital status. Such discrimination is illegal in most areas, as is discrimination against those who are physically disabled. In addition, a few areas have local laws prohibiting discrimination regarding age (applies to children as co-tenants; principal tenant must, of course, be old enough to be responsible for signing contracts), sexual orientation, source of income, personal appearance, political affiliation, place of residence, place of business, matriculation (student status), or family responsibilities.

What's left? Everything not expressly prohibited. You may still be discriminating about the tenant's ability to pay, willingness to pay, pets, waterbeds, vehicles, recommendations, number of co-tenants (even though you may not discriminate against children in some areas, you may still limit the number of people you will allow to occupy the premises), intelligence, attitude (use care with this one; I measure their attitude by whether they laugh, or at least smile, at my jokes), smoking or drinking habits, permanence, cleanliness, and the like.

Those should be sufficient criteria for tenant selection, shouldn't they? Although in the areas with the strictest discrimination laws, you may not refuse to rent a two-bedroom apartment to an applicant on the grounds that she is a lesbian who collects welfare, wears black leather hotpants and frizzy pink wigs, solicits tricks at the local tavern, lives with her bastard child and a succession of painted ladyloves, and is an anarchist student twenty-one years old, you may refuse to rent to her if she smokes cigars, and you rent only to non-smokers. It's like nailing an underworld character for tax evasion. It's perfectly legal and it's perfectly just. Furthermore, you'd have to be totally indifferent to the matter if you couldn't find some reason to refuse her.

Don't dispair about discrimination laws. They mean well. A great may people have been unfairly discriminated against in finding housing only because they were mongoloid or Puritan or black or female or Irish or Jewish or divorced. The laws merely declare that those are no longer valid reasons by themselves to refuse to rent to someone. You may not discriminate arbitrarily. That's all. You should always be able to find a valid legal reason not to rent to those who are obviously objectionable. Set your own standards well within the law, and then set about getting good tenants you can work with. Your standards for a particular rental might look like this:

Gross Income: four times rent
Income stability: at least six months with same source of income
Assets: five times rent (bank account and/or automobile equity)
Credit: nothing negative
Rent punctuality: prompt
Pets: none
Waterbed: one queen-size OK
Vehicles: one auto, no motorcycles
Personal recommendations: one available (preferably local)
Number of tenants: maximum of three
Intelligence: average or above
Attitude: cooperative
Smoking: no
Drinking: moderation (maximum of two drinks daily)
Permanence: at least six months in each of last two residences
Cleanliness: average

Naturally some of the standards you use are relative to a given dwelling, some are relative to you, and some are relative to commonly accepted rules of thumb. Be reasonable in determining those standards because if they are quite restrictive, you may well find that no one who wants to live in your rental can qualify. For most standards, you will have to determine yourself what is reasonable and what is restrictive (see Chapter 8 for ideas about accepting pets and waterbeds), but there are some rules of thumb you might follow for two of them — gross income and number of tenants.

For gross income, the commonly accepted rule of thumb is four times rent. If an applicant's income is only two or three times the rent, then you may accept or reject the applicant. The decision is yours. The point is that you don't have to accept any applicant who grosses less than four times the rent regardless of that applicant's other qualifications. You may if you want to, say, if that applicant comes with sterling recommendations from two previous landlords and landladies, but you don't have to.

Moreover, just as the Equal Rights Amendment is a two-edged sword for women, so, too, are laws prohibiting housing discrimination based on marital status. If you may not inquire into an applicant's marital status (you will notice later that the rental application included in this book makes no mention of marital status), then you have every right to require each adult

42

occupant to have gross income equal to four times the rent. After all, the living arrangements, whether sanctified by marriage vows or not, may break up, and you, dear landlord or landlady, may be stuck with the one tenant who has no income and can't pay the rent. (You don't have to be so restrictive if you don't wish to be, but you may be that restrictive legally if you do wish to be.)

Regarding an acceptable number of occupants, the rule of thumb is one fewer than the number of rooms. In other words, a studio or efficiency dwelling (2 rooms) should accommodate one occupant; one bedroom (3 rooms), two occupants; two bedrooms (4 rooms), three to four occupants; and three bedrooms (5 rooms), four to five occupants.

Exceeding these numbers increases the population density to a point where maintenance and repair costs increase considerably. Floors show more wear. The toilet flushes more frequently. The doors swing open and closed more. Faucets, switches, outlets, windows, heaters, everything gets more use and hence wears out more quickly. Besides, when the place begins to resemble a rabbit warren, exterior maintenance increases as well.

Some people may fudge on these numbers. The United States Department of Housing and Urban Development (HUD) does. Its minimums and maximums for rental occupancy are as follows: efficiency (no bedrooms), one to two occupants; one bedroom, one to three occupants; two bedrooms, two to five occupants; three bedrooms, four to seven occupants; and four bedrooms, six to nine occupants.

Fortunately, you don't have to agree with HUD. Unless local housing laws say otherwise, you are free to adopt your own guidelines for occupancy so long as you apply them consistently to all the applicants who are interested in a particular vacancy.

What does all this mean to you? It all means that you cannot be discriminating in some ways when you are selecting tenants, but you can be, and should be, discriminating in a great many others if you wish to protect your property investment. The truth is that you have to be discriminating when you're selecting tenants because you will find that some people are completely incapable of selecting their living accommodations prudently themselves. They think that a family of five, soon to be six, one dog, one cat, and a pet crocodile will fit comfortably into one of your one-bedroom apartments. You have to instruct them in the folly of their choice.

Let's take a closer look at how you can be discriminating in selecting tenants. Let's examine individually each of the ten steps for getting good tenants.

1. *Prepare the dwelling for occupancy.*

This first step in getting good tenants would appear to be totally unrelated to the overall task, but it is, in fact, just as important to getting good tenants as their payment of rent is to their staying on as tenants.

Your job at this point is to fix up, paint up, clean up, and dress up (you'll find hints for all these jobs in Chapters 8 and 14) your rental dwelling to make it attractive enough so a good prospect will want to rent it from you for the rent you want to charge. You will always attract the best tenants and get the most rent from the dwelling that shows well and smells good. (Give vacating tenants an incentive to clean well and hope that they do, but don't bank on it.)

Even so, don't become overly concerned about sanitation or perfection when you are preparing a dwelling for occupancy. Remember that you are appealing primarily to the senses of sight and smell. In this context, clean the appliances, stove hood, and cabinets (under the sink, too) both inside and out. Remove all non-adhesive shelf paper. Clean the showers, tubs, toilets, sinks, mirrors, and medicine cabinets (inside as well). Dust the ceilings (for cobwebs), baseboards, window sills, and closet shelving. Wash the kitchen and bathroom walls, and spot-clean the walls in other rooms. Dryclean the draperies. Wash the light fixtures and windows inside and out. Vacuum and steam-clean the carpets. Scrub and wax the floors. Sweep the entry, patio, storage enclosure, and garage. Remove all personal belongings of the previous tenants (including clothes hangers and cleaning supplies). Dispose of all trash. Do a good job of cleaning overall, but do not do such a good job that you get callouses on your knees from crawling all over the floors scrubbing them laboriously and polishing them to a mirror-like finish. Do not work your fingers to the bone by scrubbing the tile grout with a toothbrush. That's wasted effort.

Remember this one very important truism about each of your rentals. You, landlord or landlady, are not going to live there. Remind yourself. Remind your partner. Say it out loud while you're cleaning: "I am not going to live here." Do not give way to excessive cleaning. Clean your rentals well, but don't try to clean them any better than a maid would clean a room in a motel which is part of a nationwide chain. Your new tenants may be as fastidious about housekeeping as Felix Unger is in *The Odd Couple*, and if they are, they will probably clean everything again themselves anyway. Your thorough housecleaning efforts are a waste in that case, and they're definitely a waste if your new tenant is an Oscar Madison.

In addition to preparing the place for occupancy by cleaning, perfume it as well. No, not with Chanel No. 5. That's for people, not dwellings. You can perfume the place by cleaning the kitchen and bathroom with a pine-oil scented cleaner or you can allow the new paint odor to prevail or you can use a commercial air freshener to make the place smell of honeysuckle or you can make it smell of grandma's baking by heating two tablespoons of imitation vanilla extract on the stove.

The sense of smell is very important. It revives memories more than any of the other senses, believe it or not. Remember the wonderful aroma of homemade cookies and all the pleasant memories that go along with them? Smells bring those memories back. If tenants are charmed by agreeable odors of one kind or another, they become more willing to pay good rent for a place. You know what new cars smell like, don't you? Give your vacant rental dwelling a pleasing, memorable odor, too.

2. *Prequalify the prospect.*

This step is based mostly upon your tenant standards and consists of five or more determinations which can be made rather quickly, even over the telephone, and will save you untold time, gasoline, shoeleather, and grief. This step serves to eliminate people who are interested in renting from you but do not qualify. Here you are prequalifying them before you ever take the time to show them the rental or have them fill out an application, so you won't be exasperated to learn late in the process that they really didn't qualify to rent from you in the first place.

You can't very well determine at this stage whether someone will qualify according to all of your tenant standards. That questioning would be much too tedious and wouldn't yield useful information anyway (certain things you must observe, not ask about; can you imagine asking callers straightaway about their cleanliness and intelligence?), but you can certainly select a few important items and prequalify callers with them, devising questions suitable for this kind of situation.

To avoid wasted time, wasted effort, and possible embarrassment later on, then, you might prequalify prospects when they first make an inquiry by determining these five circumstances about them: 1) when they are ready to move in; 2) whether they have enough money to move in; 3) whether the number of people to live there falls within your limits; 4) whether they have pets; and 5) whether they have a waterbed.

If the prospects are not ready to move yet and your dwelling is ready for immediate occupancy, look for someone else. If you require $735 to move in and they have only $400 to commit right now, look further. If they are a family of four and you're looking for a maximum of three people, tell them so. If they have a pet monkey and you accept only caged birds, go no further. If they have a huge heart-shaped waterbed for themselves and a twin-sized waterbed for their four-year old and you have decided against allowing any liquid-filled furniture in this house you inherited from your favorite uncle, well, then, that's that.

Unless you have a lie detector handy, though, establishing the truth regarding these particulars may take some doing. Certain people will tell you exactly what they think you want to hear. They will move in whenever you want; they have $1000 in cash to cover move-in costs, no kids, no pets, and no waterbed, and besides, they will tell you, they're nice people. That's what they may say, but where does the truth lie? Who knows?

How do you get at the truth? At this stage, without being omniscient, all you can do is phrase your questions whenever possible in such a way that you give few clues to the answers you're looking for.

Because people seldom dissemble in answering questions about their readiness to move and their ability to pay the move-in costs, however, you can be pretty direct about the first two questions. State whether the place is available now or will be in three weeks, and ask whether the prospects' moving plans might coincide with that time frame.

Regarding move-in costs, state flatly what sum you require to be paid before they move in, and ask them whether this is within their means right now.

The next two questions are the ones which generally involve the most deceit — people and pets. These are the ones to be most wary about. To learn the truth, simply ask the prospects disarmingly how many kids they have or how many people will be living with them. Do not say, "We take only one child. How many do you have?" That approach will only elicit this response, "One's all we have." (Remember that in most areas which have laws prohibiting age discrimination, it is perfectly legal to limit the number of people you will allow to occupy your rental. There is no law anywhere which compels you to accept three people in a one-bedroom dwelling, but there are a very few local areas — Los Angeles for one — which have laws compelling you to accept as many as two people per bedroom. If your local area has no laws about age discrimination, chances are it has none about occupancy limits, and you are free to choose your own.

After establishing that the prospects fall within your definition of acceptable numbers, ask them point blank, "Do you have any pets?" Don't reveal your policy on pets before asking the question, of course, or you will likely be able to predict their answer. Reveal your policy only after you hear their answer.

Finally, now that you have prequalified the prospects on four counts, and they pass, ask whether they plan to keep a waterbed in the place they are seeking to rent. Again, reveal your policy after you hear their answer.

With all of these matters settled to your mutual satisfaction, invite them to take a look at the place.

3. *Show the dwelling.*

This step requires no great talent or skills, but you might wisely employ a number of ideas to make it less troublesome and more beneficial for you.

• After you have prequalified those who phone and express an interest in renting your available dwelling, answer whatever questions they may have while they're still on the phone, and explain exactly where the rental is located so they aren't astounded by the neighborhood if it's not quite what they had expected. Also, give them clearly understandable directions so they won't lose their way trying to get there.

• If you're one of those much maligned absentee landlords or landladies renting out a house or other dwelling located at a distance from where you live, you'll want to refrain from making repeated trips over there. Do this by encouraging people to drive by the building first and then call back for an appointment to see the inside, or do it by holding an "open house" for showing your vacancy at designated hours (should be one to two hours long). Tell those whom you have prequalified just when you intend to hold this open house and then make certain someone is there. You will save yourself many wasted trips and hours of waiting around for a specific caller who may or may not even bother to show up.

By the way, if you do make appointments to show the dwelling to specific callers, get their names and telephone numbers so they'll feel more responsible about showing up and so you can call them back if something happens and you can't make the appointment yourself.

• Never rent a dwelling sight unseen. Some prospective tenants will tell you over the phone that they want to rent your place without even looking at it. If they're that eager, don't insist that they see it, but don't rent it to them either. Something's sure to be suspect if they're that undiscriminating.

• If a dwelling coming available is still occupied and you know it's in such poor condition that it won't show well, don't show it. Instead, show another one which is similar and is occupied by a clean, cooperative tenant. Before you do so, however, be absolutely certain that the prospects are well qualified and very interested in renting from you. In other words, you should feel reasonably certain that the prospects are not really well dressed burglars casing the joint.

• Always accompany your prospects on their tour of the premises. Don't hand them a key and tell them to look it over themselves. Consider the showing as something of an opportunity to talk with the prospects and size them up.

• When you are actually showing prospects through the dwelling, you'll want to make a little sales pitch. Point out all the features of the place, including the special features of the building and the neighborhood. Be honest, though. Don't say it's quiet in the evening when, in fact, next-door there's a fundamentalist church which shakes and rolls to loud gospel music every Tuesday, Friday, and Sunday night. If you ignore the drawbacks, you may have to contend all over again with another vacancy very soon. The prospective tenants have a right to know what the place is really like and you should tell them. Of course, you may want to speak of the drawbacks as if they were advantages: "One thing I really like about this place is the great gospel music they play next-door three evenings a week. It's such a joyful sound, don't you think?"

• The first impressions you have of prospects while you show them around may tell you all you need to know to reject them outright, but there's no need to alienate them by telling them right now. Do what small claims court judges do when they don't want to anger a losing party in court. They take the matter "under submission," which simply means that to avoid fistfights in the corridors they will render their decision at a later time. Offer all your prospects applications, and tell them that you will be accepting applications over the next few days. After that, say you will check them all out and pick one. That way you avoid potential arguments over your grounds for refusing to rent to them, and everyone saves face.

• If possible, avoid mentioning whether any one prospect is the first person to submit an application. Many people believe erroneously that landlords and landladies have to check rental applications in the sequence of submission. You don't have to. The process is really quite similar to selecting someone for a job opening. Employers may not discriminate illegally in hiring any more than you may in renting. An employer interviews a number of people for an available position and considers each one equally over a period of time or until the person best suited for the job appears. The first person to be interviewed is certainly considered for the job but rates no special consideration for having shown up first.

• Get applications for everyone who wishes to submit one and don't commit yourself to rent to any applicants until you have checked them out. Not only is the information on applications essential to the selection process, but also because you have more information to base your selection on than just such obvious things as sex, race, or color, the chances of your being considered culpable of discrimination on the basis of these illegal criteria are substantially reduced. You are much more vulnerable to charges of illegal discrimination if you do not solicit applications because you have so little information to go on and the deciding factors may more easily be construed to be discriminatory.

4. *Take and scrutinize all applications.*

Your rental application should be simple to read, simple to follow, brief, and yet thorough. You don't need applicants' entire life histories to help you decide whether to rent to them. That might satisfy your curiosity, but it likely wouldn't be any more useful to you than a simple one-page application.

The application you use should have sections with information on the applicant's current and previous tenancies, current and previous jobs, fellow occupants, pets, financial status, vehicles, and driver's license. If this information is complete, you will have plenty to consider and check in the next step.

Notice that among other things the application included here asks for the name of a person to contact in an emergency. This name would not likely appear on an application unless

Rental Application

for (address) 456 Sweet St.

Name Richard Renter   Home Phone 555-1988   Work Phone 555-9686

Date of Birth 2/2/40   Social Security No. 123-45-6789   Driver's License No. A0987677

Present Address 1510 - 12th St.

How long at this address? 10 mo.   Rent $ 240-   Reason for moving Want to be closer to work

Owner/Manager Leslie Landlady, Manager   Phone 555-3210

Previous Address 1 View Circle, Apt. 105

How long at this address? 2 years   Rent $ 200-   Reason for moving got married, too small

Owner/Manager Joe Littleshoes, owner   Phone 555-1000

Name, relationship, and age of every person to live with you Mary Renter, Wife, 36

Any pets? No   Describe —   Waterbed? Yes

Present Occupation operator   Employer Bi-Lift   Phone 123-4440

How long with this employer? 2½ yr.   Supervisor B.B. Jones   Phone 123-4441

Previous Occupation operator   Employer Upstate Lift   Phone (200) 112-1160

How long with this employer? 6 yrs   Supervisor Lu Smith   Phone (200) 112-1160

Current gross income per month (before deductions) $ 1255-

Amount of alimony or child support you pay $ Ø   or receive $ Ø

Savings Account Bank Safe Savings   Branch downtown   Acct. No. 111-11-0011

Checking Account Bank Big Bank   Branch main   Acct. No. V04039586

Major Credit Card none   Acct. No. _____

Credit Reference A-Z Furniture   Acct. No. R-1345   Balance Owed $650-   Payment $79.50

Credit Reference _____   Acct. No. _____   Balance Owed _____   Payment _____

Have you ever filed bankruptcy? No   Have you ever been evicted? No

Vehicle(s)-- Make(s) Volkswagen   Model(s) Rabbit   Year(s) 1979   License(s) 222-123

Personal Reference Donna McGillicutty   Address 1516 Marina Way   Phone 555-1763

Contact in Emergency Eula Renter   Address 498-15th St, Bigtown   Phone 544-3061

I declare that the statements above are true and correct, and I hereby authorize verification of references given and a credit check.

Date 1/10/83   Signed Richard Renter

specifically requested. Yet, this information may prove vital if a tenant disappears without a trace, fails to show up to pay rent, or dies on the property. Such things do happen, you know, and it's best to be prepared for them if they do.

As mentioned before, because landlords and landladies may no longer refuse to rent to someone on the basis of marital status, you should ask every adult who expects to occupy your rental dwelling to fill out an application. Husbands and wives should fill out separate applications, and adult roommates, regardless of their relationship to one another, should each fill out an application as well. You'll use a great many applications this way, but you'll be well protected against accusations of unfair discrimination and you'll have plenty of good information for later reference.

Some landlords and landladies require applicants to submit deposits along with their rental applications. I do not. A deposit involves too much of a commitment too soon. You know nothing about the applicants and yet they assume that you are holding the rental for them, that it is as good as theirs already. If you accept deposits from applicants and you later reject their applications, then you have to face the unpleasantness of returning their deposits and explaining why you decided not to rent to them. Too often such an explanation precipitates an argument.

If you don't take deposits with the applications, you run the risk of wasting time checking out applications submitted frivolously and even losing good prospective tenants who make deposits and commitments elsewhere, but you can always keep in touch with the best prospects by telephone. I much prefer this freedom to look over a number of applications without making any commitments, either expressed or implied. Then I can pick the best applications to pursue further, regardless of when they were submitted. There are times, to be sure, when one applicant looks good from start to finish and you won't want to wait for more applications. That's no problem. You can complete all the steps in short order if you wish, and you'll still have the tenant committed with a deposit in the end.

When applicants hand you their completed applications, look them over quickly for legibility and completion, and ask to see their driver's licenses and credit cards for identification. Compare the pictures on the licenses with the faces before you, and say something kind or droll about the likenesses if you can. Then compare the numbers on the licenses and credit cards with those given on the applications to verify the information as given. If they don't match up, ask why they don't. You have no way of knowing otherwise whether the person whose name and references are listed on the application is the same person who wishes to rent from you.

Remember that whenever you rent out a dwelling, you are entrusting a valuable piece of property to a stranger. You must know whether that stranger is a proper stranger. You must know what that stranger's true identity is. Automobile rental agencies ask for identification before they will rent you a motorcar, merchants even ask for identification before they will cash a five-dollar check, and yet your property is many times more valuable than an automobile or a check. You stand to lose much more if you rent to an unscrupulous tenant, not to mention all the grief and aggravation you could suffer. Be cautious. Check the applicant's identification for certain.

If, for one reason or another, you fail to check an applicant's identification while you are looking the application over initially, don't despair. You can still check it when you visit the applicant's home. I prefer to check it at the first opportunity, however, so I don't waste any more time than I have to if an applicant proves to be impersonating someone else, someone who has impeccable references.

Unless you already know more about the applicants than what's on their applications, look at each application as if you were trying to collect an eviction judgment. If applicants have no job, no automobile, and no bank accounts to attach, then how will you be able to get any money out of them if they stop paying their rent and you have to take them to court? Many applications may be rejected at this step without further checking. You can "evict" now at the lowest possible cost. (On the backs of all applications you reject, write the reasons for your decisions and then file away each application for at least three years as proof of your fairness in tenant selection.)

Once you have scrutinized the applications to check for internal inconsistencies and obvious disqualifying factors as measured by your tenant standards, you should act promptly. Other landlords and landladies are looking for good tenants, too, and your prospects may fill out applications for more than one dwelling.

5. *Check references.*

Some people know that because few landlords and landladies bother to check out the information given on rental applications, they can lie and probably get away with it. I know it's a revelation to you that anyone would ever lie on a rental application. It isn't? Good, then you should be able to hold your own in this business. Be suspicious of the information given on every rental application submitted to you. Check the references, especially those regarding tenancy and income and maybe the credit references, too.

• Tenancy — Call the current landlord or landlady to learn whatever you can about the applicants' tenancy, but be careful. Since it is relatively easy for anyone to impersonate a landlord or landlady over the telephone, you may be talking to someone else. Say something like this when you call to check the reference: "Hello, I'm Lester Landlord, a landlord in Littletown. Richard and Mary Renter have given you as a reference on an application they made to rent a house from me. Can you tell me how you came to know them?" If you had indicated that the person at the other end of the phone line was supposed to be the one renting to Richard and Mary, then that person might have suspected that the Renters were trying to use him or her as a managerial reference and would string you along, giving you just the kind of information you'd like to hear. By not indicating that you know what their relationship is, you give that person no clues about what you already know, and you will more than likely learn what their true relationship is. Maybe they're just personal friends. Who knows?

One other danger in checking out an application is that the current landlord or landlady may be so anxious for the tenants to move that they may be recommended to you even if they are being evicted. Be wary, therefore, of glowing recommendations made by the current landlord or landlady, and weigh them with whatever else you have learned about the tenants. Compare the reasons for moving given by the tenants on their applications with the reason given by the current landlord or landlady, and if there's even a hint of a discrepancy in their stories, check with the previous landlord or landlady given on the application. That person no longer has an interest in whether the tenants stay or move and would be the most likely one to give you an unbiased appraisal.

When you have exhausted your own good specific questions about the applicants (Do they pay on time? Do they bother the neighors? Are they clean? Are they cooperative, etc.), close your conversation by asking, "If you had the chance, would you rent to these tenants again?" The answer to this question will give you a good final clue about them.

• Income — After checking into the applicants' current and previous tenancies, call the employer to verify employment, length of employment, and income. Sometimes firms are reluctant to divulge such employee information, so be sure you state who you are and why you're making the inquiry. Your call might go something like this: "Hello, my name is Lester Landlord. I'm a landlord in Littletown. Richard Renter, who says he works for you, has made an application to rent a house from me, and I'd like very much to verify some information about him so I can qualify him and his wife to move in as soon as possible." In effect, you are saying that your inquiry will benefit the employee. Small firms will assent to this reasonable request because they want to help their employees obtain housing and because you have said you are only verifying information you already have. Large firms will switch you to their personnel departments, and you'll have to repeat your speech from the top, but they, too, will generally verify the information you give them. Continue by saying, "Richard Renter says he has been working there for a year and three months. Is that about correct?" If they answer in the affirmative, say, "He has indicated that he earns a gross income of $1255 per month. Is that about right?" Phrasing your questions in this way, so they may be answered affirmatively or negatively, relieves employers of any anxiety they may feel about divulging information they shouldn't.

• Credit - Regarding credit information, you have three choices: 1) Choice one is to rely solely on the tenancy and income references already obtained to provide good clues about the applicants' ability and willingness to meet the financial obligations incurred in renting from you. 2) Choice two is to check some or all of the credit references listed on the application. Finance companies and merchants with customer charge accounts will usually divulge the information you need over the phone, but banks can no longer release any information to you unless authorized to do so by the customer, and even then it takes a few days. A letter of authorization which you might use is included here. It must be signed by the tenant-customer first and will be returned to you by mail unless you are well known at that particular bank. You may, of course, call the bank to learn whether a check for a certain sum of money would clear the applicant's checking account. 3) Choice three is to call your rental property owners' association and request a credit report on the applicant. Every association belongs to a credit reporting agency and provides its members with credit reports for a nominal charge. These reports generally take just a couple of hours to obtain and can reveal information on bad debt collections that you wouldn't otherwise learn about.

How much credit information you should obtain on applicants depends on the amount of rent involved, the percentage of their income that will be paid out in rent, and the difference between the old and new rents. If the new rent is high or equal to more than a quarter of the applicants' gross monthly income (rent, together with monthly credit obligations, should total around 40% of gross income) or if it represents a considerable increase over what they have been paying, you should check the credit thoroughly. Even though you know how much they make and that they have been paying their rent on time, you know very little about their current financial obligations and their previous credit experience. The increased cost of an improvement in housing may prove to be too great a financial burden for them right now, and you should have some clues in advance so you can advise them against renting too expensive a place. If the new rent is relatively low and amounts to less than a quarter of their income, and represents little, if any, increase over what they have been paying, then rely on the tenancy and income references alone or call just one of the credit references given.

51

BANK INFORMATION AUTHORIZATION

BANK: This request to report your direct experience and transactions is for the purpose of establishing your customer's ability to pay rent to the landlord or landlady whose name appears below. It is understood that this report is a business courtesy and is strictly confidential. Its authorship will not be disclosed nor will your bank assume any obligation for errors, omissions, or changes in this information.

	Savings	Commercial (Checking)		Loans
Date Opened	_____	_____	No Experience	_____
High	_____	_____	Date Opened	_____
Medium	_____	_____	Open Balance	_____
Low	_____	_____	Date Closed	_____
Date Closed	_____	_____	How Paid	_____
			Satisfactory___ Unsatisfactory___	

Remarks _____

Authorized Signature _____   Bank Stamp:

TENANT-CUSTOMER: Please complete all information in this section and forward to your bank along with a stamped envelope addressed to the landlord or landlady whose name appears below.

Renter   Richard   Mary
Last Name (Print)   Husband (First Name)   Wife (First Name)

Address 1510 - 12th St, Littletown

Bank Big Bank   Savings Account No. _____

Address 101 Main St.   Checking Account No. V04039586

Littletown   Loans _____

Richard Renter   Mary Renter
Tenant-Customer Signatures (His & Hers)

LANDLORD/LANDLADY: Print your name and address in the blanks provided, sign your name as acceptance of the above statement to bank, and give this form to the tenant who has applied to rent from you.

Name Leslie Landlady

Address 453 Sweet St.

Littletown   Leslie Landlady
Signature

You'll have to decide upon the right amount of credit information you need in each instance. There's a lot of information available, but you have to spend money or time to obtain it, and only you can determine how much information would be helpful to you in making your decision whether to rent to them.

Remember, though, that all the information available to you on an applicant is merely a supplement to your good judgment. You alone must decide whether to rent to someone.

• Handling a special situation — Every so often you will want to check the references of applicants who look outstanding both on paper and in person, but because it's a holiday weekend at the end of the month and you can't get a credit check or verify either tenancy or employment, you're stymied. The information you need to make your decision is simply unavailable for a few days. What might you do? You have three options.

The first is to tell the applicants to wait until you can check all their references as you normally do. Apologize that you're unable to check their references immediately, but assure them that you will check everything as soon as the holiday weekend is over. The advantage of this option is that you run no risk of renting to someone who may be a professional deadbeat. You will know with some certainty when you check them out whether they are what they appear to be. The disadvantage of this option is that you risk losing good tenants who will likely continue looking around until they find another suitable place which they can rent without having to wait for clearance.

The second option should also protect you from deadbeats, but it does have its price. Tell the applicants to find accommodations for the weekend if necessary and tell them you will deduct, say, $25 from their first month's rent for every night they have to sleep at a motel, provided, of course, that their references do check out and that you do rent to them. If you have to pay for two or three nights' lodging in order to secure good tenants, the expense is well worth it compared to the loss you would sustain if you had to evict problem tenants.

The third option is a little more creative and requires some special shrewdness to carry off, but it is almost as cautious as the other two, and it settles the matter quite sufficiently. Ask the applicants to show you their latest rent receipts and their latest payroll stubs. If current, a rent receipt will verify an applicant's tenancy, and a payroll stub will verify both employment and wages. Since few people carry these two items around with them and since the rent receipt could be forged pretty easily if the applicants were to leave your sight after you made the request, refrain from requesting the rent receipt unless you are visiting the applicants at their current residence in the next step. A payroll stub, on the other hand, is more difficult to forge, so have no qualms about asking to see one when you first decide to try this option. If the applicants claim to have stubs at home, tell them you'll meet them there shortly. When you arrive, follow the procedure outlined in the next steps and ask to see both payroll stubs and rent receipts. Be sure to check driver's licenses and credit cards at some point and make no exception to your normal method of payment for move-in costs. In other words, accept only cash, gold, money orders, or cashier's checks for payment. Accept no personal checks for the first payment from this or any other new tenants.

6. *Make a visit to the applicants' current home.*

If everything about the applicants checks out satisfactorily so far, call them on the phone and arrange to visit them shortly at the place where they are currently living. Don't show up without calling first. You simply want to make sure they're home to save yourself a wasted trip. You are not trying to catch them completely off guard, only slightly off guard. You might want to invent an appropriate pretext for the visit, that you need more information about the credit and personal references given on the application for example, but the main reason for this visit is to see how the applicants live and to meet all those who would become your tenants. If the applicants presently live too far away for you to make a visit, you may have to skip this step, but do so reluctantly.

Once you arrive, say a few pleasantries and then begin asking questions such as these: "I see here that you work at Dario's Pizza Parlor. What are your hours there? Do you receive any commissions in addition to your regular salary? How long have you been banking at Midtown Bank? Is Cash Smith still the manager there? Did you attend school in this area? How long have you lived around here? What keeps you living in this area?" and so on.

While you're conversing, look around for various indications of how well these prospective tenants care for the place where they currently live. Is there a motorcycle in the living room? How many holes are there in the walls and doors? Are there burns in the carpets? What shape is their furniture in? How's the housekeeping? How closely does this place resemble the dwelling they wish to rent from you? The closer the resemblance, the better they will be as your tenants.

Also, look and listen for pets and people likely to make the move with the household. You might expect that the springer spaniel sleeping on the sofa will make the move. If he doesn't appear on the application, ask why he doesn't. If they say they're planning to get rid of old Rufus, make a note of their answer and judge for yourself whether they're telling the truth or not. If you hear two kids raising Cain somewhere out of sight and it appears to be the kind of dispute that siblings usually have, you can assume that the offspring will both probably be accompanying their parents in the move. If only one kid appears on the application, inquire into the matter. If the parents say they're trying to get rid of one of the kids, try to contain yourself and make a note of their answer. Who knows, maybe they have sold one already and the purchasers just haven't taken delivery yet.

At some time during your visit, if you haven't done so before, say that you'd like to see the applicants' driver's licenses and credit cards to verify the numbers. When you have them in hand, check to see whether the numbers match those given on the applications, note down the full names (including middle names), and verify the birth dates.

If you have any doubts about the applicants after this interview, say only that you want to check the applications further and leave, but if everything meets with your approval, proceed at once with the next three steps.

7. *Review your rules, requirements, and policies.*

Before you finally commit yourself to accept any applicants as your tenants, review your rules, requirements, and policies with them in order to avoid possible ambiguities and prevent later misunderstandings. Remember that at this time, while you are talking with the tenants before they move in, you can get them to agree more readily to strict terms than you can at any later time.

Discuss your rules, requirements, and policies regarding the following: deposits, rent collections, rent payment, first month's rent, last month's rent, guests, parties, quiet hours, parking, utilities, garbage, pets, waterbeds, hanging things on the walls, changing locks, painting, maintenance, emergencies, window breakage, drain stoppages, lockout, and insurance. Add to this list any special considerations which apply to your situation. Mention, for example, that rerenting is contingent upon the existing tenants' vacating, if they still occupy the premises. Mention that the pool is heated only by the sun's striking the surface of the water (it's unheated). Be candid. You want them to have realistic expectations about living there.

Indicate that you are especially concerned that they keep the dwelling clean, that they be relatively quiet, and that they pay their rent promptly. Tell them that you are quick to evict tenants who do not abide by the rules and ask them whether they think they can live there in your rental under those circumstances. If they agree, and you believe them, then commit yourself to rent the place to them.

8. *Fill out and sign the Rental Agreement.*

Now put in writing most of what you have already agreed upon verbally. Use a simply worded rental agreement (see "Should You Use Rental Agreements or Leases?" in Chapter 8), one which most tenants can easily understand. In fact, you should use agreements written not only so they can be understood, but also so they cannot be misunderstood.

Explain every bit of your agreement to your new tenants, word for word. Give them blank copies and read everything to them as you are filling in the blanks. Many adults can't read, and many others won't read an agreement thrust at them for signatures. Because the rental agreement is so important to your relationship, read it to them now and you will avoid misunderstandings later.

Explain that the monthly rental figure used in the agreement is higher than what you advertised because this gross rent includes an amount, usually between $10 and $20, which is deducted as a discount when the rent is paid on or before the late date. Tell them you advertise the net rent because that's what most people pay. Make sure they understand this discounted rent policy before you continue.

Explain that the first month's rent is higher than the usual rent to cover some of the many costs connected with a new tenancy, costs such as cleaning the carpets and drapes (tell them they won't have to clean the carpets or the drapes or wax the floors when they move out; tell them that move-in costs are borne by those who cause them, new tenants; otherwise the rents would have to be higher for everyone), advertising, showing the dwelling, checking credit, and changing locks.

Explain that there is a deposit of one dollar per key which is refundable after the keys have been returned.

Tell them how much notice they should give you before they plan to vacate. Thirty days is most common, but I use fifteen because that's all the time I really need to prepare for a vacancy, and fifteen days is much more realistic for tenants. It has another important side

Rental Agreement

Dated _January 12, 1983_

Agreement between _Lester Landlord_ , Owners, and
Richard Harvey + Mary Louise Renter , Tenants, for a dwelling located at
456 Sweet St., Littletown, Calif. .
Tenants agree to rent this dwelling on a month-to-month basis for $ _275-_
per month, payable in advance on the _1st_ day of every calendar month to
Owners or to their Agent, _XXXXX_
When rent is paid on or before the _4th_ day of the calendar month, Tenants
may take a $ _20-_ discount.

The first month's rent for this dwelling is $ _355-_ . _(Waterbed Agreement)_

The security/cleaning deposit on this dwelling is $ _200 + $25_ . It is
refundable if Tenants leave the dwelling reasonably clean and undamaged.

A deposit of $ _3.00_ for _3_ keys will be refunded after the keys
have been returned.

Tenants will give _15_ days' notice in writing before they move and
will be responsible for paying rent through the end of this notice period
or until another tenant approved by the Owners has moved in, whichever
comes first.

Owners will refund all deposits due within _7_ days after Tenants
have moved out completely and returned their keys.

Only the following persons and pets are to live in this dwelling:
Richard + Mary Renter XXX
No other persons or pets may live there without Owners' prior written per-
mission, and it may not be sublet.

Use of the following is included in the rent: _Carpets, drapes,
Shades and stove. Refrigerator on loan temporarily._

Remarks: _Water and garbage paid. Tenants pay other utilities. Parking
in space 2. Occupancy contingent upon existing occupants' vacating premises._

Tenants agree to the following:

1) to keep yards and garbage areas clean.
2) to keep from making loud noises and disturbances and to play music
   and broadcast programs at all times so as not to disturb other people's
   peace and quiet.
3) not to paint or alter their dwelling without first getting Owners'
   written permission.
4) to park their motor vehicle in assigned space and to keep that space
   clean of oil drippings.
5) not to repair their motor vehicle on the premises (unless it is in an
   enclosed garage) if such repairs will take longer than a single day.
6) to allow Owners to inspect the dwelling or show it to prospective
   tenants at any and all reasonable times.
7) not to keep any liquid filled furniture in this dwelling. _ll oor. RR_
8) to pay rent by check or money order made out to Owners. (Checks must
   be good when paid or Owners will not grant discount.)
9) to pay for repairs of all damage, including drain stoppages, they or
   their guests have caused.
10) to pay for any windows broken in their dwelling while they live there.

Violation of any part of this agreement or nonpayment of rent when
due shall be cause for eviction under appropriate sections of the applicable code, and the prevailing party shall recover court costs and reasonable attorney's fees involved.

Tenants hereby acknowledge that they have read this agreement, understand it, agree to it, and have been given a copy.

Owner _Lester Landlord_   Tenant _Richard Renter_

By _____   Tenant _Mary Renter_

_pg 1 of 3_

Lease

Dated *April 26, 1984*

Agreement between *Leslie Landlady*_____, Owners, and
*Tina Oldtimer)*_____, Tenants, for a dwelling located
at *350 Boondocks Lane*_____. Tenants agree to lease this
dwelling for a term of *one year*_____, beginning *May 1, 1984*_____
and ending *May 31, 1985*_____ for $ *470—* per month, payable in advance
on the *first* day of every calendar month to Owners or to their Agent,
*XXXX*_____. When rent is paid on or before the
fourth day of the calendar month, Tenants may take a $ *20—* discount.

The first month's rent for this dwelling is $ *550—* . *(see Pet Agreement)*

The entire sum of this lease is $ *5720—* .

The security/cleaning deposit on this dwelling is $ *350+75=425* It
is refundable if Tenants leave the dwelling reasonably clean and undamaged.

If Tenants intend to move at the end of this lease, they agree to
give Owners notice in writing at least 30 days before the lease runs out.
Otherwise they will be regarded as automatically switching over to a month-
to-month tenancy.

A deposit of $ *2.00* for *2* keys will be refunded after
the keys have been returned.

Owners will refund all deposits due within *10* days after Tenants have moved out completely and have returned their keys.

Only the following persons and pets are to live in this dwelling:
Tina Oldtimer) and Fang XXX .
No other persons or pets may live there without Owners' prior written
permission and it may not be sublet.

Use of the following is included in the rent: *carpets, drapery rods,*
built-in stove and built-in refrigerator.

Remarks: *owner pays water and garbage. Tenants responsible*
for all other utilities)

Tenants agree to the following:
1) to keep yards and garbage areas clean.
2) to keep from making loud noises and disturbances and to play music
   and broadcast programs at all times so as not to disturb other people's
   peace and quiet.
3) not to paint or alter their dwelling without first getting Owners'
   written permission.
4) to park their motor vehicle in assigned space and to keep that space
   clean of oil drippings.
5) not to repair their motor vehicle on the premises (unless it is in an
   enclosed garage) if such repairs will take longer than a single day.
6) to allow Owners to inspect the dwelling or show it to prospective
   tenants at any and all reasonable times.
7) not to keep any liquid-filled furniture in this dwelling.
8) to pay rent by check or money order made out to Owners. (Checks must
   be good when paid or Owners will not grant discount.)
9) to pay for repairs of all damage, including drain stoppages, they or
   their guests have caused.
10) to pay for any windows broken in their dwelling while they live there.

Violation of any part of this agreement or nonpayment of rent when
due shall be cause for eviction under appropriate sections of the applicable code, and the prevailing party shall recover court costs and reasonable attorney's fees involved.

Tenants hereby acknowledge that they have read this agreement, understand it, agree to it, and have been given a copy.

Owner *Leslie Landlady*_____ Tenant *Tina Oldtimer*_____

By_____ Tenant_____

benefit for you as well, one which is explained in step nine.

Ask for the names of all persons and pets who will be living in the dwelling, and write them into the agreement. Explain that no other persons or pets may live there without your written permission. Tell them that their "guests" become tenants after two weeks and will have to be approved and added to the agreement at a slight increase in rent.

List briefly the appliances and furnishings which are included in the rent. Indicate whether they are on "loan" (see "Should You Furnish the Major Kitchen Appliances?" in Chapter 8.) Explain that you and the tenants together will make a complete on-site survey of the dwelling using the Condition & Inventory Checksheet as a record.

Explain which utilities you pay for and which parking space or garage the tenants may use, and indicate this information under "Remarks." Also, if the rental is still being occupied, stipulate here that rerenting is contingent upon the other tenants' vacating the premises.

Review the ten requirements on the agreement. Explain that they will be strictly enforced and that after fair warning, you will evict the tenants for any violations.

If applicable, complete pet and waterbed agreements at this time.

Finally, sign the Rental Agreement yourself and have the tenants sign.

9. *Request rent or a deposit.*

Think back for a moment to Step Two, prequalification, and remember two of the questions you asked then to determine the following: when the prospects would be ready to move in and whether they would have the money necessary to move in. These two considerations become very important now that you are preparing to conclude this initial phase of your renting relationship.

At this point you have a signed agreement in hand and you have taken the dwelling off the market, so as far as you are concerned, the place is now rented and the rent should begin the very next day, but if the tenants cannot move in for a week or so, you might consider splitting the rent with them for this short period as a good-will gesture. For example, if you come to terms with them on Monday, March 10th, and they can't move in until Wednesday, March 19th, you might begin their rent from March 14th. Whatever you do, though, don't split rents for more than two weeks, don't do it if the tenants are moving in immediately, and don't do it at all around the first of the month. Above all, don't come to terms with prospective tenants, tie the place up for a week or two while they are preparing to move, and then begin the rent from the day they actually move in. That's not a good-will gesture at all; that's a foolish gesture, for you suffer the full loss of rents due to circumstances which are beyond your control. It's their problem that they can't move in, not yours. You're ready for them to move in now. Share the loss, if you're inclined to, but don't assume it all yourself.

If you and the Richard Renters agree that their rent should begin March 14th, then their rental period for that first month is March 14th through April 13th. Since you probably want their rent to be due on the first (see Chapter 5 for the advisability of having rents due on the first) of the month, prorate their rent the second month, not the first. Request the full month's rent when they move in as a full commitment from them and a kind of insurance for you. On April 1st, collect rent to cover the period April 14th through April 30th. Make a point of telling them that the prorated rent for the balance of April is due on the first of April, not on the fourteenth, the same as it would be if they owed rent for the entire month. Keep them a full month ahead during this crucial early period of tenancy when you are just getting to know them and you don't know how dependable they are.

Be careful when you prorate rent. You can cheat yourself quite easily if you calculate that the period April 14th through April 30th, for example, is 16 days rather than 17. It may seem to be 16, that is, the difference between 30 and 14, but it isn't. It isn't because this period includes both the 17th and the 30th, as well as the days in between. To calculate the number of days correctly, subtract 14 from 30 and add one. If that doesn't make sense to you, count the days on your fingers and toes and you'll see that 17 is correct. Then divide the monthly rent by the number of days in the month and multiply that figure, which is the rent per day, by the number of days the tenants are occupying the premises. Tell them what this amount is even before they move in so they will know how much to set aside to pay you on the first of the following month.

You should request as much advance money as you can get from new tenants — the first month's rent, last month's rent, and combined deposits for security, cleaning, pets, waterbed, and keys equal to one month's rent (some local laws restrict advance money for unfurnished dwellings to the equivalent of three months' rent and for furnished dwellings to four months' rent). You can't always get that much, however, so you should have a minimum, too. The minimum amount to request before letting tenants move in under a month-to-month agreement, no matter which day of the month they do so, is the sum of the first month's rent, a security/cleaning deposit equal to the higher first month's rent (to avoid the problem of tenants' using their deposits for last month's rent, that is, if they haven't specifically paid last month's rent in advance, make the deposits equal to sums higher or lower than the regular monthly rent, and stress that these deposits are not to be considered last month's rent; another solution to this problem is to require less than thirty days' notice to vacate; if you require only a fifteen-day notice, the tenants' rental period and the notice period do not coincide, and tenants are far less likely to use deposits for rent; in most cases, when they do decide to give notice, they will already have paid their last month's rent two weeks before and can't be tempted to use their deposits for rent), and a one-dollar deposit for each key. Consider that the minimum. I've tried requesting less but have wound up losing too much to unscrupulous tenants. Of course, the more advance money you request, the better you're protected, but the harder it is to find new tenants with a large advance sum. To help you decide how much to request, you might inquire into the prevailing practice in your rental area and then follow suit.

Few people keep money lying around the house, so it would be understandable if Richard and Mary Renter did not have on hand all the money they need to move in. If they cannot pay you all the rent and deposits immediately, accept a minimum of a half month's rent. Do not hold the dwelling without receiving some payment at this time, and under no circumstances should you issue keys or let them move a "few things" in until every last cent has been paid. Too many landlords and landladies get burned by allowing tenants to move in some belongings without their having paid the full amount owed. Once they're in, the tenants pay not a cent more and have to be evicted. Don't get burned with this little ruse, and don't accept anything but greenbacks, gold, money orders, or cashier's checks from brand-new tenants without first verifying it. Only when you know their money is as good as what the government prints should you issue keys.

Be sure to issue a receipt for whatever money they pay. If you don't have a receipt book with you, use the back of the Rental Agreement to write up an itemized receipt, making at least an original and one copy.

Condition & Inventory Checksheet Dated January 15, 1983

Tenant Name **Richard + Mary Renter**   Address **456 Sweet St.**

Date Moved in **January 15, 1983** Date Notice Given _____ Date Moved Out _____

Abbreviations:

Air Conditioner, A/C	Dinette, Din	Hood, Hd	Shades, Sh
Bed, Bd	Dishwasher, Dish	Just Painted, JP	Sofa, Sfa
Broken, Brk	Disposer, Disp	Lamp, Lmp	Stove, Stv
Carpet, Cpt	Drapes. Drp	Lightbulbs, LtB	Table, Tbl
Chair, Ch	Dryer, Dry	Linoleum, Lino	Tile, Tl
Chest, Chst	Fair, F	Nightstand, Ntst	Venetian Blinds, VB
Clean, Cl	Good, G	OK, OK	Washer, Wsh
Cracked, Cr	Heater, Htr	Poor, P	Waxed, Wxt
Curtains. Ctn	Hole, H	Refrigerator, Ref	Wood, Wd

Circle applicable rooms and enter appropriate abbreviations:

	Walls, Doors cond.	chgs.	Floors cond.	chgs.	Windows, Screens, Coverings cond.	chgs.	Lt. Fixt. cond.	chgs.	Inventory: Appliances, Furniture item	cond.	chgs.
(Liv. Rm.)	ok		Cl Cpt		wind cr, scrn ok, Cl Drp		ok LtBG		⊖		
(Kitchen)	ok		wxt lino		Scrn ok Sh G		ok LtBG		Stv Ref (on loan) Hd	Cl Cl Cl	
(Bath)	JP		wxt Tl.		Scrn ok Sh G		ok LtBG		⊖		
Dining											
(BR 1)	ok		Cl Cpt		Scrn ok Cl Drp		⊖		⊖		
BR 2											
BR 3											
Other											

Charges   _____   _____   _____   _____

Total Itemized Charges   _____

Other Charges Not Itemized
(Broken Locks, Dirty Garage, etc.
Explain on Backside)   _____   Total Deposits   **$228⁰⁰**
Deduction for Improper Notice   _____   Less Deductions & Charges   _____
Deduction for Missing Keys   _____   Deposit Refund or
Total Deductions & Charges   _____   (Amount Owed)   _____

Tenants hereby acknowledge that they have read this Condition & Inventory Checksheet, agree that the condition and contents of the above-mentioned rental dwelling are without exception as represented herein, understand that they are liable for any damage done to this dwelling as outlined in their Lease or Rental Agreement, and have received a copy of this checksheet.

Owner **Lester Landlord**   Tenant **Richard Renter**

By _____   Tenant **Mary Renter**

page 3 of 3

10. *Fill out and sign the Condition and Inventory Checksheet.*

"The palest ink is better than the most retentive memory," says an old Chinese proverb. Because you and your nice new tenants will surely differ in your recollections of the rental as it was when they moved in compared with its condition when they finally do move out, you should have a written record (if you want a photographic record, too, take some instant pictures in the tenants' presence) of its condition and contents to protect both yourself and them.

To fill out the checksheet properly, go through each room of the dwelling with the tenants, circle the applicable rooms, and fill in the "condition" and "item" columns with the appropriate abbreviations. Do not put anything in the "charges" columns. They're for you to fill in after the tenants have moved out. Now add up the tenants' security, pet, waterbed, and key deposits and write down that sum as the total deposits. Date the checksheet, sign it yourself, and have the tenants sign it. Keep the original and one copy and give one copy to the tenants.

Then when the tenants have moved out and are demanding their deposits back, take your original and your copy and make a comparison inspection of the dwelling, marking the charges for broken shades, dirty carpets, etc. (see Chapter 6).

Only after you and your new tenants have signed the Rental Agreement, filled out the Condition & Inventory Checksheet, and settled all your accounts, should you issue keys and change the mailbox label. Both of you are then completely committed to each other, having created that special landlord/landlady-tenant relationship.

Even after you have completed all ten steps with Richard Renter and have created that special relationship, you and he will still be conjuring up strange mental images of each other, but you will have done all you can do to assure yourself of a good tenant. Give him a chance to prove that he is what he seems to be, at the same time you're proving to him that you are what you seem to be.

REJECTING APPLICANTS

Rejecting those applicants you believe would be poor tenants for one reason or another is a corollary to this whole process of getting good tenants. Rejection is hard for some people to take, and it is still harder for others to give. Some landlords and landladies rent to the first person who expresses an interest in renting their place because they just can't say "no." That kind of timidity you can ill afford. You have to get used to saying "no" in this business periodically, and one of the most important times you'll ever say it is when you refuse to rent to an applicant.

The trick is to say "no" in a kindly way. If you have more than one applicant for a vacancy and you have rented it to the one you consider the best, saying "no" is relatively easy, for you are merely informing the unsuccessful applicants that you have rented the place to somebody else. In that case, you might call them and say something like this, "Hello, Gulley Jimson, I just wanted to let you know that sombody else rented the house on Sixth Street that you were interested in. We had four applications for it and I sure do wish we had four places to rent because all four applicants would have made fine tenants, but unfortunately we had only the one vacancy and we could accommodate only one tenant. We'll certainly keep your application on file in case something else comes up, and we'd like to wish you good luck in finding something else even more suited to your needs." This kind of rejection sounds sympathetic enough to be acceptable to practically anybody. It's inoffensive and it's entirely plausible. It works well.

If your dwelling has not been rented, however, such a rejection would be very risky and very foolish. Never say a place has been rented to somebody else unless it actually has been. Never say it has been rented in order to dissuade a persistent inquirer or anyone else, for that matter. Such a simple-minded ploy will only cause you trouble. Even when you are not actually discriminating against someone illegally, this falsehood, if discovered, could be construed to be a sign of blatant discrimination, and it could be all the evidence needed by those who thrive on suing unsuspecting landlords and landladies for discrimination.

Be more cautious than that. Even when you have yet to find a suitable tenant and you are being pestered for acceptance by undesirable applicants, don't say the place has been rented. Stall if need be. Say that you turned the applications over to a tenant-checking service and that they are a little slow at times in notifying you of the results. It's not the best approach, but it will suffice for a few days while you pray for good acceptable applicants to come along so you can rent to them and then use the kindly rejection approach on the others.

Sometimes the best approach, though, is an honest and direct approach. It may not appear to be kindly on the surface, but it is, because it deflates the applicant's hopes for your rental so they can realistically assess their prospects and won't waste any more time waiting to hear from you. Tell the applicants by phone, if possible, that you're sorry they just don't fit your tenant guidelines and that they should begin looking further for housing. If you want to, give them the precise reason for the rejection and be as polite as you can while they argue their case, recount their sad story, bang the receiver in your ear, or string together a few profanities. Don't budge from your decision, no matter what they do or say. You know you don't want them to be your tenants. Let them rent from someone else who has different standards.

Endure the few unpleasantries right now that your rejection might cause in order to avoid having to cope with them later as unsuitable tenants.

RENTS

"What do you think your landlady does with the rent money you pay her?"

"Oh, I suppose she buys fancy clothes, makeup, and stuff, and she goes on trips every summer, love-boat trips, I think someone told me. The rest of it she probably sews inside her mattress or puts in the bank. She's a rich lady to own this building. That's for sure."

Many tenants believe that you pocket either their entire rent payment or a substantial portion of it. They cannot understand what else you might do with it, for they are mostly oblivious of loan payments, property tax bills, garbage bills, utility bills, advertising bills, maintenance bills, repair bills, vacancy losses, replacement reserves, and insurance bills, not to mention management costs (your time included). They regard rent as a kind of legal extortion or a tax levied by the rich directly on the poor, and thus, some of them feel justified in depriving you of the rent money or, if that's not possible, in depriving you of the prerogative to charge more rent to meet your increasing expenses (rent control).

Short of turning over the property completely to your tenants and letting them try to pay all the bills themselves out of what rent they are able to collect, you may find that convincing them that their rent money pays bills directly related to their tenancy is just as hard as convincing the devil that whiskey and holy water, taken internally, helps even the most devilish of colds. Old, old notions about landlords and landladies and rents are deep-rooted indeed.

Try educating your tenants little by little whenever you have the opportunity, though. Sometime when you're out collecting the rent, ask them what they think the rent money goes for, and be prepared for some very astonishing answers. Tenants haven't a clue what you do with their rent money. Of course, you might not know yourself exactly what percentage of a $450 rent check goes to pay utilities, what to insurance, and so on, and you should certainly calculate those percentages (use expenses for the previous tax year and include as an expense at least 5% of the income to represent your own time contribution for overall property management alone) before you ever broach the subject to your tenants. (On an average, the percentages are as follows for multiple-family dwellings: expenses, 25%; taxes, 25%; interest, 35%; debt retirement, 2%; vacancy factor, 5%; overall property management, 5%; cash flow 3%.) Once you have calculated your percentages, you may be quite surprised by how little of their rent you do pocket (positive cash flow) or, more likely by how much you have to contribute (negative cash flow) to keep a roof over your tenants' heads. Like any teacher preparing a class lesson, you may learn much more about rents while preparing to teach your tenants than you ever knew before.

Don't be too hopeful that your students will learn their lessons, however, for you have some very reluctant learners. Neither these informal discussions nor formal disclosures with copious explanations will enlighten your tenants about their rent so thoroughly that they will volunteer to pay their "fair share" of the expenses, but at least through such attempts, you *might* find them a *little* more understanding about rent collection, rent raises, and rent control, all subjects of this chapter.

COLLECTING RENTS

You may have your tenants trained to pay you their rent two weeks before it's due. If so, skip this section and the next. Everyone else, read on.

Collecting rents on time requires persistence, consistency, and firmness. You can't expect tenants to pay promptly if you aren't trying to collect from them, or if they never know whether you will be coming on the third or on the tenth of the month to collect, or if you give them the impression that you're an old softy. Be persistent. You earn that rent money and you shouldn't be the least bit timid about collecting it. Be consistent. Rent collecting is so important to landlording that you must learn to subordinate everything else when rents are due so you can pursue rent collection in the same way month after month, year after year. Be firm. Convince your tenants that rent is your top priority.

Remember that paying rent is just as unsatisfying to tenants as paying taxes is to you. Neither rent nor taxes pay for anything that the payer didn't already have before, or so it would seem. Few would pay if they didn't believe that they would be penalized somehow. You have to establish yourself, therefore, from the very beginning as a threat, like the I.R.S., a landlord or landlady who expects the rent to be paid promptly, no matter what. When it isn't, you become menacing, a force to contend with.

All too frequently it is easier not to pay the landlord or landlady than it is not to pay the bookie, the dentist, the grocer, the utility company, the haberdasher, the finance company, the barber, the gasoline company, the insurance company, or even the news carrier. Who then gets paid last, if at all? You, that's who! Why? You're not firm enough when you should be. Be like that family dog which is faithful and loving except when anyone tries to take away its food. Then it growls and bites. There's no reason you can't be considerate to your tenants either, except where rents are concerned. Then you have to be menacing (I.R.S. K-9 Corps?). After all, you and your rental properties live on rent money just as dogs live on Gravy Train.

Make it more difficult for your tenants not to pay you than not to pay anyone else. Explain precisely what your policy is regarding rent collection. Tell them before you ever rent to them that your rent is due on the first, it is late on the fifth, and if it's not paid by the fifth, you'll give them just three days to pack up and leave. Talk tough. Be tough when you collect rents. You won't be understood otherwise.

Besides persistence, consistency and firmness, collecting rents on time requires a reasonable, lucid, and strict rent collection policy more than anything else, a policy which should include a mutually agreed upon collection procedure, a specified form of payment, set due and late dates, and a definite penalty for late payment.

• Which collection procedure you use will depend upon what kind of tenants you have, where you live in relation to the units, how many units you have, how much you want to be involved, and whether you have a manager. Some landlords and landladies prefer to collect the rent by mail, some have the tenants visit them or the manager, and some actually go themselves to their tenants' dwellings to collect rents. There are merits to each procedure.

Collecting the rent by mail is certainly the easiest and most efficient for you. You don't have to waste time going to the tenant's dwelling or waiting around for the tenant to come to you. You don't have to listen to the latest gossip about the neighbors, and you don't have to hear the inevitable complaints. It's quick, it's easy, but it's also impersonal, and it separates you from your source of income to the point where you may lose touch and eventually control. If you keep in touch with your tenants at other times and in other ways, by all means, have your tenants mail their rent to you, but if rent collection day is the only chance you have all month to see your property, then maybe you'd better collect the rent on the spot. You might see something that should be remedied and you might see it while it still can be remedied easily.

Having the tenants come to you or to your manager, if either of you lives close by, is surely the most common collection procedure. It's personalized and it's pretty efficient, but it may make you feel confined to one place while you wait for tenants to come to you. It's best used in combination with the third procedure.

Despite some very real disadvantages of the third procedure, its inefficiency and its placing the burden of the transaction on you, there are advantages to collecting rents on the tenant's doorstep or inside the tenant's dwelling itself. It's as personalized as possible. It shows that you care enough to take the time to look after your property. It shows that rent collection is important to you. It lets you know straightaway whether a tenant will be late and, if so, what the tenant's excuse for late payment is, and it allows you more freedom of movement because you don't have to wait around for the tenant to call on you.

Whether you use the first, the second, or the third procedure, or any combination, you should be absolutely certain that your tenants understand how you expect to collect their rent. You don't want them to be waiting around for you to knock on their door to collect it while you're expecting them to come to you.

• Since you want to be certain that your rents will reach the bank intact, stipulate in your rental agreement that all rents are to be paid by check or money order. If you don't, you could be carrying large sums of cash around with you at rent collection time and be a tempting mark for a mugger. (See "The Little Old Rubber Stamp Trick" in Chapter 10 for another safety precaution.)

And since you want to keep good income records which brook no argument, take the precaution of receipting all rents in duplicate if you collect the rents yourself or in triplicate if you have someone else collecting them (one copy for the tenants, one for the manager, and one for you). The negligible expense and trouble involved in writing receipts for every rent collection, even for those paid by check or money order, have paid off for me more than once. Neither you nor your tenants should have to rely on your memories to verify dates, amounts paid, and rental periods. Put it in writing.

• You may have noticed I stated above that rent is due on the first. My rents all are. Why the first? There are several reasons. Rents traditionally are due on the first. Tenants are in the habit of paying on the first. They associate the first of the month with rent payments, and consequently they are more likely to remember to pay without having to be prompted. Busy as you are, you remember, too, that rents are due on the first and late on the fifth. You can then concentrate all your energy on those tenants who haven't paid by the fifth. You can identify and handle the delinquencies more readily if the rents are all due at the same time and late at the same time.

Once I bought a 41-unit residential property which had rents due all through the month. This interminable series of rent due dates confused the tenants as much as it did the manager and me. So we changed all the due dates to the first. Collections immediately became easier, and delinquencies declined. The tenants remembered to pay, and we remembered to collect.

Just as important as a realistic due date is a realistic late date. This is the day when rents are considered delinquent and penalities are assessed. I give my tenants a four-day grace period, considering their rent late only if it's paid on the fifth or thereafter. Why? There are two good reasons, one legal and one practical.

Legally the rent due date must be a banking day, that is, a weekday when the banks are open. Tenants must have had an opportunity to visit their bank to cash a check, buy a money order, or withdraw funds to pay the rent. If the rent due date falls on a Saturday, Sunday, or holiday, days when they cannot get to the bank, you may not consider the rent late until the day following the next available banking day. If rent day falls on the Saturday of a three-day weekend, for example, the rent may be paid on Tuesday without penalty, and it is not considered late until Wednesday. Now if that Saturday were the first, your normal rent due date, that Tuesday would be the fourth. Four days would be the longest possible legal period of time that tenants would ever have to pay the rent without incurring a penalty. To be entirely consistent, I use this same period throughout the year. There are no exceptions.

In practice, this four-day grace period works well. You no longer have to listen to those hackneyed excuses tenants have for not having paid on or before the first. You know and they know that if the rent hasn't been paid by the fourth, there's either a serious excuse or there's a conscious attempt to avoid paying altogether. You save innumerable calls and trips on the second or third or fourth of the month to inquire after the rent, and you can feel entirely justified collecting more from a tenant who's missed the due date by at least four days. days.

• To encourage prompt payment, I use a discounted rent policy. My gross rents are set $20 higher than the rent advertised for a place. If tenants pay on or before the third day following the due date, that is, by the fourth of the month, they may take a $20 discount from the gross rent. In other words, they pay the net advertised rent. This method is legally defensible and it works. When I first adopted it, I was requiring tenants to pay on or before the first of the month, but I kept feeling guilty about charging a late paying tenant $20 more

if that tenant were only a day or two late. Sometimes I'd just tell the tenant to forget it, or I'd allow some tenants to get away without paying the additional sum and not say anything about it because I knew that collecting it from them would be difficult anyway. Such inconsistency in my collections made the whole process too subjective, too open to negotiation. On the one hand, I wanted to be reasonable and, on the other hand, I wanted to be tough and collect rents promptly when due. My first-of-the-month due date became as well enforced as the 55 mile-an-hour speed limit. So, I changed my definition of lateness and adopted a policy that the tenants and I could live with.

Late fees, which you assess tenants if they pay their rent after a certain date, work almost as well to encourage prompt payment as the discounted rent policy, but fees of $15 and more have been challenged as excessive in the courts, and some judges have ruled that rent late charges must not exceed the damages you sustain when tenants pay late. Since the discount for paying on time represents a reduction in rent, rather than an addition to it, you may deduct whatever you please if they pay on time without having to prove what your damages are. The approach you take makes the difference.

The one other late fee you may find in some agreements stipulates that tenants are to pay so much a day for each day of delinquency. Although penalizing late payers more and more for each day they are late sounds like a good idea, it may work against you, for one court has held that so long as tenants have agreed to pay the accumulating penalty, they must be allowed to retain possession even though they are in arrears. I don't claim to understand such legal thinking, but I prefer to avoid the difficulties it could cause. Instead of chalking up increasing penalties against nonpaying tenants, penalties which you have a slim chance of collecting anyway, you might as well use one penalty tied to one late date, and beyond that, you should use the various means described in Chapter 7 to get nonpayers to move.

Collecting rents requires an effective, pragmatic rental policy with teeth in it and someone to carry it out who is both firm and quick. You are in business and you should mean business when you collect rents.

Always treat late rents with gravity but also treat late payers with understanding, depending upon your past experience with them as tenants. Sometimes the unexpected will cause even the most diligent tenants to pay a few days late, and they will advise you voluntarily in advance just why they expect to be late and when they will pay. Such tenants deserve your patience while they cope with a calamity or a disruption in their income, and you would do well to accommodate them if you believe their explanation for the delay and if you believe the rent will be forthcoming in a couple of weeks.

If, however, by the third day after the rent due date, normally the fourth of the month, the tenants have neither paid their rent nor have advised you that the rent will be delayed for some good reason or another, you should make plans to visit them the very next day to deliver a notice to pay rent or quit. Listen to their explanation sympathetically; talk with them about rental assistance programs available, if appropriate; and then have them make a definite commitment to pay on or before a certain date, not over two weeks hence for the best of tenants and within just a few days for those doubtful ones. Tell them that you will sue for eviction if they do not pay by the promised date. Have the notice already filled out so you can hand it to them before you leave, and tell them, "We give everyone one of these notices if the rent isn't paid by the fifth, regardless of who it is. We treat everyone the same way."

Giving them the notice on the fifth strengthens your case should you have to go to court because you would have waited a reasonable period before giving the notice and you would have waited longer than required before filing the court papers. You would not appear hasty to the court, but more importantly, you would already have begun your court case. If you fail to give the tenants a notice on the fifth, and they don't pay on the appointed day, you'll have to deliver the notice then and you'll have to wait the required number of days following service of the notice before you can file your court papers. That wastes precious days, whereas, if you deliver the notice on the fifth and the tenants don't pay on the appointed day, you can go right ahead if you wish and file your court papers that very same day because you have already served the notice and you should already have waited the required number of days.

Sometimes your tenants will offer to pay you part of the rent and promise to pay the balance before the month is out. If they do, hesitate a little and then take the money. Tell them you prefer not to accept just part of the rent but that you will do it this time under the

NOTICE
to Pay Rent or Quit

TO __CHESTER & CATHY CAREFREE__, TENANT IN POSSESSION:

You are hereby notified that the rent is now due and payable on the premises now held and occupied by you, being those premises situated in the
City of __LITTLETOWN__, County of __SADDLEBACK__,
State/Province of __CALIFORNIA__, commonly known as
__460 SWEET ST.__

Your account is delinquent in the amount of $__250.00__, being the rent for the period from __MARCH 1__ to __APRIL 1, 1984__.

You are hereby required to pay said rent in full within __3__ days or to remove from and deliver up possession of the above-mentioned premises, or legal proceedings will be instituted against you to recover possession of said premises, to declare the forfeiture of the Lease or Rental Agreement under which you occupy said premises and to recover rents and damages, together with court costs and attorney's fees, according to the terms of your Lease or Rental Agreement.

Dated this __5TH__ day of __MARCH__, 19__84__.

Lester Landlord
Owner/Manager

PROOF OF SERVICE

I, the undersigned, being at least 18 years of age, declare under penalty of perjury that I served the Notice to Pay Rent or Quit, of which this is a true copy, on the above-mentioned Tenant in Possession in the manner(s) indicated below:

☑ On __MARCH 5__, 19__84__, I handed the Notice to the tenant.

☐ I handed the Notice to a person of suitable age and discretion at the tenant's residence/business on _____, 19____.

☐ I posted the Notice in a conspicuous place at the tenant's residence on _____, 19____.

☐ I sent by certified mail a true copy of the Notice to the tenant at his place of residence on _____, 19____.

Executed on __MARCH 5__, 19__84__, at __LITTLETOWN, CA__.

Lester Landlord

circumstances, provided they understand that they must pay either the full gross rent or the full late fee (whichever you use) and that they must pay the balance within two weeks. Much as I dislike the extra trouble involved with collecting partial rent, I would rather get some of the rent money than risk getting none at all.

Whenever you accept partial rent, give the tenants a receipt which does not cover a specific rental period. Only the receipt you write for the balance should include the rental period covered by both payments. It's too confusing to try to figure out exactly how many days in a 31-day month are covered by 56% of the rent money. Don't bother.

It can also be confusing to write receipts for past due rents. Just remember that you should never write a receipt for a current period if the tenant is in arrears for a previous period. All rent monies paid should apply to the earlier period. Here's why. Suppose some tenants are one month behind in their rent and you sue them for nonpayment. Suppose also that on July first they pay June's rent, but you give them a receipt covering the month of July. In court the tenants produce your receipt for the current month of July and tell the judge they lost the receipt for June. The judge has to assume they are telling the truth, and you will lose one month's rent.

When tenants do get behind on their rent, the chances are good that they're behind on other bills as well and they'll be shaping up a list of payment priorities mentally or on paper. See that yours is on top. Pressure them. Credit experts rank most people's priorities for paying their bills in descending order as follows: 1. Rent/mortgage 2. Utilities
3. Telephone 4. Car payments 5. Insurance 6. Taxes 7. Heating fuel 8. Cleaning/ laundry 9. Schools 10. Doctors 11. Dentists 12. Dues. Even so, remember that landlords and landladies are fair game to some people. They think there's nothing wrong with trying to beat you out of your rent money. They think they can string you along with one promise after another and that you'll just be so beguiled by their ruses that you will neither collect rent from them nor evict them for a long time to come.

What do you wish to allow your tenants to get away with? It's up to you. I have seen a middleaged schoolmarm, 4 feet ten and all of 90 pounds, keep supposedly incorrigible, hyperactive high school boys under her complete control. Another teacher, marveling at the situation, asked one of the boys why he never misbehaved in Miss Cheever's class. The boy replied, "Oh, she doesn't allow it." You can allow your tenants to pay late if you want to, but you'll be the one who pays in the long run. Don't allow it!

If tenants don't have one month's rent when it's due, they're surely not going to have two months' rent in 30 days. The longer they stay without paying, the harder it is for them to pay and the less desire they have to pay. Staying without paying becomes easier and easier. Why should they pay for time they have already spent under your roof? By allowing them to stay rent free, you are only postponing the inevitable.

Remember, too, that tenants who aren't paying their rent are actually stealing from you. They might as well be picking your pocket or snatching your purse, but the law doesn't quite see it that way. The law gives you no immediate recourse. You can't call the cops for help. You have to rely on yourself to get them to pay up or move out, and if you do something drastic, you're the one who'll be in trouble. Only after you have resorted to a legal eviction procedure can you get the law behind you to settle the matter.

In all my experience as a landlord, I have never been pleased when I have allowed any tenant to stay more than fifteen days beyond a rent due date. It has always cost me money or time or both. Even so-called good risks, teachers, policemen, apartment managers, college student body presidents, have moved out owing me money when I have permitted them to get more than fifteen days behind. I have collected lots of promises and a sheaf of letters. In some cases I managed to collect the past due rent in full, but it always required more of my time, and I had to become a bill collector to do it. Bill collectors generally charge 50% to collect judgments. They know how much time and effort such work requires. You aren't charging enough rent to include bill collecting among your services, and you really do become a bill collector when you have to scurry around collecting late rents. Your rents should be paid voluntarily. They shouldn't require more than ten minutes' work per month. That's all.

Collecting your rents swiftly and doggedly on a scheduled basis will prevent evictions for nonpayment of rent more than anything else. Your tenants will know full well what to expect of you. They may test you once, but they won't do it again. It's too costly. If they have to, they will borrow the money from someone else to pay their rent rather than risk your wrath and risk being evicted.

SETTING RENTS

Because rents used to be tied fairly closely to property values, setting rents was simple. The rule of thumb for an unfurnished house or duplex was that the monthly rent should equal one percent of its fair market value. A $25,000 house, for example, would rent for $250 a month, and the tenant would pay for all the utilities and tend to the minor repairs. For multiple-family dwellings larger than duplexes, the rule of thumb was that the monthly aggregate of rents would approximate 1.2% of the value of the property, a figure which is the reverse of the common yardstick that the value of multiple units should equal seven times the annual gross rents. Each apartment in a $40,000 fourplex, then, would normally rent for $120 per month.

Those old rules of thumb, which took into account a decent cash flow return on the investment, simply do not apply now as much as they once did, for property values have outstripped rents significantly in most areas. Today, an $80,000 house may rent for any sum of money, from $400 to $800, from one-half of one percent of the property value to a full one percent, and a multiple-family dwelling may rent for as little as one-half of one percent to as much as 1.4% of its value. Rents no longer guarantee landlords and landladies a cash flow return, and setting them is no longer a simple calculation using percentages or multipliers.

Since the residential real estate market, which is measured by property values, and the rental housing market, which is measured by rents, have diverged appreciably over the past ten years so that they no longer are bound together by time-honored rules of thumb for setting rents, you must look to the rental housing market itself when you set rents today. In other words, with rents no longer contingent upon the value of your investment or upon your costs for maintaining the property, you have to familiarize yourself with what other people are getting for their rentals and charge accordingly. You can't expect to get $800 a month for your

$80,000 house if other owners are renting similar houses for $500, and some of those are going begging. The market isn't there.

Setting rents nowadays involves learning about the rents charged for dwellings similar to yours in location, amenities, and upkeep. To find out what they are, you have to do a market survey of sorts. Check newspaper advertising periodically, ask people at your rental property owners' association, ask other owners you know, and inspect other properties yourself in the area. When you have done all that, you will know what constitutes a competitive rent for your dwelling, and you won't have to wonder after it's rented whether you could have charged more.

Remember that when you set any rent, you are virtually fixing it at one level for a 12-month period, so do treat this process with the seriousness it deserves. Don't be afraid to set your rent high, because anyone who looks at the place will tell you if the rent is too high, whereas they won't say a word if it's too low. You can easily lower the rent any time you want, but you can't always raise it so easily.

The decision to charge a certain rent is yours, and if it is a deliberate, informed decision, you can trust yourself to find the right rent.

RAISING RENTS

If you are at all like most landlords and landladies, you dislike rent raises more than any other aspect of this business because of the tenant dissatisfaction and resentment they frequently cause. Statistics show that landlords and landladies have an aversion to raising rents, for not only have rents failed to keep pace with percentage increases in property values over the years, they haven't even kept pace with the consumer price index. In other words, no matter what people in general think about rent levels, no matter how shrill their cries for rent control, landlords and landladies have actually been both lax and restrained in raising rents. Consequently, the profitability of rental property is shrinking perceptibly, and residential income property is becoming less attractive as an investment.

There's no good reason for you to stop disliking rent raises, but you should come to accept them as a necessary element in the conduct of your landlording business, an element made absolutely necessary by the impact of inflation on your expenses. Since your very business survival depends upon your being able to meet these increased expenses with increased revenues, you have no choice but to raise your rents.

You must expect that any raise may expose you to charges of profiteering and may precipitate a whole host of tenant complaints, but you must learn to cope with these problems unless you have some perverse desire to subsidize your tenants, in effect, for the dubious privilege of serving as their landlord or landlady, or unless you wish to invest your money and time in a business venture which only loses money. You are in this business to make a profit, aren't you? It certainly is not worth the worry, the risk, the trouble, the time, or the expense otherwise.

To have the desired effect, raising rents requires a policy as carefully outlined as your rent collection policy, one which is calculated to minimize tenant dissatisfaction and resentment. Rent raises under this policy should occasion neither a mass revolt nor a mass exodus of your tenants because they should come to understand that your rent raises are fair, and therefore, acceptable. This policy should involve five elements: careful preparation, proper timing, reasonable increments, amicable notices, and personal delivery.

• Careful preparation for rent raises consists of much more than merely preparing the notices to change terms of tenancy. That's the smallest part of preparation and the least time-consuming. Actually, careful preparation should continue year-round. As soon as you give one increase, you should already be preparing for the next one. Here's what you do to prepare — Prepare by keeping up with your bookkeeping every month so you know how much your expenses are and how much you need to raise the rents to operate profitably and also so you can refer to your expenses knowledgeably when you must discuss with your tenants your reasons for raising the rent. Prepare by keeping track of market conditions in your area so you know what current rents are for other similar rentals. Prepare by beginning a rumor that the rent will increase to a level higher than what you anticipate, so the tenants are relieved when they learn later how small the increase was in comparison to what they had expected. Prepare by telling your tenants exactly when they can expect the rent to increase. Prepare by charging new tenants at the anticipated higher rents so that when the rents are raised for everyone else to those market levels, or close to them (because good long-term tenants are hard to find and cost you far less in many ways than short-termers do, give them special consideration when you're raising rents; keep their rents $5–20 below market levels), you can indicate to your old tenants that new tenants have already been paying higher rents. With such preparation, you should be able to forestall most charges tenants might make that your increase was unfair and irresponsible.

• The proper time to raise rents is always when tenants are expecting an increase. More than at any other time, they expect increases when there has been a change of ownership, so give them an increase then if one is justifiable, but take a month first to become acquainted with the building and determine whether an increase is, in fact, justifiable.

Once when I was a new student of landlording and reluctant to raise rents at all, I waited twenty months after buying a building before making a well warranted increase, from $165 to $185, and when I did so, one irate tenant called to complain. She said she had expected me to raise the rents when I bought the building almost two years before, but coming when it did, the increase was a complete surprise to her and therefore totally unfair. How do you argue with that kind of reasoning? You don't. Clearly, though, I had done things wrong. I had assumed that an impersonal increase notice and all that elapsed time since their last increase would be sufficient for the tenants to accept a new rent raise unquestioningly. Of course, they weren't sufficient because tenants were not expecting an increase.

You should raise your rents when tenants expect increases, and you should condition them to expect increases like clockwork one year after the rents were last raised. Following this policy, you might want to stagger the increases throughout the year by scheduling them to coincide with the anniversary of each tenant's arrival; that way you manage to spread the repercussions. If possible, time your rent increases to coincide with some improvements you are making to the property so the tenants will believe they are getting something more for their money and will complain less at having to pay more.

Proper timing refers to the cycle of increases and to tenant conditioning, and it also refers to the actual moment when the official written rent increase notice is timed to reach the tenants. That best time is just after they have paid their rent, at least 30 days before the increase goes into effect, or, if possible, 60 days before (give lessees similar notice before their lease expires). Your tenants will appreciate 60 days' notice, for they will feel far less threatened when you give them that much time to consider their alternatives. They will have a whole month to look around before they even have to give notice that they intend to move. Such a strategy will lessen the tension and win as much of their cooperation as you can possibly expect it to.

• Having carefully prepared for the increase, you will know what rents are reasonable for your rentals and you will also then know approximately how much the raise should be. Because you have to take many factors into consideration when you calculate any rent increase and because your final figure will usually be the result of numerous compromises, you may want to select an increment which is psychologically more acceptable to your tenants. The more acceptable numbers are those which are not multiples of five. $12, for example, is better than $10 or $15. $18 is better than $15 or $20. Such figures lead tenants to believe that their increases have been carefully calculated to match actual increases in operating expenses rather then to include still more arbitrary profit for the owners.

You are taking a calculated risk of creating vacancies with any raise you give, but that risk increases somewhat if the rent increase exceeds either 10% or the consumer price index, whichever is greater. If you have timidly lagged behind the marketplace and you now have to raise your rents higher than those guidelines to approach a reasonable rent schedule, you may want to do so even knowing full well that some tenants are going to vacate. Wish them well, and then don't get yourself into the same bind again.

Raise your rents on an annual basis from then on.

• Besides preparing carefully, timing properly, and calculating reasonable increases, you should announce your raises officially in writing using honest, sympathetic notices. The notice itself is the culmination of all your work, and it should reflect the great care you have put into all the preparation thus far. The notice should soften the blow with some reasons for the raise and an expression of your personal concern about the possible hardships the increase might cause.

Use a cold, impersonal, legal notice like the "Notice to Change Terms of Tenancy" in the back of the book if you want, but add to it your own personal message. Mention the tenant

Richard and Mary,

Sorry we have to raise your rent. We want to continue maintaining your place as best we can, but with prices going up the way they are, we just have to raise it. I am giving you two months' notice to give you an opportunity to look around at other places. I hope you'll decide to stay here, of course.

— Lester

NOTICE TO CHANGE TERMS OF TENANCY

To RICHARD & MARY RENTER , Tenant in Possession

456 SWEET ST.

LITTLETOWN, CA

YOU ARE HEREBY NOTIFIED that the terms of tenancy under which you occupy the above-described premises are to be changed.

Effective APRIL 1 , 19 84 , your rent will be increased by $23 per month, from $275* per month to $298* per month, payable in advance.

Dated this 1ST day of FEBRUARY , 19 84 .

Lester Landlord
Owner/Manager

* *When rent is paid on or before the third day following the rent due date, you may take a $20 discount.*

by first name in a handwritten aside and apologize for the increase, saying that you are trying to maintain the tenant's dwelling as best you can, but that it is impossible to do so unless you raise rents.

Or you might want to type up your own complete notice using personal wording like this: "As you know, we are living in a period of runaway inflation, and even though I do my best to keep costs down, there's no way I can reduce the expenses of this building back to what they were a year ago. I have absorbed these increases as long as I could, but now I am forced to increase your rent by $_____, or _____%, from $_____ per month to $_____ per month, effective _____, 19 ____."

Remember that if you use any rental agreement or lease form which has a discount provision as do those in the back of this book, the increase should be based on the gross or non-discounted rental figure and not on the discounted amount that you are accustomed to collecting when the tenant pays on time. You might want to remind the tenant of this situation by stating it directly on the notice, asterisking the rental figures and explaining below as follows: "*When rent is paid on or before the third day following the rent due date, you may take a $_____ discount."

Remember also that if you collected your tenants' last month's rent when they moved in, the sum you originally collected will be insufficient to cover the increased rent which will be in effect during their last month of tenancy. To avoid misunderstandings later, advise them that they should pay the increase for that last month's rent as soon as the new rent becomes effective.

• You may deliver a rent increase by mail or in person, but personal delivery is certainly preferable because you can attest to the delivery having been completed yourself and you can discuss the reasons for the increase with your tenants on a personal level.

Your raising rents doesn't suddenly metamorphose you into a greedy, unscrupulous monster of a landlord or landlady. Rather, it means that you are a good business person who understands the nature of the business you are in. You understand that you can lose money in this business if you want to, just as you can in any other business, and that no one will care, least of all your tenants. You understand that no one is going to nominate you for the Landlord or Landlady of the Year Award just because you leave your rents low and that no one is going to tell you that your rents are too low, either.

When was the last time one of your tenants told you the rent was too low and offered to pay more? Don't wait for it to happen. It won't. Just because tenants don't volunteer to pay more, however, doesn't mean that the dwellings they occupy aren't worth more rent and that they can't pay more rent. You are the only one to judge, and you alone must take the initiative necessary to raise your rents.

CONTROLLING RENTS

Can you imagine any politician proposing wage controls without price controls (trade unions might bicker among themselves about some matters, but this would unite them like filings on a lodestone) or proposing ceilings on the prices of single-family dwellings (homeowners would take up their Saturday-night specials to defend their right to sell their castles at fair market value)? Both are such absurd proposals that any politicians espousing them today would be stripped of their brown shirts and whisked off to asylums to babble and cavort with the other lunatics.

Yet, how many politicans are there who seriously propose rent control as the solution to the rising cost of rental housing, a scheme every bit as illogical as controlling wages without controlling prices and as utterly ridiculous as putting a ceiling on the prices of houses? In effect, rent control does both. It limits the landlord's and landlady's "wages" without affecting their expenses, and it limits artificially the value of their rental property.

Politicians who support rent control don't see it that way, however, and they don't see themselves as fascists, either. They see themselves as Robin Hoods, championing the cause of impoverished, victimized renters in the interminable and righteous struggle against wealthy landlords and landladies. That's you, remember. They hear the caterwauling of their tenant constituents lamenting the hardships of living on a fixed income and decide that the simplest way to appease these people is to limit the obscene profits, fix the income of the monopolistic property owners. You again. Although do-gooder politicians are only greasing the squeaky wheels in their communities when they act to control rents and are ignoring the long-term ramifications of what they are doing, they are in truth attempting to silence those noisy tenants the only way they can, with a specious solution to a large and complex problem.

The problem we all face, tenants, politicians, and rental property owners alike, is not constantly increasing rents, and the solution to constantly increasing rents is not rent control. The real problems are a shortage of housing and an increase in the many expenses involved in landlording, from toilet parts to interest rates. The solutions are to build more housing, to control inflation, and to subsidize the housing of those who are truly poor, but obviously these are formidable solutions, ones which local politicians cannot effect easily or inexpensively, if at all. Rent control, on the other hand, is easy to enact and relatively inexpensive to administer, and it provides immediate relief. So what if it does exacerbate the real problems. So what if it does victimize those who own rental property. So what if it does favor all tenants regardless of their financial need. It appeases the people with the votes. Therefore, it is an ideal political solution for harrassed politicians struggling to cope with what appears to be a local problem they can handle, and it is a solution which appears to be gaining more and more vocal proponents.

Whenever it becomes an issue in your area, you would be wise to become involved in the political process which will determine whether rent control will be adopted, and if so, what form it will take. Any talk of rent control should bring you to your feet before rent control itself brings you to your knees. Support the political efforts of your rental property owners' association. Attend hearings. Ask the reference librarian at your local library to help you find some of the many studies on the subject. Write letters to your politicians and to the editor of your local newspaper citing certain rent control case studies and outlining your own views relative to the local situation. If, at last, you sense that some form of rent control is inevitable, become involved with the shaping of the measure so it will be easier to live with. Face the fact that we live in a world which is more consumer-oriented then ever before, and expect to have to give a little.

Odious as rent control sounds to us landlords and landladies, conjuring up images of abandoned properties and bankruptcy, it may be written as a compromise to everyone involved. Tenants fear quantum leaps in rents, increases of 30% and 50% a year, and you can hardly blame them. Landlords and landladies fear being forced to maintain rents at current base levels *ad infinitum* and eventually losing their buildings. But some form of rent control might assuage both those fears.

Would you balk, for example, at rent control which would apply only to buildings with six or more units and would allow owners to pass through all increased expenses and prorations of improvements, as well as to increase rents no more than 15% per year? That wouldn't be hard to live with, would it? Well, that is rent control just as much as is a measure which requires you to roll back your rents to what they were twelve months ago and then to keep them there forever. Compromises are possible, even desirable at times, in order for everyone involved to save face.

Finally, if rent control is adopted in any area where you own rental property, take the time to learn all you can about it. Are certain sizes of rental dwellings exempt from controls? Under what circumstances may you raise rents? What procedures are there for grievances? How are evictions affected by the controls? The rent control regulations and the bureaucrats who administer them will answer these and other pertinent questions you might have. Be more familiar with these regulations than your tenants are. Be cooperative with the authorities, work within the law, seek to change it, and buy more properties in anticipation that the controls will be lifted when people come to their senses.

Don't panic. Don't give up. Shrewd owners study such predicaments thoroughly and learn how to profit from them. There's always a way.

HELPING TENANTS MOVE OUT

Tenants come and tenants go with some degree of frequency every year (turnover averages 45% for unfurnished rentals), and when they do either, you as the landlord or landlady involved have certain responsibilities you should be aware of and be prepared to carry out. You know pretty well what those responsibilities are when tenants move in and you probably pay close attention to them then, but chances are good that you know only superficially what your responsibilities are when tenants move out and you pay little attention to them.

Except in the most perfunctory ways, we all tend to neglect helping tenants when they move out because we are generally disappointed at their moving and regard it as a desertion of sorts and also because their moving is overshadowed by our simultaneous preparation for new tenants, something we regard as much more important. While the pitfalls you face when tenants move in may indeed be more momentous than those you face when they move out, pitfalls do exist when they move out, too, pitfalls which can cause you unnecessary aggravation and cost you wasted time and money.

Ask small claims court judges about the landlord-tenant cases they hear, and they will tell you that almost all such cases involve disputes arising from tenants' moving out. Sometimes the landlord or landlady is bringing the case and sometimes it's the tenants, but almost always the cases are related to the tenants' moving out. Either the deposits weren't refunded as they should have been, or the deposits were insufficient to cover the charges due, or there were misunderstandings about the condition of the dwelling before the tenants moved in as compared to its condition after they moved out, or there were misunderstandings about the meaning of the expressions "reasonably clean and undamaged" and "normal wear and tear," or there were misunderstandings about ownership of certain contents of the dwelling, or there were misunderstandings about whether the deposits could be used for rent. That's altogether too much misunderstanding, if you ask me, and even though it cannot all be avoided, much of it can be with some preparation and some pointed communication.

You may lessen the chances of misunderstanding every time your tenants move out by following these six steps:

NOTICE OF INTENTION TO VACATE   Date __9/13/85__

TO: __LESTER LANDLORD__

FROM: __RICHARD AND MARY RENTER__

Please be advised that on __SEPTEMBER 30, 1985__ we intend to move from our residence at __456 SWEET ST., LITTLETOWN__ .

We understand that our rental agreement calls for __15__ days' notice before we move and that this is __17__ days' notice. We understand that we responsible for paying rent through the end of the notice period called for in the rental agreement or until another tenant approved by the management has moved in, whichever comes first.

We understand that our deposits will be refunded within __7__ days after we have moved out completely and returned our keys to the management, so long as we leave our dwelling reasonably clean and undamaged.

Reasons for leaving: __WE BOUGHT A DUPLEX!__

Forwarding address: __1610 DURANT, LITTLETOWN__

In accordance with our rental agreement, we agree to allow the management to show our dwelling to prospective tenants at any and all reasonable times.

Tenant __Richard Renter__
Tenant __Mary Renter__

Received 9/13/85 LL

Prepare at move-in time for the move-out.
Provide a written "Notice of Intention to Vacate" for tenants to sign.
Advise tenants how to get their deposits back.
Inspect the dwelling and itemize its deficiencies.
Calculate the charges.
Return the deposits promptly.

• *Prepare at move-in time for the move-out.*

Avoid this kind of misunderstanding: "Mrs. Landlady, we're moving to Houston next Tuesday and we'd like to use our deposits to pay for the rest of the rent we owe you from last month." "You can't use your deposit for rent, Mr. Renter. That's money I'm supposed to return to you after you leave the place clean." "Oh, don't worry, we'll leave everything spic 'n' span."

When your tenants moved in, you were already preparing for them to move out, whether you ever thought about their moving out at some future time or not. You stipulated the notice period necessary for them to advise you they were moving; you asked for proper notice in writing; you inspected the dwelling with the tenants before they moved in and you noted its condition and inventory in writing; you collected adequate deposits; and you informed the tenants that those deposits were not to be considered as last month's rent. You did each of these things for one very good reason — to avoid misunderstandings when they were ready to move out.

Should you fail to establish these rules at the very beginning of your relationship, you will have to expect misunderstandings later, for you cannot expect tenants to know what they should and should not do when they move out unless you inform them. Isn't it logical for them to think that their deposits should cover their final rent payment, especially if the two are identical sums? Isn't it logical for them to expect all their deposits back as soon as they move out? And why should they have to give you any notice? You'll only rerent it the very next day anyway. Discuss the end-game rules with tenants before you ever rent to them and put those rules in writing.

• *Provide a written notice for them to sign.*

Avoid this kind of misunderstanding: "Hello, Lester? This is Richard Renter. I just called to tell you we're all moved out and we'd like to get our deposits back." "That's news to me, Richard. You never gave me any notice. You only told me you might be moving sometime soon. You didn't say exactly when." "Don't you remember last month when I told you we were planning to move before school started? Isn't that notice enough?"

The primary reason for requiring written notice from your vacating tenants is to tie them to a specific moving date so you can begin making preparations to rerent the dwelling without delay. Verbal notice may be satisfactory in some cases, but written notice is always better. It's definite, it's incontestable, and it's useful in court.

Some tenants will take the time to compose a letter of their own to advise you dutifully of their plans to move out. Accept it so long as it includes the anticipated moving date, the address of the place they're renting from you, and the signatures of those who signed the rental agreement. But because few people know how to communicate in writing anymore, you should provide a ready-made form for your tenants to fill out in order to make your written notice requirement easier to satisfy. When they give you verbal notice, supply them with one of your forms and ask them to fill it out.

The form I use also includes space for tenants to indicate why they are leaving, information

September 13, 1985

Dear *Richard and Mary,*

Moving time is always a busy time, and you will have lots of things on your mind now that you have given notice you are moving. One of those things undoubtedly is how to get your deposits back promptly. In your case, they amount to $ *225.00* .

Contrary to what some tenants believe, we WANT to return your deposits, and we WILL return them to you so long as you leave your place "reasonably clean and undamaged." That's what your rental agreement says and that's what we will do. You're probably wondering, however, what "reasonably clean and undamaged" means, so we'd like to tell you how we interpret it and tell you also what you should do to get your deposits back.

"Reasonably clean" to us means as clean as you would leave your dwelling if you knew your best friend or favorite aunt were going to move in after you. To get it that clean, we expect you to clean the appliances, stove hood, and cabinets (under sinks, too) both inside and out; remove all non-adhesive shelf paper; use an appropriate cleanser on the showers, tubs, toilets, sinks, mirrors, and medicine cabinets (inside as well); dust the ceilings (for cobwebs), baseboards, window sills, and closet shelving; wash the kitchen and bathroom walls, and spot-clean the walls in other rooms; wash the light fixtures and windows inside and out; vacuum the floors; scrub the floor tile or linoleum; sweep the entry, patio, storage enclosure, and garage; remove all personal belongings (including clothes hangers and cleaning supplies); and dispose of all trash. PLEASE DO NOT CLEAN THE DRAPERIES, SHAMPOO THE CARPETS, OR WAX THE FLOORS. We prefer to do those cleaning chores ourselves, and you will not be charged for our doing them.

"Reasonably undamaged" to us means that items which we have supplied should not be missing (including light bulbs) or broken; that there should be no new burns, cracks, chips, or holes in the dwelling or its furnishings; and that the paint on the walls should be sufficient to last at least two years from the time they were last painted. PLEASE DO NOT REMOVE ANYTHING YOU HAVE ATTACHED TO THE WALLS OR CEILINGS WITHOUT FIRST TALKING TO US, and please try to avoid nicking the paint in the halls and doorways as you move things out.

After you have returned the keys, we would like to inspect your dwelling with you to check it for cleanliness and damage, and unless we have to get prices on special work or replacements, we will refund all deposits owed to you at that time.

We expect you to have moved out completely by *September 30, 1985* . Because we are making arrangements for new tenants to move in soon after that, we would appreciate hearing from you immediately if your moving plans should change.

We hope your moving goes smoothly, and we wish you happiness in your new home.

Hate to lose you!

Sincerely,

Lester Landlord

which might prove useful to you in case there's something you might do to get the tenants to stay, should you be so inclined.

• *Advise them how to get their deposits back.*

Avoid this kind of misunderstanding: "What do you mean you're going to deduct $35 from our deposit? The place is spotless. We spent $15 on supplies and cleaned in there for six hours." "I admit it's clean, but just look at these drapes. They were new only last year and now they've shrunk so much I couldn't even use them at a toga party. You weren't supposed to wash them." "Well, how were we supposed to know? You never told us what to do."

Some of the conditions you impose on your tenants for the return of their deposits are necessarily subjective and open to interpretation. You may have explained what they were way back when the tenants first moved in, but since time tends to muddle recollections and since the tenants were hardly thinking then about moving out, you should review your conditions once more while they are thinking much more specifically about moving out and are more concerned about getting their deposits back.

Discuss your conditions with them in person or send them a letter like the form shown here outlining your conditions or, better yet, do both. Whatever you do, remind them of the amount of their deposit which is at stake and convince them that you will refund it promptly. Even if they have failed to meet certain conditions already and you are legally entitled to keep most of their deposits, you should establish some amount they will receive if they return the place to you reasonably clean and undamaged. Give them an incentive to do just that.

Because tenants will seldom clean the draperies, shampoo the carpets, wax the floors, or remove their wall and ceiling attachments to your satisfaction, you would be wise to give them very precise instructions for performing these jobs or tell them not to bother at all (include the cost of doing this work in a higher first month's rent for each incoming tenant). Well-meaning tenants may attempt a job and bungle it so badly that you will have to spend extra time and money setting things right, and the tenants, for their part, will expect a full refund regardless of the extra work they have caused you. That kind of situation frustrates everyone involved and can easily be avoided.

• *Inspect the dwelling and itemize its deficiencies.*

Avoid this kind of misunderstanding: "That oven was dirtier when I moved in." "I know it was clean because I remember cleaning it myself." "Well, I cleaned it after I moved out and I say you aren't going to charge me for a dirty oven! I'll take you to court! You can't prove anything anyway. It's your word against mine."

If you can possibly arrange for the vacating tenants to accompany you as you inspect their dwelling to determine deposit refunds, do so. You can then explain precisely what is wrong with the place, and you can give them the choice of correcting those deficiencies themselves or paying for the corrections.

Tenants' conceptions of what their dwellings looked like when they moved in are as likely to be mistaken as yours, but from quite the opposite viewpoint. That's why a proper move-out inspection requires a record of a prior inspection attested by the tenants. If one is lacking, there is no standard for comparison. Did the vacating tenants put twelve burns in the carpet or only nine? Did they break the toilet tank top or did their predecessors do it? Were there working lightbulbs in every fixture when they moved in or were the bulbs mostly burned out?

There are two good ways to prove whether the current tenants are at fault. One is to take an extensive array of "fat-farm" (before and after) photographs and then to play "hocus focus" with them, and the other is to use a form like the Condition & Inventory Checksheet which lists the defects and contents of the dwelling when the tenants moved in and can be used again when they move out to determine the final reckoning.

If you use photographs for comparison, take enough of them beforehand, at least two per room, and date them. Then repeat only those shots which show evidence of damages after the tenants move out. If they leave the place in good condition and you expect to return the deposits, don't waste film taking any more photographs.

The Condition & Inventory Checksheet should have been filled out in triplicate before the tenants moved in, one copy for the tenants to keep, and two for the landlord or landlady to use at move-out time. Retrieve those same two sheets from the tenants' file and itemize in duplicate all the various deficiencies you notice this time during your tour of inspection, from holes in the screens to holes in the walls. Then you can make direct line-by-line comparisons of the previous condition with the current condition and analyze the discrepancies.

• *Calculate the charges.*

Avoid this kind of misunderstanding: "How come you kept $30 from my deposit? What was it for?" "You didn't leave the place clean." "We did too." "No, come to think of it, you did leave it pretty clean. Well, you must have broken something then." "Why should I pay you $30 for something when you can't even remember exactly what it was? Don't you have a receipt or anything?"

Having itemized the rental's deficiencies, you can begin calculating approximately how much to charge the departing tenants to restore their dwelling to its original splendor minus normal wear and tear, of course. These calculations will be estimates, naturally, but they should suffice for determining deposit refunds in most cases, especially since you are trying to expedite the refunds. Those tenants who request calculations based upon actual, rather than estimated, expenditures will just have to wait longer for their refunds.

Most of the time you will be able to calculate what the deductions and charges should be without ever having to contact a contractor or supplier. You'll have a pretty good idea how much things such as towel bars and lightbulbs cost and you'll know approximately how long chores like cleaning an oven take.

Be reasonable with your estimates. Lightbulbs don't cost $2 apiece just yet and oven cleaning shouldn't take twelve hours to do. Remember, too, that you should charge tenants only for the useful life remaining in an item which is broken or missing, not for its replacement cost. If two-year-old draperies are missing, charge tenants for only half, rather than all, the cost of replacement. Likewise, because interior paint jobs should last two years when

Condition & Inventory Checksheet Dated January 15, 1983

Tenant Name *Richard + Mary Renter*   Address *456 Sweet St.*

Date Moved in *January 15, 1983* Date Notice Given *9-13-85* Date Moved Out *9-30-85*

Abbreviations:

Air Conditioner, A/C	Dinette, Din	Hood, Hd	Shades, Sh
Bed, Bd	Dishwasher, Dish	Just Painted, JP	Sofa, Sfa
Broken, Brk	Disposer, Disp	Lamp, Lmp	Stove, Stv
Carpet, Cpt	Drapes, Drp	Lightbulbs, LtB	Table, Tbl
Chair, Ch	Dryer, Dry	Linoleum, Lino	Tile, Tl
Chest, Chst	Fair, F	Nightstand, Ntst	Venetian Blinds, VB
Clean, Cl	Good, G	OK, OK	Washer, Wsh
Cracked, Cr	Heater, Htr	Poor, P	Waxed, Wxt
Curtains, Ctn	Hole, H	Refrigerator, Ref	Wood, Wd

Circle applicable rooms and enter appropriate abbreviations:

	Walls, Doors cond.	chgs.	Floors cond.	chgs.	Windows, Screens, Coverings cond.	chgs.	Lt. Fixt. cond.	chgs.	Inventory: Appliances, Furniture item	cond.	chgs.
(Liv. Rm.)	OK		Cl Cpt		Wind Cl Drp, new Cl rod, Cl Drp W 12.00	Brk	OK LtB G		⊖		
(Kitchen)	OK		Wxt Lino		Scrn OK, Sh G		OK LtB G		Ref (on loan) Stv Hd	Cl Cl Cl	
(Bath)	JP		Wxt Tl		Scrn OK, Sh G		OK LtB G		⊖		
Dining											
(BR 1)	OK		Cl Cpt		Scrn OK, Cl Drp		⊖		⊖		
BR 2											
BR 3											
Other											
Charges	⊖		⊖		12.00		⊖				⊖

Total Itemized Charges ___12.00___

Other Charges Not Itemized
 (Broken Locks, Dirty Garage, etc.
 Explain on Backside) ___⊖___
Deduction for Improper Notice ___⊖___
Deduction for Missing Keys ___⊖___
Total Deductions & Charges ___12.00___

Total Deposits **$228.00**
Less Deductions & Charges 12.00
Deposit Refund or
 (Amount Owed) **$216.00**

Tenants hereby acknowledge that they have read this Condition & Inventory Checksheet, agree that the condition and contents of the above-mentioned rental dwelling are without exception as represented herein, understand that they are liable for any damage done to this dwelling as outlined in their Lease or Rental Agreement, and have received a copy of this checksheet.

Owner *Lester Landlord*   Tenant *Richard Renter*

By ___*page 3 of 3*___   Tenant *Mary Renter*

people are moving in and out, charge those tenants whose one-year-old paint job needs repainting for just half of a new paint job. After all, you had half the use out of those drapes and that paint job before they were ruined.

• *Return the deposits promptly.*

Avoid this kind of misunderstanding: "Where's our deposit, Les? It's been three days since we moved out." "I've been so busy I haven't had a chance to check your apartment. Is everything all right there?" "Everything's perfect." "OK, I'll send you the money tomorrow." — "But, your honor, I sent them back their deposit right away and later I found all this damage." "Mr. Landlord, you are to be commended for returning your tenant's deposits so promptly, but you should have inspected the apartment first. I can't possibly award you a judgment because when you refunded your tenants' deposit, you actually acknowledged that you were accepting the condition of their dwelling and were settling all debts with them, whether you understood that or not. Be more careful next time."

Do not return tenants' deposits until you are absolutely certain that you have calculated everything that might be deducted. If you have returned the deposits and you later learn that the tenants have broken a $25 refrigerator door shelf, you have no legal grounds for collection, and as a practical matter, you might as well forget it, too. Once you have inspected the dwelling, however, and have subtracted all the deductions and charges, there's no sense in procrastinating about the matter any longer. Even though most state and provincial laws which govern rental deposit refunds allow you a very reasonable 14 days' time to return and account for the deposits after tenants move out, you should try to return them sooner if you can. Tenants who are moving likely need the money more than you do and they appreciate receiving it without delay.

Remember that all those tenants' deposits you hold are not yours. They have been entrusted to you in good faith to insure tenants' compliance with the terms of their rental agreements. If they have indeed complied, then there's no reason to keep the money any longer. Refund it promptly. Whenever possible, combine the inspection calculation, and refund steps together and do them both at one time.

You'll have to forgo an acquaintance with your local small claims court judge if you follow these six steps for fulfilling your responsibilities when tenants move out, but you'll be well compensated. You'll be saving yourself a great deal of aggravation, as well as both time and money, and you'll be earning yourself a reputation as a fair landlord or landlady, too. That's good business. People will remember your fairness and will recommend your rentals to others, and the tenants you have will feel relieved of any worry about their own deposits.

GETTING PROBLEM TENANTS OUT

Problem tenants are the bane of the landlording business. They are always testing you. They are the last ones to pay and the first ones to gripe. They're the ones who change their locks, paint their walls flat black, adopt animals, or invite their friends to move in with them, all without saying a word to you. They can be noisy, contrary, destructive, malevolent, or hypocritical all at once or bit by bit. They enjoy their music loud, especially between midnight and sunup, and they can cuss as well as any guttersnipe, but what they seem to enjoy most of all is misquoting landlord-tenant laws to you. They love those incredulous looks on your face when they tell you what your legal responsibilities are as their landlord or landlady.

Have you ever encountered such people?

Unless you inherit them from a previous owner, you never will encounter them if you practice prevention whenever possible, if you select tenants carefully, enforce agreements assertively, and collect rents promptly. Remember that in landlord-tenant relations, an ounce of prevention is worth many pounds of cure, for cures are costly, agonizing, time-consuming, crisis-oriented, and sometimes downright dangerous to life, limb, and property. Prevention methods, on the other hand, are not cheap either, but neither are they costly. They may cause dyspepsia at times, but they are hardly agonizing. They do take some time to do, but they save much time in the long run. What's most important, though, is that they serve to eliminate crises altogether, and they never endanger anyone or anything.

When you recognize that you do have problem tenants with some of the characteristics mentioned above, however, you cannot think in terms of prevention. You have to think in terms of cures. You have no choice really. Either you get rid of them or you prepare yourself for complaints from the neighbors, deterioration of your property, departures of your good tenants, your bankruptcy, your capitulation, or all five. Humor them, ignore them, pacify them no longer. Marshall your forces, steel your will, and think in terms of getting them out. When you do, be mindful of the following:

• Be more interested in getting problem tenants out than in teaching them a lesson. They don't learn.

NOTICE
to Perform Covenant

TO HENRY & GLADYS ANGEL , TENANT IN POSSESSION:

PLEASE TAKE NOTICE that you have violated the following covenant(s) in your Lease or Rental Agreement:

TENANTS AGREE NOT TO PAINT OR ALTER THEIR
DWELLING WITHOUT FIRST GETTING OWNERS'
WRITTEN PERMISSION

You are hereby required within __3__ days to perform the aforesaid covenant(s) or to deliver up possession of the premises now held and occupied by you, being those premises situated in the City of LITTLETOWN , County of SADDLEBACK , State/Province of CALIFORNIA , commonly known as 460 SWEET STREET .

If you fail to do so, legal proceedings will be instituted against you to recover said premises and such damages as the law allows.

This notice is intended to be a __3__ day notice to perform the aforesaid covenant. It is not intended to terminate or forfeit the Lease or Rental Agreement under which you occupy said premises. If, after legal proceedings, said premises are recovered from you, the owners will try to rent said premises for the best possible rent, giving you credit for sums received and holding you liable for any deficiencies arising during the term of said Lease or Rental Agreement.

Dated this __6TH__ day of __APRIL__ , 19 __84__ .

Lester Landlord
Owner/Manager

PROOF OF SERVICE

I, the undersigned, being at least 18 years of age, declare under penalty of perjury that I served the Notice to Perform Covenant, of which this is a true copy, on the above-mentioned Tenant in Possession in the manner(s) indicated below:

☑ On __APRIL 5__ , 19 __84__ , I handed the Notice to the tenant.
☐ I handed the Notice to a person of suitable age and discretion at the tenant's residence/business on _____ , 19 _____ .
☐ I posted the Notice in a conspicuous place at the tenant's residence on _____ , 19 _____ .
☐ I sent by certified mail a true copy of the Notice to the tenant at his place of residence on _____ , 19 _____ .

Executed on __APRIL 5__ , 19 __84__ , at LITTLETOWN, CA.

Lester Landlord

• Be pragmatic and businesslike with nonpaying tenants rather than feeling wronged and challenged. You will either lose their challenge or pay a big price to win. Suppress your feelings. This is a business matter.

• Try to stop losing rent money as soon as possible instead of relying solely on the certainty of an eviction to cut your losses later. Be relentless. Hound those tenants.

• Do follow the adage, "Spare the evictions, spoil the tenants," but recognize that "evictions" can mean alternative eviction methods as well as conventional ones.

LEGAL ALTERNATIVES TO EVICTION

You can always hope that a Notice to Pay Rent or Quit (used when tenants are in arrears — see Chapter 5), a Notice to Perform Covenant (used when tenants break their rental agreement), or a Notice to Terminate Tenancy (used when you wish to terminate a rental agreement for any reason at all — check its legality in your area) will precipitate the response you desire, but don't bet any big money on it. Like all consumers nowadays, tenants are better informed than ever before, and many know that you simply cannot legally put them out in just a couple of days. Consequently, they tend to linger beyond the period specified in the notice, and you then seemingly have only one alternative — eviction.

Even if you handle an eviction yourself, it will cost you around $50 in out-of-pocket expenses for filing and process-serving fees, not to mention what the lost rent will amount to. It will take you time to prepare all the papers and time to present the papers to the court, too. Finally, when it's all over with, after you have painstakingly followed every obligatory legal step, from serving the proper notice to accompanying the marshals as they put the widows and orphans out on the street, you begin to believe that you and your tenants have been duped because all of you have wound up losers in one way or another.

Take heart. There are other alternatives you might try to get problem tenants out without ever going to court, alternatives which seem to be unreliable at first because they follow neither a clear-cut procedure nor a precise timetable and they require a somewhat artful approach. Some might even say they require a bit of chicanery. Yet they work surprisingly well and, what's more, they don't make losers of everyone involved. These other alternatives you might try are talking, bribery, intimidation, and throwing a temper tantrum. On third thought, forget the last one. It's legal all right, but generally it's not very effective. Let's consider just the first three: talking, bribery, and intimidation.

Remember that with any of these methods you are trying essentially to convince your tenants that it is more advantageous for them to leave than to stay put. After all, if it is more advantageous for them to stay put, they will do exactly that, wouldn't you?

Talking — All right, how do you convince tenants to vacate by talking? Go to their dwelling. Do not summon them to yours and do not talk with them by telephone. Make sure when you arrive that the decision-maker of the group is there. Ask them to explain first of all what has happened, why they have broken their agreement with you. Then outline the situation matter-of-factly as you understand it and suggest some alternatives. After that, ask them what they would do if they were in your shoes. If they offer up some unacceptable solution, tell them frankly why it wouldn't work and pose your own. Try to be understanding and try to reach an agreement that allows them to save face. Give a little, take a little. Be both reasonable and businesslike.

If you cannot reach an agreement you consider fair, tell them you are left with no alternative but to evict them in court. Tell them you are loathe to go to that extreme because they

30-DAY NOTICE
to Terminate Tenancy

TO ___ERNEST PEABODY_____, TENANT IN POSSESSION:

PLEASE TAKE NOTICE that you are hereby required within 30 days to remove from and deliver up possession of the premises now held and occupied by you, being those premises situated in the City of ___LITTLETOWN___, County of ___SADDLEBACK___, State/Province of ___CALIFORNIA___, commonly known as ___462 SWEET ST.___.

This notice is intended for the purpose of terminating the Rental Agreement by which you now hold possession of the above-described premises, and should you fail to comply, legal proceedings will be instituted against you to recover possession, to declare said Rental Agreement forfeited, and to recover rents and damages for the period of the unlawful detention.

Please be advised that your rent on said premises is due and payable up to and including the date of termination of your tenancy under this notice, that being the ___30TH___ day of ___APRIL___, 19 ___84___.

Dated this ___31ST___ day of ___MARCH___, 19 ___84___.

Lester Landlord
_____
Owner/Manager

PROOF OF SERVICE

I, the undersigned, being at least 18 years of age, declare under penalty of perjury that I served the 30-Day Notice to Terminate Tenancy, of which this is a true copy, on the above-mentioned Tenant in Possession in the manner(s) indicated below:

☑ On ___MARCH 31___, 19 ___84___, I handed the Notice to the tenant.

☐ I handed the Notice to a person of suitable age and discretion at the tenant's residence/business on _____, 19 _____.

☐ I posted the Notice in a conspicuous place at the tenant's residence on _____, 19 _____.

☐ I sent by certified mail a true copy of the Notice to the tenant at his place of residence on _____, 19 _____.

Executed on ___March 31___, 19 ___84___, at ___LITTLETOWN, CA___.

Lester Landlord

will be identified to the local property owners' association as having been evicted, and it will be more difficult thenceforth for them to rent in the area. Their credit rating will suffer because you report all such matters to the credit bureau, and the bill collecting agency will begin hounding them. In addition, they will never again be able to answer honestly on rental applications that they have not been evicted. After stating these consequences candidly, see if the tenants still persist in being unreasonable. If so, depart and say, "I'm disappointed that you have left me no choice. I had very much hoped we could work something out." Don't get into an argument. Don't leave in a huff. Just go.

Your success or failure in using this maneuver will depend upon the kind of relationship you have already developed with your tenants, as well as upon your skills of persuasion. Tailor the appeal to the people you are dealing with. Above all, be firm and polite. Don't antagonize them. Don't call them names or impugn their ancestry. You may believe very strongly that they are doing you wrong, but keep your head. Swallow your pride. Keep the dialogue open-ended. If you cut off the dialogue, your impending eviction suit will be all the more difficult to pursue. You want the tenants to be available to be served with court papers as the cases progresses. You don't want to alienate them so much that they will avoid service and thereby delay your case.

Talking can work well for some people. I know a landlord who successfully convinced a motorcycle gang leader and his retinue to vacate a house they had rented under false pretenses. One evening the landlord brought over a case of beer and gingerly persuaded them that he was sympathetic with their wanting to remain but that he was being harrassed so much by the neighbors who were telephoning at all hours to tattle about what was happening at his house that he was falling asleep at work and was in danger of losing his job. He apologized about asking them to move out, but he said he just couldn't see any other way to end the neighbors' wee-hour phone calls. The gang moved out the following weekend. When the neighbors called to report that the motorcyclists were moving their things out, he rushed over there with two more cases of beer. They left the place spotless.

Perhaps you have already tried talking your tenants into leaving or you feel that talk just wouldn't work. Well, how about bribery?

Bribery — Bribery has several real advantages. It is quick and, comparatively speaking, it is inexpensive. If you required enough in deposits from your tenants before they moved in, you should, if you act fast, have money enough available from these deposits to pay the tenants for leaving. This was one of the reasons for requiring a deposit in the first place, wasn't it? Obviously, should you succeed in suing to evict them, the money judgment, including court costs, would be subtracted from their deposits, and they could expect to receive little or no money back. In fact, they'd probably owe you some. An offer to return what's left of their deposits after you deduct for the rent they owe you might be enough to get them moving.

Calculate approximately how much an eviction and lost rent would cost you (especially if an attorney is handling the case) before making your offer, and you'll likely find that a bribe will cost you far less. Even if you do have to sweeten the offer somewhat out of your own pocket because you have delayed so long that there's only a paltry deposit balance remaining of, say, less than $100 (few tenants would move for less), you will come out ahead by bribing them to leave and so will they.

There are some good variations on the bribery gambit, too. You might offer to store the tenants' goods in one of your garages or pay the rent at a miniwarehouse for a few months.

The tenants would then be free to stay with friends or relatives until they get back on their feet, and you'd have a dwelling available for a paying customer.

You might offer to arrange and pay for a U-Haul van and a small crew to move the tenants' possessions anywhere within fifty miles or so.

You might cut a $100 bill in half right before the tenants' eyes, give the tenants half, and keep half yourself until they have moved out completely on or before a designated date, or you might leave the entire $100 bill with a neutral party who has instructions to give it to the tenants if they move by a certain date. This ploy is dramatic enough to work, and it also circumvents many tenants' natural skepticism about whether you will really pay off or not. Naturally, you should never pay off until you have verified that they have in fact vacated.

You might offer to buy the tenants' TV, stereo, appliances, and furniture if they have fallen on hard times. This would unburden them enough so the move would be easier and so they would have the funds needed to pay their other wild-eyed creditors. Before consummating your purchase, however, you would be wise to determine whether the tenants' possessions are paid for or are being used as collateral for a loan. If they are paid for, ask for a bill of sale.

Intimidation — Another maneuver which is perfectly legal and ofttimes prompts tenants to vacate without your ever having to resort to the courts is intimidation. I don't mean hiring gorillas to scare your tenants out. I mean hiring the sheriff, marshal, or constable to scare your tenants out. How? Have the local law-enforcement officer serve your notices. Sure, you can serve the notices yourself, but you're too familiar a face to your tenants. You're simply not intimidating enough. You cannot possibly impress them with the gravity of the matter as much as can an armed and uniformed law-enforcement officer who's handing out a notice signed by you stipulating that the tenants have a fixed number of days to clear out. That is quite intimidating to most people. They simply do not want to get mixed up with the law if they can help it, and they frequently will mistake your notice for one which actually announces their eviction. It all looks so official and imperative.

For about $10 you can arrange to have a notice served by the law-enforcement officer who customarily serves process papers in your area. The officer will understandably take a few days longer to get around to serving the notice than you would if you were to do the serving yourself, but official service is more effective in getting action out of the tenants, and the nominal delay may be worth it.

A variation of this method involves the direct hiring of an off-duty law-enforcement officer to serve your notices. In most areas, officers may wear their uniforms while off duty and may act as process servers on their own. Inquire whether officers can and will moonlight doing this in your area. If you can find someone who does perform this service, your notices will be served more promptly than if you have to hire a bureaucracy as well.

ILLEGAL ALTERNATIVES

It some respects it's fortunate that there are laws to keep us landlords and landladies from acting rashly when we're trying to force bad tenants to move out. After being frustrated repeatedly, some of us might be driven to near distraction and feel compelled to take the law into our own hands. We might lock tenants out, toss them out, turn off their utilities, take their belongings, poison their animals, threaten them with bodily harm, harrass them, or even damage the dwelling we own in order to render it uninhabitable for our tenants.

Why do laws keep us from carrying out such perfectly reasonable acts? These acts disturb the peace. That's why. They enrage tenants and endanger the lives and limbs of everyone concerned, yours too, to say nothing of the possible property damage they might cause. People get hurt when they're being tossed out. People become infuriated when their belongings are peremptorily confiscated. People become incensed when someone locks them out of their homes. They strike back. Tempers flare. Problems grow out of all proportion, and the police have to be called in to quell the disturbances.

Self-help eviction methods are to be avoided. Yet, I know some landlords and landladies who resort to such methods when they believe the circumstances are right for self-help to work, that is, when they anticipate no complications. The secret to using self-help methods successfully, they say, is to keep a low profile, be unobtrusive and canny.

One landlady told me how she locked out a tenant several months ago, seemingly a dangerous and illegal act. Maybe it would have been dangerous in other circumstances, but she thought otherwise. You be the judge. It so happened that one of her tenants was two weeks in arrears, and at great inconvenience to herself, she had been trying several times a day for the previous ten days to find him. Upon making inquiries, she learned that none of the neighbors had seen him during that period, and she was unable to reach any of the contacts listed on his rental application. To determine whether he had indeed flown the coop or whether he was just being evasive, she peered through the windows, and seeing what appeared to be little but trash inside, she decided to enter with her passkey. Strange to say, from what she saw in this house which she had rented out unfurnished, she couldn't tell whether he was still living there or not. There was a mattress on the floor in the bedroom and a table and one chair in the kitchen. That's all there was for furniture. On the back porch was a fair-sized heap of trash, and the usual junk one finds in a recently vacated rental was scattered throughout the rooms. The place looked abandoned.

It was then that she decided to change the locks, using old replacements exactly like the originals so her locking out the tenant would not appear obvious to him if he did return. His key would fit into the keyway, but it wouldn't turn. That night at 2 o'clock the tenant called to let her know that he couldn't get his key to work. Apologizing for the "defective" lock, she let him in after pretending to have trouble opening the lock herself. They talked cordially. He apologized for not contacting her earlier about the rent. All kinds of things had happened to him lately, he said, and he had just forgotten, but he promised to move out within two days, and he did.

She believed he was eluding her all that time, coming in late and leaving early, and that he would have continued playing cat and mouse, occupying the premises rent-free much longer, if she had not forced him to meet with her. Her strategem had worked. She had outsmarted her tenant. She had recovered possession of her house, and she had done it quickly, much more quickly than if she had gone to court.

Do the ends justify the means? It's an age-old question. This landlady believed that they did in her case. Otherwise she would never have gambled and she never would have won. You will have to decide for yourself whether you might use certain pragmatic, quasi-legal (quasi-illegal?) methods to accomplish your objectives in a given situation quickly, cheaply, and painlessly. I do not necessarily advocate the use of any methods which skirt the law because they can be dangerous, they must be carefully chosen and carefully executed, they require extra-careful judgment, they don't always work, and they may backfire, but I think you should be familiar with them and their drawbacks nonetheless, just as you should be familiar with the applicable legal eviction procedure in your area.

LEGAL EVICTIONS

When you have tried and failed to rid yourself of problem tenants by hook or by crook, you have no alternative but to try an eviction by the book. You need legal clout to get them out.

Before you begin, however, you should know that in most areas evictions are handled in small claims courts as well as in other courts, but small claims courts have one major disadvantage. In a word, they are slow. Whenever you hear of a case involving a landlord or landlady who has been trying to evict a tenant for three months or more, chances are good that the case was filed originally in small claims court.

Each day tenants spend in your dwelling costs you money. Figure it out. A house renting for $360 a month is costing you $12 a day in lost rent, money you will never see again. Four days of that rent would pay all your costs in other courts which expedite evictions. If it's summary justice you want, don't go to small claims court. Go instead to whatever other court acts on such cases in your area, be it municipal court, justice court, county court, or circuit court.

You should also know before you begin that you may represent yourself in an eviction case or you may be represented by an attorney. Most of the time you'll be able to handle everything yourself because evictions are little more than a formality requiring that certain forms be filled out properly and that certain time limits be observed carefully. Attorneys seldom do this work themselves anyway. They delegate it to their secretaries, and their secretaries select the appropriate form from a form book (Californians may use *The Eviction Book for California*), which, by the way, you may consult free in your court's law library, and then they fill in the blanks. That's all they do, and you can surely do the same.

Besides, you will devote more attention to your own eviction case than will attorneys who may have 50 to 150 other cases vying for their attention. You will certainly get the tenants out sooner yourself because you have an incentive. You are losing money every day a non-paying tenant remains. Attorneys aren't. Regardless of how long an eviction takes, they will charge you the same sum for their services.

Be shrewd enough, though, to recognize when you do need to engage the services of an attorney. Generally you need one when your tenants have hired an attorney themselves, when your tenants in an apartment house have organized against you, when your tenants have filed a written answer to your complaint or affidavit, or when there are any complications you don't understand. That's when you should hire yourself an attorney, and remember that even though you have begun an action on your own, you may always hire an attorney to assist you whenever you feel you need one as the case progresses.

Because the procedures and time limits for evictions vary considerably from region to region, you will have to research that information in publications written specifically for your area, but here is some information on evictions which should prove useful to you as you wend your way through the legal maze to get problem tenants out, no matter where you live.

Notices — Every legal eviction must begin with a notice advising the tenants of your intentions. It must be properly filled out and properly served. The notice should include the number of days the tenants have in which to comply (minimums are set by law), the tenants' names (those who signed the rental agreement; if there is no agreement, use the names of the responsible adults living there; if you don't know their names, call them Does I through V), the address of the rental dwelling, the amount of rent due through the current rental period (applicable only in evictions for nonpayment of rent), the period for which this rent is due, and your signature.

Personal service is better than what attorneys call "nail and mail" (affixing the notice to the door and mailing a copy) because longer waiting periods apply in such substituted service situations. Serve the notice yourself or hire an intimidator to do the job for you.

Waiting periods — In some regions, you may count weekends and holidays when determining the waiting periods in an eviction, but the final day for the tenants to pay the rent, vacate, or answer the complaint must be a day when the court is open. Find out from the court clerk whether you may count weekends and holidays. If you may count them, you will save quite a bit of time in expediting your case.

Best times to serve — Whenever weekends and holidays may be counted in determining the waiting periods, there are certain good days to serve 3-day notices in order to take advantage of weekends and holidays in the count. Those best days are Sunday and Monday. Delaying service of a 3-day notice until Tuesday will, believe it or not, cost you at least five extra days in the whole process.

In those areas where weekends and holidays do not figure into the count, there are no "best" days for serving 3-day notices. They're all good.

The best time to serve a Notice to Perform Covenant or a Notice to Terminate Tenancy is always right after rent has been paid. After being served, the tenant's will to pay rent diminishes drastically, and you may actually create an eviction for nonpayment if you serve the notice at a "wrong" time.

Copies — Spend a few cents more to produce enough extra copies of all your eviction papers, including the notices, and you will avoid much disappointment and aggravation later. The copies needed will vary, depending upon the type of form and the number of defendants to be served. If you produce an original and three copies of each, though, you will be reasonably certain to have enough of every form to go around.

Accepting rent — You must accept rent offered to you by someone who is responding to your Notice to Pay Rent or Quit within the period specified in your notice. After that time you may accept rent if you want to but you don't have to. If you accept so much as one dollar at any time before the eviction has run its course, however, you will have to begin all over again by serving another notice. For this reason, do not accept partial rent after you have spent the money to file your complaint or affidavit unless the tenant agrees to pay back rent plus your expenses.

Records — Whether or not you expect the tenant to appear, carry with you into court all the records you possess on the tenant you are evicting. These should include whatever is applicable from the following list: rental agreement or lease, pet agreement, condition and inventory checksheet, waterbed agreement, correspondence, certified mail receipt, invoices covering repairs of damage, collection records, and photographs.

Such records will strengthen your case much more than anything you are likely to say in court.

Lessons — A final eviction notice on one door of an apartment building serves as a convincing lesson to other tenants that you know how to evict and will evict when necessary. Leave the notice on the door long enough for at least one other tenant to see it and then remove it yourself. The word will spread quickly. Don't leave the notice up longer than an afternoon, however, because you don't want other owners in the area to see it. They will wonder what's wrong with your building and will depreciate its value in their minds.

The final eviction notice on the door of a single-family dwelling should be removed as soon as the tenants' belongings are cleared out. It serves no useful purpose after that.

Remember that an eviction is in one respect like buying merchandise on sale. It will not make you a cent; it will only save you money.

Remember, also, that not evicting problem tenants is much more aggravating than all the aggravations of evicting them.

DECISIONS, DECISIONS

Solomon's decisions may have been more momentous, but they were certainly no more numerous than the landlord's and landlady's. There's always some decision or other to make, and there always seems to be so little help when each decision has to be made that you might as well be plucking daisy petals or flipping nickels. Hopefully the alternatives presented in this chapter will contribute something towards helping you make a few of those many decisions sensibly, so you'll be able to improve your profitability and may even begin to enjoy landlording.

SHOULD YOU DO IT YOURSELF?

Do-it-yourself books never discuss whether you should consider hiring someone else to do it for you. Why should they? That's a subject beyond their province, and besides, they're too involved with explaining *how* you can do things yourself to discuss *whether* you ought to be doing them yourself at all. They assume that doing things yourself is more enjoyable and less expensive than hiring help, and such assumptions will generally prove correct for most do-it-yourselfers unless they botch a job so badly that they only add to its complexity and have to pay that much more for professional help or unless they cut off an ear and have to pay big medical bills.

This do-it-yourself book is different, however, because landlording is different. In landlording it is often good business, for a variety of reasons, not to do everything yourself, and you can even ask yourself a few questions when you are trying to decide. Here are some questions, some obvious and some not so obvious, which take into account the special nature of this business and may help you decide whether to do certain things yourself or hire them done.

Are you able and knowledgeable enough to do it yourself? You know what expertise you have, and you know what you're capable of doing physically and mentally. Can you do this job? It may necessitate climbing up the side of a two-story building on an extension ladder that sways in the wind. Are you afraid of heights? It may involve knowledge of the latest tax laws about exchanging. Have you been keeping abreast of the field? It may mean testing electrical connections with the power on. Do you know enough about electricity to avoid electrocuting yourself? If you suspect that you can't do the work properly or at all yourself, hire it done.

Do you want to do it yourself? Some jobs are tedious or repetitious or mundane or loathsome and you may have no desire to do them yourself even though you are able to do them. If you don't want to do them yourself, hire them done.

Do you have the time to do it yourself? There are only 168 hours in a week, and even though you may be superhuman, you still cannot create more time. If you don't have the time to do a job, hire it done.

How much would this job cost relative to the other landlording work you have to do? You can figure the relative cost of a job by the type of work involved. Plumbing generally costs more than painting, and painting costs more than housecleaning. If you have a kitchen gusher on a Sunday morning, don't call the plumber and pay the $45 per half hour minimum for weekend work, fix it yourself unless you figure your own time is worth more. Sometimes the work you do yourself and the work you hire done should be determined strictly on the basis of cost so long as you are able to do both and have the time to do one or the other. Painting, gardening, yard maintenance, and housecleaning are all relatively inexpensive to hire done, whereas work such as plumbing, electrical, and appliance repair are relatively expensive. If you have a choice, do the expensive work yourself and hire the inexpensive work out.

Do you have the money to pay for help? In the beginning of your landlording career you will have more time than money and you will have to do much more work yourself. If you don't have the money available to hire work done, do it yourself.

Will you lose any additional rental income by doing certain work yourself? Some landlords and landladies refuse to hire help because "it costs too much" and "you can't trust workers nowadays," or they think of any other reason that suits their fancy. There are plenty.

If preparing a vacated unit for renting will take you three weeks to do yourself in your spare time, however, and the rent you may expect for the place is $300 per month (30 days), then your rent penalty (lost rent) for doing the work yourself is $210. If, on the other hand, you hire the work done for $192 (labor only) and it takes three days, your rent penalty is only $30. Adding the rent penalty to the labor costs in each case yields sums of $210 and $222, a difference of $12. In other words, you would be spending three weeks of your spare time, say, 48 hours approximately, and you would be earning all of $12 or 25 cents per hour. That's below the minimum wage. Report yourself to the Department of Labor and go directly to jail. Do not pass GO. Do not collect $192 in savings.

The advantage of hiring help would vary somewhat, of course, if there were no immediate demand for your rental, if the rent were more or less than $300, if the work took more or less than 48 hours, or if your helpers demanded more or less than $4 per hour, but this example serves to illustrate just how shortsighted some landlords and landladies can be when they ignore the rent penalty and try to do everything themselves to save a few dollars. If your rent penalty approximates the cost of hiring help, then hire the help.

Is the work tax-deductible? Every expense related to your landlording business is tax-deductible, of course. If the labor for a landlording job will cost you $200 and you're in a 35% tax bracket, you might say that the job is really costing the equivalent of $130 in taxable dollars.

Now suppose you have two jobs to do, one involving some exterior painting at your rental property and the other involving some exterior painting at your own home. You have a $550 bid on the rental property paint job and a $450 bid for the home paint job. You're capable of doing them both and you are willing to do them both, but you have time enough to complete only one. Which one should you do?

Do the one at home. Why? It will cost you more to hire out that job because it is not tax-deductible. Your home paint job would cost you $450, while the rental property job, because it is tax-deductible, would actually cost you around $360 if you were in a 35% tax bracket.

If you must choose between doing several jobs, figure out their tax consequences before you hire either of them out.

Is there anyone available to do the work? Sometimes you will have decided to hire help, but because it's the first day of elk season, Big Game Weekend, New Year's Eve, or Mardi Gras time, there's just no one available to work for you. If there is indeed no one available, cry, stall until someone is available, or do it yourself. What else can you do?

Is there much traveling required? Those rental properties you own which are located at a distance from your home require a certain amount of time and expense to reach, and you should calculate approximately what both of them are. If they are anywhere near the sums necessary to hire a job done and if you have no other good reason to visit the property, pick up the phone, hire it done, and save yourself the travel expense and the bother of doing it yourself.

Are personal relationships going to suffer if you do it yourself? A divorced landlord once told me that no marriage could survive more than ten rental buildings, be they houses or high rises. His number may or may not be accurate, I don't know, but he knew from first-hand experience that his own marriage couldn't survive the fourteen rental houses and two sixplexes he and his wife had accumulated. It couldn't survive because he was trying to do everything himself. Looking back on his own experience, he felt that ten would have been the magic number to keep his own marriage intact. Ten may be the correct number for some people and it may be two or twenty-six for others. The number is relatively unimportant. What's more important are the demands which you allow your rentals to place on your time. Spending all your spare time and energy on your rental properties would strain any personal relationship to the breaking point and would probably strain you, too, even if you could draw your family into the business to help. If you persist in accumulating rental properties, you must begin to hire help in order to preserve your personal relationships and your own sanity as well. Don't try to do it all yourself. You'll only succeed in becoming a lonely millionaire.

SHOULD YOU OWN UP TO BEING THE OWNER?

Shortly after I purchased my first fourplex, a friend mentioned in casual conversation that he knew a landlord who would never admit to his tenants that he was, in fact, the owner. He would always call himself the manager, and never, never, the owner. To someone who had just become a landlord, such a posture was inconceivable. I was proud of my units and denying ownership would have been tantamount to denying paternity of a first born. I not only felt I couldn't do it, but I couldn't see the point of the ruse unless, perhaps, one owned tenements and didn't want to be bothered with all the attendant problems.

Years later, I came to understand the value of this polite fiction, and I have come to use it at some buildings successfully myself. What it does is enable you to pass the buck.

Invariably something will come up that a tenant wants to do which you know you don't like, but you're on the spot and you can't think of a good reason for refusing the request outright. Tomorrow you will think of a good reason in hindsight, no doubt, and you'll kick

yourself for not having thought of it when you needed it, but then it will be too late to do anything about it. If you are known as the "manager" or as one of the "partners," though, you merely say that you will have to consult with the owner or your partner. Then you will have the time necessary to think up a good excuse, or, if you wish, you can simply refuse the request after having consulted with the "owner" and not offer any excuse at all for the refusal. When asked for detailed reasons, you simply say you're awfully sorry but there's nothing you can do about the matter. You tried, but your partner could not be budged.

It can even work when you live on the premises. You are the manager, aren't you?

SHOULD YOU USE RENTAL AGREEMENTS OR LEASES?

You'll notice that there are only two choices given in the question above — rental agreements and leases. In truth, there are three choices — oral rental agreements, written rental agreements, and leases (leases have to be written), but oral agreements, while they may be binding, are seldom used anymore because people don't trust their memories or each other as much as they once did. Forget about oral agreements altogether yourself (after all, some people nowadays even put their nuptial agreements in writing to remind their spouses of certain obligations), and you'll avoid the many misunderstandings which can be caused by people's foggy recollections of what was agreed upon initially. Consider only whether you should use a written agreement, hereinafter called simply a "rental agreement," or a lease, and bear in mind the difference between the two.

Basically the difference is a simple one, but it is an exceedingly important one. Rental agreements cover time periods which are either indefinite (month-to-month) or short (a day), whereas leases cover a definite and longer period of time (generally a year for residential property). Although they may be written to contain rent escalation and thirty-day termination clauses, in which cases they are essentially rental agreements anyway, leases bind both parties to the terms of the agreement so that no changes may be made by either party until the lease expires or unless one party breaks it.

Lease breaking occurs every day and you don't have to think too much about the matter to figure out who usually breaks them. Tenants do. In theory, if tenants move before their lease expires and they do not have good cause, that is, they have not entered active duty with the U.S. military or taken employment in another community or lost the main source of income used to pay rent, then they are responsible for paying rent covering the entire lease period, so long as you have been unsuccessful in a reasonable effort to find new tenants at the best rent possible. In practice, however, even if you do make a reasonable effort to rerent the place and find nobody, you would have a difficult time collecting all that rent owing on the lease unless the tenants had sufficient assets, and even then you'd probably have to sue them every month in separate small claims actions to recover.

Leases are like those treaties which the U.S. so naively signs with Russia every so often. They bind the U.S., just as leases bind landlords and landladies, while Russia and tenants do as they please, impudently enjoying the limitations they have placed upon their foolish adversaries.

Leases bind only those who have some assets and want to be bound. Tenants generally have little to lose by breaking a lease, but woe be unto you, landlord or landlady, if you should try to break a lease! That "Clark Kent of consumerism," Ralph Charell, in his book, *How I Turn Ordinary Complaints into Thousands of Dollars,* boasts of collecting a $25,000 payoff from his landlords for dispossessing him before his lease was up, and his was a lease which the new owners inherited.

Remember that any and all rental agreements, leases included, which are in effect at the time of a property transfer become the responsibilities of the new owners to uphold. Covering extended periods of time as they do, leases can affect the transfer of property substantially if the new owner wants to assume possession of the dwelling or change the terms of an agreement. If you are renting out a house, for example, on a one year's lease which has four months to run, and you have found a buyer who wants to move in upon close of escrow, you may lose the sale entirely unless you can somehow convince your renters to move before their lease expires.

All of these considerations appear to reflect so negatively on leases that you may wonder why any landlord or landlady would ever use one. There are a few circumstances, precious few, where leases may prove favorable to the landlord or landlady, and even then they should be limited to periods of a year or less (except for commercial properties, which vary according to area and market conditions). Those circumstances include student rentals (to assure year-round occupancy), luxury rentals (to encourage tenant improvements), established tenancies (to ease good long-term tenants' fears), high vacancy areas (to offer security from rent increases as an incentive), and commercial properties (to facilitate business cost projections and encourage stability and improvements).

Unless you can conceive of some obvious advantage to you for using leases, use written month-to-month rental agreements instead, and you'll stay out of trouble.

SHOULD YOU RENT IT FURNISHED?

There is extra money to be made in renting furnished dwellings, no doubt about it, but it requires extra effort and investment, and sometimes it brings extra grief. Actually it adds another business, furniture rental, to the one you're already conducting, and it presents numerous advantages and disadvantages for you to consider, too.

Advantages:

more income
lower vacancy factor
increased depreciation available for tax purposes
less redecoration required when people move (furnished dwellings, when vacant, still look lived in and distract the eye from the walls)
less wear and tear on the buildings caused by tenants' careless moving of their own heavy furniture

Disadvantages:

greater investment required
more tenant turnover
muscles needed for moving furniture about
more repairs
more maintenance (excluding redecorating)
increased risk of damage
greater theft potential
storage area required for surplus furniture
added recordkeeping and bookkeeping
purchasing time needed (you have to select the furniture)
obsolescence (furniture goes out of style)

Seemingly, the disadvantages of renting furnished dwellings outweigh the advantages. They certainly outnumber the advantages. What's more important, though, in this comparison is whether you would be adequately compensated for assuming the burden of all the disadvantages, and that comes down to numbers. If the added furnishings can produce, say, a

100% return on the investment over a twelve-month period, then renting furnished dwellings might actually be an attractive proposition. It can be done. Such a return can even be surpassed.

One landlord friend of mine has found that renting one-bedroom apartments furnished with his own sturdy homemade furniture, including waterbeds, yields a 100% return in six months and more than compensates him for the extra effort and investment. His turnover is slightly higher, but his vacancy factor is nil, and his cash flow is phenomenal. Renting furnished apartments has paid off handsomely for him.

If you are fully cognizant of both the advantages and the disadvantages of renting furnished dwellings, and your own rentals lend themselves to being rented furnished, such as those catering to singles, armed services personnel, students, or vacationers, you might try furnishing one rental as an experiment before you furnish them all. See for yourself if you like the furniture rental business and see if you can make any money at it. Then either buy out Levitz or call Goodwill.

If you'd rather not experiment at all, recommend to those people who come to you to rent furnished dwellings that they contact a furniture rental company (listed in the Yellow Pages under "Furniture Renting & Leasing") and rent their furniture separately.

If you happen to buy a building which has old furniture that obviously isn't adding enough income to compensate you for the trouble of looking after it, get rid of the furniture. Don't let the frustrations of handling a furniture rental business interfere with your more important activities. Give the furniture away to a charitable cause and deduct its agreed-upon value from your landlording income.

SHOULD YOU ALLOW YOUR TENANTS TO SLEEP ON WATER?

We landlords and landladies tend to be protective of our property and to resist anybody and anything that might pose a threat. We don't want pets. We don't want teenagers. We don't want motorcyclists. We don't want children. We don't want attorneys. We don't want welfare recipients. We don't want students. We don't want rock musicians. And we certainly don't want waterbeds. We seem ornery, suspicious, misanthropic, negative.

Yet, we become that way honestly. We start out as innocents determined to be trusting and determined to be unlike any grouchy, greedy landlord or landlady we ever knew. Then we have experiences. We learn slowly, incredulously, but we learn. After we have cleaned up the filth and repaired the damage left behind by more than one unscrupulous tenant who has vacated owing us rent, we become less trusting of people and more protecting of our property. We tend to regard people and things guilty until proven innocent.

So when waterbeds first swept into faddish favor in the late 60's, we landlords and landladies considered the perils of allowing one-ton water balloons to lie on the floors of our bedrooms, and we acted quickly to protect our interests. We banned them.

Inevitably some tenants sneaked them in, and just as inevitably our worst fears were realized. Those early waterbeds stained our carpets and buckled our hardwood floors, necessitating expensive repairs. We swore never to allow them, and we wrote into our rental agreements carefully worded clauses to cover future developments, too. We prohibited not only waterbeds but any and all liquid-filled furniture. We fought waterbeds in the courts, and, believe it or not, we won. Even today we do not have to rent to waterbed tenants.

But waterbeds are no longer a fad. They are here to stay, for there are many people who find them essential to get a good night's sleep. Nor are waterbeds any longer the flimsy water bags they once were. They have become thick (20-mil) water containers adequately safeguarded against accidental spillage, so that today a properly designed and installed waterbed is perfectly safe for use in most rental dwellings.

What's a landlord or landlady to do then? Strike that "no liquid-filled furniture" clause from the contract? Absolutely not!

Waterbeds are still capable of damaging your building. Flimsy waterbeds and waterbeds without frames or liners are still around, and they could cause you the same grief today that they caused people years ago.

What should you do? Above all, be protective. Either continue banning all liquid-filled furniture from your rentals (remember that you are well within your rights in doing so), or adopt a well-considered policy which will enable you to rent to waterbed tenants at minimum risk.

Communicate this decision, to ban waterbeds or to accept them on well-defined terms, clearly to both your prospective tenants and your existing tenants. Begin when you first qualify prospective tenants by determining whether they even expect to have a waterbed. Make no assumptions about what they will be sleeping on. Bring the matter into the open for frank discussion, and you will virtually eliminate unauthorized waterbeds that tenants try to sneak in, beds which expose you to damages you're not protected against.

Before you ever adopt a policy to admit waterbeds, if you choose to, you should determine whether your building can indeed support their weight structurally. Residential buildings built to current construction standards will withstand around 60 pounds per square foot on suspended floors and can safely support most any waterbed. Poured concrete floors, of course, pose no problem at all. If you have any doubts, first read the Waterbed Manufacturers' Association report called "An Analysis of Waterbed Floor Loading," which is available for the asking from the WMA, 1411 West Olympic Blvd., Los Angeles, CA 90015. Second, check with your local building department about the floor loading limits for your building. Third, if you still have reservations, hire a structural engineering firm (look in the Yellow Pages under "Engineers-Structural") to determine the weight per square foot your building can safely support. Compare that with the weight per square foot of each waterbed in question, and you will be able to tell whether your building can take the weight.

Waterbeds vary significantly in total weight, from around 360 pounds for a twin-sized hybrid (urethane foam and water combination) bed to about 2500 pounds for the large round all-water variety. You can estimate the total weight of any waterbed yourself by making some simple calculations. Multiply the water capacity in gallons by 8.33 pounds and then add 4% for the miscellaneous waterbed parts if it's an all-water type or 20% if it's a hybrid.

More important than total weight, though, is floor loading or weight per square foot, for these are the figures which structural engineers use to determine the stress the waterbed places on the floor. Again you can estimate the weight per square foot quite accurately yourself. Simply divide the total weight of the bed by the square footage of its base (unless the bed rests on a pedestal base which is smaller than the surface, the base and the surface dimensions will be the same).

Let's take, as an example, the most common size of waterbed, the queen size (60″ × 80″), and we'll figure its weight per square foot. The all-water type (9-inch fill) has a water capacity of 196 gallons; the hybrid, 72 gallons. 196 gallons times 8.33 pounds per gallon plus 4% equals 1698 pounds total weight for the all-water queen-size waterbed. 72 gallons times 8.33 pounds per gallon plus 20% equals 720 pounds, total weight for the queen-size hybrid. To find the pounds per square foot for a queen-size waterbed, assuming that the base and surface dimensions are the same, multiply the length (80″) times the width (60″) and divide by the number of square inches in one square foot (144). Thus, we calculate that a queen-size waterbed has 35 square feet. Divide 1698 by 35 and you get 48.5 pounds, which is the weight per square foot of an all-water queen-size waterbed. Divide 720 pounds by 35 and you get 20.5 pounds, which is the weight per square foot of a hybrid queen-size waterbed. That wasn't hard, was it? You can do the same for any size waterbed.

Once the weight question is answered to your satisfaction and you know the floor loading limits for your building, you may want to consider renting to tenants who sleep on water. If so, take these seven items into consideration for each individual waterbed: specifications, components, installation, inspection, insurance, deposit, and agreement.

Specifications — Waterbeds differ considerably. Learn the size, weight, and type of each waterbed your tenants wish to have. Using these specifications, calculate whether or not each bed falls within the floor loading limits for your building. Reject those which might seem perilous to you, and suggest that the tenants consider lighter beds.

Components — The minimum allowable components, as far as you are concerned, are a mattress at least 20 mil thick with lap seams (preferably less than three years old so it has more flex-fatigue resistance), a safety liner at least 8 mil, and a frame enclosure which meets WMA standards. If made of wood, the frame should be at least 2″ × 10″, the deck should be at least 1/2″ thick, and neither the deck nor the pedestal should have any particle-board components (plywood or solid natural wood only).

Installation — To prevent floods and minor catastrophes when they are most likely to occur, insist that professional installers (every waterbed store has its own service department) do the installation, and insist that you supervise the eventual dismantling. If, for some reason, professional help is unavailable and you feel confident enough in your own abilities, help the

Waterbed Agreement

Dated __January 12, 1983__

(Addendum to Rental Agreement)

This agreement is attached to and forms a part of the Rental Agreement dated __January 12, 1983__ between __Lester Landlord__ , Owners, and __Richard Harvey + Mary Louise Renter__ , Tenants.

Tenants desire to keep a waterbed described as __queen size, Combination, foam and water__

in the dwelling they occupy under the Rental Agreement referred to above, and because this agreement specifically prohibits keeping waterbeds without the Owners' permission, Tenants agree to the following terms and conditions in exchange for this permission:

1) Tenants agree to keep one waterbed approved by Owners for this dwelling. Waterbed shall consist of a mattress at least 20 mil thick with lap seams, a safety liner at least 8 mil, and a frame enclosure which meets the Waterbed Manufacturers' Association standards.

2) Tenants agree to consult with the Owners about the location of the waterbed. They agree to hire qualified professionals to install and dismantle the bed according to the manufacturer's specifications and further agree not to relocate it without the Owners' consent.

3) Tenants agree to allow Owners to inspect the waterbed installation at any and all reasonable times and Tenants agree to remedy any problems or potential problems immediately.

4) Tenants agree to furnish Owners with a copy of a valid liability insurance policy for at least $100,000 covering this waterbed installation and agree to renew the policy as necessary for continuous coverage.

5) Tenants agree to pay immediately for any damage caused by their waterbed, and in addition, they will add $ __25⁰⁰__ to their security/cleaning deposit, any of which may be used for cleaning, repairs, or delinquent rent when Tenants vacate. This added deposit or what remains of it when waterbed damages have been assessed, will be returned to Tenants within __Seven__ days after they prove that they no longer keep this waterbed.

6) In consideration of the additional time, effort, costs, and risks involved in this waterbed installation, Tenants agree to pay additional rent of $ __3⁰⁰__ , which /includes/~~does not include~~ the premium for the waterbed liability insurance policy referred to in item 4.

7) Tenants agree that the Owners reserve the right to revoke this permission to keep a waterbed should the Tenants break this agreement.

Owner __Lester Landlord__   Tenant __Richard Renter__

By _____   Tenant __Mary Renter__

Page __2__ of __3__

tenant yourself by overseeing the installation while you consult the manufacturer's printed instructions. Proper installation will validate the insurance policy and give you peace of mind.

Inspection — Make your first inspection just after the waterbed has been installed. Check its location, which should be along a load-bearing wall and away from intense heat sources. Check its problem potential, which should include feeling the frame for protrusions which might puncture the mattress. Check for water spillage from the installation, and direct the tenant to clean up any water immediately. After that, you might wish to check the waterbed periodically, say, every six months or so, for possible damage and signs of potential damage.

Insurance — Responding to popular demand, the Maryland Casualty Company now writes waterbed liability insurance designed specifically for tenants and makes it available through waterbed stores. The annual premium is $25 per year, with a $25 deductible clause and a liability limit of $100,000. Require your tenant to secure such a policy. The policy covers damage to the building and to the property of other tenants, but it specifically excludes fire damage; damage to buildings which do not conform to governing building codes; and damage resulting from failure to follow the manufacturer's specifications for assembling, installing, filling, emptying, locating, and maintaining the waterbed. Because the policy expires after twelve months, make certain that the tenant renews for continuous coverage.

Deposit — Require at least an extra $25 deposit from the waterbed tenant to cover the deductible should the insurance policy have to cover damages. Add this deposit to the total security/cleaning deposit so it need not be restricted in use to waterbed damages alone. That way it could be used for any kind of damages, for cleaning, or for rent.

Agreement — Cross out and initial the liquid-filled furniture exclusion, if any, in the rental agreement you use, and add to the agreement the terms under which you are allowing the waterbed. These terms could be included in a remarks section of the agreement; they could be written or typed on the back of the agreement and signed by all parties concerned; or they could be written as a separate agreement and referenced to the main rental agreement. Written succinctly into the remarks section, the wording might be as follows: "Tenants have one waterbed approved by Owners for this dwelling. Waterbed shall consist of mattress, liner, and frame; shall be kept insured for liability to $100,000; and shall be installed according to manufacturer's specifications."

This entire waterbed-acceptance procedure involves additional time, effort, costs, and risks which other tenants should not have to subsidize. Therefore, consider adding a nominal sum to the waterbed tenant's rent to compensate you for all this, and consider including in the sum enough to pay the premium (a little more than $2 a month) yourself on the tenant's waterbed liability policy so you are certain the policy is kept current.

Waterbeds may not be what you want in your building, but if you do, and if you follow these guidelines, you will be able to rest well at night no matter what you sleep on.

SHOULD YOU ALLOW PETS?

Just as there is no law compelling you to rent to tenants with waterbeds, there's none compelling you to rent to tenants with pets, seeing-eye dogs excepted, and you might be perfectly correct in excluding both waterbeds and pets. It's your prerogative, but in adopting a dogmatic, hidebound approach to these questions, you are excluding not just waterbeds and pets but also all the people who go along with them, some of whom make very good tenants. You are almost halving the number of people who can qualify to rent from you, and consequently, you are making the task of finding good tenants that much more difficult.

If finding good tenants without accepting pets is easy for you, then continue excluding pets altogether because pets undeniably do pose problems, but if you are having problems finding good tenants and if you have a building which is suitable for pets (buildings suitable for dogs and cats have little carpeting and may have yards or patios), consider accepting good tenants who have good pets.

Such tenants save you money because they tend to be more permanent residents, and they make you money because they will pay higher rent for their accommodations than will tenants without pets. Set the rent high, advertise that you accept pets, and you'll be inundated with applicants who have pets because pet owners' options are more limited (avoid pet surcharges because they tempt pet owners into believing that pet damages are already paid for; charge higher rents and higher deposits instead). My own experience with an admittedly small sample has shown that tenants with pets stay an average of twice as long as those without and that they will pay $5 to $25 more per month for a place to live where they can keep their pets. They realize that finding another place which accepts pets is difficult at best and is sometimes altogether impossible, so once they move in, they stay a long time and they pay more in rent while they stay there.

Whether you choose to rent to these people with pets or not, you must have a pet policy. Actually you have one already, but you may not have formalized it very well. You may have been telling your tenants all along that you do not accept pets, and they may be interpreting that to mean no fish, fowl, mammals, insects, or reptiles. Then again they may interpret it to mean that certain fish, fowl, and insects are acceptable, but not mammals or reptiles. What do you mean by "no pets"? Would you allow someone to have a twenty-gallon aquarium or three parakeets in one cage? They are all pets. Would they violate your policy?

Spell out what you mean when you say "no pets" or "pets OK" by putting your policy in writing, and make it fair to your tenants, their pets, the neighbors, and yourself. Specify in your policy the type, size, age, and number of pets you will accept or not accept and outline these specifications clearly.

```
                        PET POLICY

    Subject to approval, tenants may have pets in any one
    of the following categories:

        1)  Caged birds (maximum of two)

        2)  Fish (as many as can live happily in a fifty-
            five gallon aquarium)

        3)  House cats (one, not to exceed 12 pounds, at
            least three months old)

        4)  Dogs (one, not to exceed 25 pounds or 15
            inches at the shoulders when full grown, at
            least nine months old)

        5)  Other animals (permitted only on a case-by-
            case basis)

    Tenants shall bring all prospective pets to management
    for approval beforehand.

    Tenants shall have a Pet Agreement covering the keep-
    ing of their pet.
```

You may wish to include in your list of acceptable pets only caged birds or only house cats, or you may wish to exclude every conceivable animal, no matter what it is. That's your decision to make. You have great flexibility in determining your policy and you have some flexibility in applying it, but you should be astute enough to recognize that whatever pet policy you adopt will have to apply equally to everyone in a building or at least to everyone in a very distinctly designated area. You cannot extend a privilege to some tenants and not to others. They won't stand for it.

Inadvertently I happened to inherit a situation once where an old lady had been allowed by a previous owner to have a small house dog. It was her constant companion, her security system, her confidant, and her first love, and I was averse to giving her the choice of dog or dwelling since she had lived there for fifteen years already. Still, I was adamant about allowing anyone else to keep a dog there because the building was being improved with new carpeting. Three of the thirteen other tenants who lived there defied me by getting their own dogs, and when confronted with my no-pets policy, which I had already discussed with them, all three referred to the little old lady's dog. "If she can have one, why can't we?", they asked almost in unison. Indeed, why couldn't they? The crucial difference between them and the little old lady as far as I was concerned was that she had had the dog before I assumed ownership and before I instituted the no-pets policy, but as far as the tenants were concerned, there was no difference whatsoever between her and them. If she were allowed a dog, then they should be as well. One of those tenants had to be evicted over this matter. The other two finally relented and gave their pets away, but they struggled hard.

By the way, if tenants ever do break your rental contract by acquiring a pet which you distinctly prohibit, you should confront them about the matter immediately and give them no more than three days to get rid of it. If you give them any more time, they will only dillydally in getting rid of the pet and become attached to it in the process, and you'll wind up having to evict them. If you fail to approach them at all when you first learn about the pet, you have in effect given them your tacit approval, and you'd better be prepared to fend off your other tenants. They'll want one, too. This is just another one of those small landlording crises which only becomes more difficult to deal with if you procrastinate in handling it.

Having a pet policy you can enforce when necessary is one thing, but finding good pet owners with good pets is another. It is a process for circumspection and deliberation. You will want to determine whether the pet owners you interview are devoted enough to their pet to care for it faithfully. Check them out by asking questions such as "Will you rent this place if we do not allow you to keep your pet?" and "Who will be taking care of your pet in your absence?" and "Will you pay a larger refundable security/cleaning deposit of $100?" and "Can you live by our pet agreement which says the following . . . . ?" Their answers to these questions will indicate fairly clearly how important their pet is to them and how faithfully they will care for it after they move in. The pet itself, which you ought to meet at some point before you agree to accept it, should fall within your pet policy guidelines and should be reasonably friendly, healthy, and well behaved. If this preliminary screening of the owners and their pet raises any doubts in your mind about their ability and willingness to respect your property, refuse to rent to them. You have every right to be discriminating in this matter, and furthermore, you should be discriminating.

Refusing applicants with pets is pretty straightforward, and refusing existing tenants who want a pet is much the same, even when you suspect that they might prove to be indifferent toward the pet they choose. The only way to determine that is to impose upon them the same set of conditions which you impose upon newcomers with pets. Caution your tenants that you will allow them to have a pet only if they discuss the matter with you in advance and only if you approve. When they approach you, review your pet policy with them first to make certain that they understand what kinds of pets you allow, and then go over the entire pet agreement point by point. Tell them that you treat all pet owners alike and that they all have submitted their pets for approval, signed pet agreements, and increased their security/cleaning deposits, and so long as your existing tenants will do likewise, they too will be allowed to have a pet. Emphasize that your refusal of any particular pet has nothing to do with their own tenancy but that keeping an unauthorized pet will certainly result in an eviction of both the tenants and the pet.

All of your tenants should understand that they have no right to have a pet on the premises unless you grant them the privilege under well-defined conditions. If they should fail to live up to those conditions, you will be forced to withdraw the privilege.

Should you allow pets? Considering your building and its vacancy factor, what do you think?

Pet Agreement

Dated **APRIL 26, 1984**

(Addendum to Rental Agreement)

This agreement is attached to and forms a part of the Rental Agreement dated **4-26-84** between **Leslie Landlady**, Owners, and **Tina Oldtimer**, Tenants.

Tenants desire to keep a pet named **Fang** and described as **Lhasa Apso** in the dwelling they occupy under the rental agreement referred to above, and because this agreement specifically prohibits keeping pets without the Owners' permission, Tenants agree to the following terms and conditions in exchange for this permission:

1) Tenants agree to keep their pet under control at all times.

2) Tenants agree to keep their pet restrained, but not tethered, when it is outside their dwelling.

3) Tenants agree not to leave their pet unattended for any unreasonable periods.

4) Tenants agree to dispose of their pet's droppings properly and quickly.

5) Tenants agree not to leave food or water for their pet or any other animal outside their dwelling.

6) Tenants agree to keep pet from causing any annoyance or discomfort to others and will remedy immediately any complaints made through the Owner or Manager.

7) Tenants agree to get rid of their pet's offspring within eight weeks of birth.

8) Tenants agree to pay immediately for any damage, loss, or expense caused by their pet, and in addition, they will add $ **75 -** to their security/cleaning deposit, any of which may be used for cleaning, repairs, or delinquent rent when Tenants vacate. This added deposit or what remains of it when pet damages have been assessed, will be returned to Tenants within **Seven** days after they prove that they no longer keep this pet.

9) Tenants agree that Owners reserve the right to revoke permission to keep the pet should Tenants break this agreement.

Owner _Leslie Landlady_   Tenant _Tina Oldtimer_

By _____   Tenant _____

Page **4** of **4**

SHOULD YOU FURNISH THE MAJOR KITCHEN APPLIANCES?

You don't always have a choice of whether to supply your tenants with stoves and refrigerators in your unfurnished rentals because sometimes these appliances are already built in. When you do have a choice, however, either don't furnish them at all or tell your new tenants that you no longer supply these appliances in unfurnished rentals but that you would be willing as a favor to supply them on loan for a few months.

Tenants are far less likely to complain about the minor faults of their appliances when they are using a stove or refrigerator "on loan" than if you tell them the appliances are included in the rent. Tenants fear that each time you see the appliances you'll be reminded of the loan agreement and may ask for them back, so they keep mum about the little problems. Fiddling with temperamental stoves that bake lopsided cakes and explaining why the milk freezes while the ice cream melts in some crazy refrigerators takes far too much of your valuable time.

SHOULD YOU LEAVE THEM PLAIN OR FIX THEM FANCY?

Cosmetics people market hope. Automobile people market youth. Wine people market status. Appliance people market freedom. Vitamin people market health. What do you market, landlord and landlady? A place to live with plain white walls. How pedestrian! Shame on you! You could do better, much better.

Don't get me wrong now. There's nothing wrong with renting clean, functional dwellings with heating, electricity, carpets, drapes, and indoor plumbing, but it's just so, well, so practical. That's all. And "practical" doesn't sell for very much. Checker automobiles are practical, too, but they don't sell for what Sevilles do. People will rent your functional dwellings in tight housing markets no matter what, to be sure, but they will always pay more in any market if they believe they are getting more for their money, and you can give them more for very little.

With a little extra work and very little investment, you could be marketing the same kinds of illusions that Seville customers so willingly pay extra money for. What illusions? Individuality, chic, warmth, luxury. "All that in my rental, and with very little investment?" Yes! Here's how.

Hire yourself as an interior decorator and make these three alterations to your rental — wallpaper one wall, put up at least one woven shade, and mount a shower-bath curtain rod valance. You could dream up other alterations if you wanted to, but they should be few, uncomplicated, inexpensive, and easy to care for.

Wallpapering only one prominent wall either opposite the front door or opposite the entrance to the kitchen makes a very big impression on prospective tenants as they walk in and begin visualizing themselves living there. Yet, vinyl-coated, prepasted wallpaper costs surprisingly little, is easy to apply, and is easy to care for, too.

A woven shade on any window which requires some kind of window covering anyway creates much the same impression as the wallpaper. It's an unexpected splash of color, a welcome departure from all those boring white walls so prevalent in rental dwellings, and it dazzles the beholders into believing they are getting something special for their money. Although Roman shades made of wood are available, they're costlier and no more decorative than the vinyl variety, which sell for approximately what you'd pay for ordinary window shades. Sears catalog offers both.

A shower-bath curtain rod valance made of 1″ × 6″ fir or pine and painted with a simple design or covered with fancy Contact Paper spruces up drab bathrooms as if by magic. Mounted just in front of the rod itself, the valance hides the curtain rod and lends a special illusion of warmth and luxury to the place.

All three of these dazzlers together should cost the do-it-yourselfer no more than $50, and yet they should yield around $10 more a month in increased rental income. Think of what that does to the value of your property! At seven times the annual gross, $10 of additional rental income increases the value by $840. Try these dazzlers, or be imaginative and think up others of your own, and capitalize on people's willingness to pay extra for illusions.

SHOULD YOU OUTFIT THE LAUNDRY?

An apartment-house laundry room can be a blessing or a curse. It can pay off as handsomely as a small casino full of slot machines, or it can simply be another welfare case for you to support. Mostly there are two factors which determine whether you will win or lose in your laundry room: how much the machines are used and who owns them.

Use — All things considered, your laundry room will pay off handsomely if it's used enough, and though you cannot tell for certain whether your tenants will indeed do their laundry there or how many loads they will wash per week, you can make an estimate based on the number of people or the number of bedrooms. If you have a fourplex, for example, and you have four families with two children living in each apartment, you have sixteen people living there, and they will surely produce the laundry to support one pair of machines. On the other hand, a fourplex tenanted by singles and couples, no matter how clean they are, just will not support machines. The rule of thumb I use is sixteen people or twelve bedrooms (even the smallest dwelling counts as one bedroom). If a building meets either of these minimums and if its laundry machines are set to charge competitive rates, those machines should produce liberal returns.

Ownership — Some landlords and landladies feel they have better things to worry about than laundry machines and would rather let someone else handle them completely. They have that choice and so do you if you have an apartment-house laundry room. If you contract to have vendors supply the machines on a lease or commission basis, you will be relieved of all the ownership worries. Vendors will supply and service the machines while you supply the wash house itself, the necessary plumbing and electrical hookups, and the utilities. They will write a one- to five-year contract to assure themselves of a profit and then split the leavings with you.

If you supply the machines yourself, you will have to take care of the repairs and maintenance, count the coins, worry about vandalism and other calamities, and you'll have to pay for the machines with a sum of money which cannot be charged directly to expenses, but you'll have the only access to the coin boxes, you'll get depreciation on the machines, and you'll get a 10% investment tax credit.

Which choice should you select? That depends. If you are clumsy, if you don't think you'd enjoy the business, if you own an apartment building with fewer than sixteen occupants or twelve bedrooms, *or* if you intend to dispose of your building within three years, don't buy your own machines. Contract with someone else to supply them.

Should you decide to install someone else's machines, ask other landlords and landladies for their recommendations of trustworthy companies and then shop around for the best available terms. If it's a small building, consider the laundry more of an amenity than a moneymaker and hope that you'll be able to recover the utility costs. A straight commission should net you more than a lease-commission arrangement because some money will accrue to you with each load washed, regardless of how many. Under the lease-commission arrangement, the machine supplier retains a fixed sum each month and splits the balance with you, so if the machines produce only enough to cover the supplier's fixed sum, you get nothing. Lemons, oranges, and grapes. Tough luck.

If you are the least bit handy, if you believe you'd enjoy looking after your own coin-operated laundry machines, if you own an apartment building with at least sixteen occupants or twelve bedrooms, *and* if you intend to keep your building at least three years (naturally you can take them with you if you want to; specify that in the property sales agreement), then, by all means, install your own machines. You will be pleasantly surprised to see just how much money they can make, and soon you will understand why so many firms are in the business of supplying laundry machines on a commission basis, why they offer to paint laundry rooms "free," why they invest in non-resettable load counters, why they advertise so heavily in apartment association publications, and why they offer various inducements to managers and owners of large complexes. It can be a lucrative proposition for them.

Should you decide after due consideration to install your own laundry machines in your apartment house, you need to know something about buying laundry machines, setting and changing rates, and counting coins.

Buying laundry machines — Consult *Consumer Reports* for the best information about the reliability and operating costs of various brands of domestic washers and dryers. Commercial machines, one old codger many years in the business told me, have innards exactly like the home machines. "Only the tops are different," he said. "When my bottoms wear out, I junk 'em and put my old tops on the cheapest new home machines made by the same manufacturer. They last just as long as new commercial models." I've never tried it because my bottoms haven't worn out yet, but I suppose he's right.

If the two are that similar, then the manufacturers of good home machines also make good commercial machines, and you'll have no trouble finding the right machines for you.

My machines are all Kenmore commercial models purchased through Sears' Contract Sales Department, which sells them for less than a regular Sears store's appliance department. In fact, Contract Sales sells the machines for less than the wholesale price to my local Whirlpool dealer for commercial Whirlpool machines, and as you may know, Kenmore machines are made by Whirlpool.

Besides being inexpensive to purchase, Kenmores wash and dry well, are sparing on the utilities, are quite reliable, and are easy to repair. The one drawback they do have is that Sears' local parts cache for commercial machines is such slim pickin's that Sears usually has to send away for parts. Fortunately, however, the machines seldom need parts, and they seldom need repairs either.

Commercial Kenmores are not covered by lengthy guarantees as are the domestic models. Sears does sell maintenance contracts for nervous Nellies, but my own experience has shown that these contracts are priced higher than the repairs themselves would cost without a contract, so I don't bother.

My biggest problem with commercial laundry machines couldn't be solved with a maintenance contract anyway. Every so often I get calls that washers or dryers won't work and find that the only thing wrong with them is that I had forgotten to empty the coinboxes, so I "fix" them by collecting $160 in quarters and dimes from each pair of machines. Jackpot!

Setting and changing prices — Since you are actually providing a service for your tenants rather than competing directly with coin-operated launderettes in the area, set your machines at rates slightly higher, say, 5 cents, than the prevailing scale for local launderettes. Your machines will need more repairs and wear out faster with frequent use, so you don't want to stimulate use by keeping the charges too low. Keep them just low enough so the machines will be used fairly often, yet not so high that they won't be used often enough to justify your investment.

Income from the machines should cover your utility costs (because heat for hot water accounts for between 75% and 90% of the energy used to wash clothes, consider changing the laundry room to cold water washing only and, if you do, posting a sign to that effect), purchase of the machines, repair service, and a fair return on your investment.

The return should be very fair. One of my eightplexes, all two-bedroom units, paid for its washer and dryer and all its overhead in just eleven months, and ever since, those machines have simply churned profits, never missing a beat.

My first laundry laundry machines charged 25 cents to wash and 10 cents to dry, and if I were to charge that today, I'd barely break even. As it was, I kept those rates much too long because the coin slides were fixed to accept only quarters and dimes, and it took me a while to find adjustable coin slides. Adjustable slides enable you to change the amount charged to any one-, two-, three- or four-coin combination in minutes with only a screwdriver. Order any new laundry machines you buy with these slides rather than the fixed slides, to allow you the flexibility of adjusting your income to offset leaping utility costs. Adjustable slides may be purchased by themselves and retrofitted to most existing machines. For your nearest dealer, call ESD, one manufacturer, at (800) 523-1510, except in Pennsylvania, where they can be reached collect at (215) 877-5042.

Counting coins — Those coins you remove from your laundry machines are all mixed up and require sorting, counting, and wrapping before being deposited. It's a pleasant chore, counting stacks of your very own coins, one which you can do almost without thinking while you watch TV, but if you find the laundry business profitable enough to install more than one washer and dryer, you will notice that counting coins becomes increasingly tedious. When that happens, buy a coin sorter for your counting house and restore some of the old pleasure to the chore.

There are coin sorters which whirl and tinkle and even tally their coins digitally, and they cost pretty pennies, too. You'd certainly need such a machine if you had a vending machine route or a casino, but you don't need the fanciest sorter available to help you count a few hundred dollars in coins every month. You need just a simple, inexpensive sorter to help out with the chore.

Fortunately, there is one. It enables you to sort, count, and wrap coins quickly and accurately, and it works without moving a single part. Gravity makes it work. After you feed the coins in at the top, they sort themselves by following tracks of varying widths until they wind up sorted into calibrated stacks at the bottom. Little nubs in the stacking tubes raise the 41st or 51st coin, depending on the denomination, to mark full rolls, which can then be removed, checked with the instant count verifier, and wrapped (banks provide coin wrappers free of charge).

This marvel of simplicity and utility is called the Nadex Coin

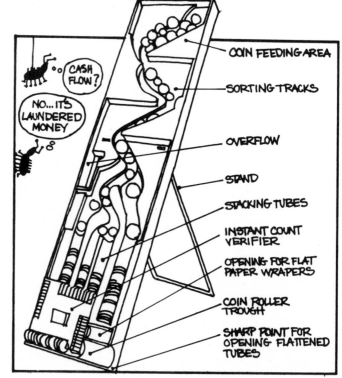

Sorter and Packager, Model 607. It sells for $45 and may be purchased in stationery stores

or directly from the manufacturer, Nadex Industries, 220 Delaware, Buffalo, NY 14202, (716) 845-6910.

SHOULD YOU PAY THE GARBAGE AND UTILITY BILLS?

Landlords and landladies frequently pay the garbage and water bills themselves for their single-family rental properties rather than leaving that responsibility to their tenants, and with good reason. Paying the garbage bill means that the garbage will positively be picked up and the property will be kept reasonably tidy. Paying the water bill means that the yard will probably be watered and the landscaping won't die of thirst. Paying both means that the tenant can offer no excuse for poor groundskeeping at least, and the place should look reasonably presentable when you drive by.

These arguments make sense for the house rental, but what about the apartment house which has no yard? Whenever I'm lucky enough to have separate water meters for each apartment, I require that the tenants pay their own bills. They should know what their water usage costs. Garbage is another matter, however. Personally, I prefer to pay the garbage bill for all my rentals unless some other satisfactory precedent was established by a previous owner. Some tenants either forget to pay or discontinue service claiming that they would rather haul it to the dump themselves to save paying the bill, and then their cans begin overflowing and there's a constant mess for you to look after. Control of the garbage area is always easier if you pay. If you don't pay, there's bound to be friction caused by the invasion of one tenant's garbage can by strange garbage. It gets tossed aside and then begins a great garbage battle. Finally, there's more of a mess than you can cope with. You pay and you control. Make them pay and you're likely to be plagued by a continuous garbage war.

As for the utilities in an apartment house, my practice is to have the tenants pay for their own so long as they are on separate meters, and if they are not on separate meters, I try to effect a conversion.

One situation that had me puzzled for a while involved a big, old fourplex with steam heat produced by one boiler connected to a gas meter with dials that spun faster than a moon rocket's altimeter. I was paying the bill for that one meter myself, and with today's sharply rising utility rates, the bill soon rose to equal a fourth of the building's total rental income. As if that weren't bad enough, one tenant kept complaining that he never had enough heat, and I had to turn the controlling thermostat up to 80 degrees just to keep his place around 68. Every unit but one then had to keep the windows open night and day to avoid being bathed in steam heat, and so, much of the heat that I was paying dearly for was going out those windows.

What could I do? I knew that I couldn't raise the rents to a level where the increased utility costs would be covered. That would have necessitated an increase substantially higher than market conditions warranted. Fortunately, because each unit had its own gas meter for an individual stove and water heater, I could install new direct-vent heaters in each unit and connect them to the individual meters. In less than twelve months, those heaters paid for themselves in utility-bill savings and my tenants' heating complaints vanished.

Tenants are more interested in lower rent, I believe, than in the inclusion of utilities, and when they have to pay their own utility bills, they conserve energy as they should.

SHOULD YOU ALLOW NAILS IN YOUR WALLS?

When you come across tenants who don't want to attach your walls to their pictures because they don't want to damage your walls, let me know, and I'll recommend that they be enshrined in the Tenants' Hall of Fame. The Hall still has lots of room.

For all those other tenants, you have several decisions to make: What should you allow them to use to attach your walls to their pictures, clocks, and other lighweight stuff? And should you let them hang the heavy stuff at all, stuff like birdcages, planters, bookcases, wall systems, and bulletin boards?

First, about the lightweight stuff — Remember the olden days when tenants could cause

their landlord or landlady to have a crying jag if they tried banging a nail into the wall and got caught? Why the concern? Because one nail in a plaster wall would sometimes cause a tiny crack which would grow into a fissure, and then chips and chunks of the plaster would start falling down, and finally there would be a lath wall showing where once there had been one of plaster. Fortunately, along came some nice person who invented stickem wall hangers, and the problem was solved. The stickem hangers would hold light burdens without disturbing the plaster wall at all. Landlords and landladies invariably recommended them and most tenants dutifully used them.

But things changed again with the advent of sheetrock, also known as plasterboard, wallboard, and gypsum board. A nail wouldn't crack the sheetrock as it would the plaster, but the stickem wall hangers, when removed, would peel off both the paint and the paper surface of the sheetrock, leaving a broad, ugly scar underneath which was difficult to conceal.

Since we now have both plaster and sheetrock walls in general use, landlords and landladies need to offer their tenants recommendations which vary according to wall type. For plaster walls, recommend that your tenants use stickem hangers whenever possible, and if they must use a nail, recommend that they drill a pilot hole first to avoid any cracking which might be caused by banging too hard on the wall. For sheetrock walls, recommend that your tenants use nails tapped in carefully and that they avoid using those stickem hangers or tapes altogether. Holes left by nails in sheetrock can be filled neatly with spackling compound and do not even have to be painted in most cases.

And now about the heavy stuff — Here you should think as much about the psychological aspects of the heavy stuff as you should about the damage that hanging it could possibly cause. Because tenant turnover is costly, you want your tenants to feel well rooted in your units so that, all things being equal, they will stay a long time. If they are comfortably ensconced in one of your rentals midst all their hanging plants, their swag lamps, their wall systems, and their pet canaries, they likely will stay awhile. Swallow hard and let them hang these things.

There is the danger, certainly, in their hanging this heavy stuff from your walls, that they'll use an inadequate fastener and that chunks of your walls will come tumbling down when their heavies and your walls part company, but you may avoid this danger by recommending that they first try to find a concealed stud to screw or nail into. Show them how to do it. This is by far the best way to hang any heavy things from either plaster or sheetrock walls. If this is absolutely impossible to do, recommend that they use an anchor (show them what you mean by an "anchor") designed to support at least twice the weight of their hanging.

By all means, discuss your hanging policy thoroughly with your tenants before they move in because few of them will approach you for permission or advice later on. They'll just go ahead and hang things any old way, but if you have discussed the matter with them in advance, most of them will try to follow your advice and hang their things your way.

SHOULD YOU HAVE DRAPERIES, SHADES, OR VENETIANS?

Every type of window covering has its place, of course. A fancy dwelling which rents for a handsome sum should have handsome appointments, to include fine draperies. You wouldn't want anything else for those places. For average rentals, you may find that contract draperies (see Maintenance & Repair Hints, "Measuring for Contract Draperies") are necessary to enhance appearances and generate additional revenue.

But don't overlook roller shades as a window covering possibility for any rental dwelling. They help to insulate. They are cheaper than drapes, longer lasting, easier to install, and easier to keep clean. They never need to be taken down for dry cleaning, they don't get threadbare, and except on sliding patio doors, shades and drapes can even fit on the same windows at the same time. You might consider supplying shades and drapery rods yourself and letting your tenants supply their own drapes, for those tenants who do supply their own draperies tend to stay put a lot longer.

Consider yourself lucky if you already have Venetian blinds in your rentals, and unless they are too dated, leave them right where they are because they should last a long time without requiring any further capital outlay. When kept cleaned and repaired by professionals, Venetians cost surprisingly little to maintain

Above all, do use some window coverings when your rentals are vacant. The obviously vacant dwelling with bare windows is a prime target for vandals and squatters, both of whom are on the increase these days.

SHOULD YOU CARPET THOSE FLOORS?

Understand, first of all, that there is no such thing as a perfect floor covering for rental dwellings. Each one has its disadvantages, but there is one floor covering which has fewer disadvantages and more advantages for most rentals, excluding kitchen and bath areas, than all the other floor coverings you might consider, and that one is wall-to-wall carpeting.

Besides the other attributes it has, carpeting adds tremendously to the soundproofing and income of any rental, and I can testify that it adds to the warmth and rentability as well. After working two weeks on one apartment unit installing a new kitchen counter, sink, oven, and vanity, and painting the walls and doors throughout, I thought I'd really made great changes, but all that work was nothing compared to the change that my carpet installer made in only three hours. Wow! That apartment was transformed from stark, cold, colorless housing into an inviting, warm, cheerful place which someone would want to call "home," and it rented easily for a substantial sum. It's no wonder tenants prefer wall-to-wall carpeting and will pay more for it.

Before you buy any carpeting, however, make a few important approximations to determine whether you ought to make the investment at all — Consider roughly how much the carpeting will cost (draw and measure the floorplan, determine the yardage required, and multiply that by a telephone quote); consider how much additional rent you can expect if you add carpets (make a brief marketing survey); consider how much your income property will increase in value if you add carpets (use prevailing rules of thumb for determining the market value of income property and see whether the addition of carpets will more than offset the cost); and consider whether the condition of the present floors warrants either adding carpets or recarpeting right now (look them over carefully).

After you have considered those investment questions and have decided to go ahead with the carpeting, you'll still have decisions to make about areas, colors, patterns, piles, yarns, pads, prices, suppliers, and installers. Read on and then make your decisions with deliberation.

Areas — Since one of your major concerns is the overall expense, you might save by carpeting only a portion of a unit, perhaps just a living room, because it will cost a mere fraction of a fully carpeted installation and yet you will have "wall-to-wall carpet" to tout to prospective tenants. Another possibility for savings involves laying durable sheet goods (linoleum, tile, or vinyl) by entrances (usually in a three-foot square) and in hallways where traffic is heavy and the carpet tends to wear and spot quickly. You won't notice any savings by doing this right away, but you will in time because you won't have to replace an entire room full of carpeting to eliminate the eyesore of small worn areas.

Colors — Carpets come in all the colors God made and in some that only man could concoct, many of which you can summarily reject for use in rental units. No matter what color you choose, you'll manage to choose one that clashes with some tenant's taste, so don't worry too much about it. In general, avoid light and bright colors and choose those which are relatively neutral. Medium shades of gold and brown are the most neutral, but greens and blues work well, too. Darker colors naturally show less dirt and fewer spots, while lighter colors are more cheerful and make rooms look larger. Select darker colors for rentals where you expect kids and less responsible tenants, and use lighter colors in places where you expect sun fading and more responsible tenants.

Patterns — There may be some doubts about what carpet color is best, but there's no doubt about what pattern of carpet is best for most rental units. Tweed is. Stains, wear areas, crumbs, toenail clippings, ashes, swatted flies, and swift cockroaches just don't show up as much on tweed. They blend right into its randomness.

Piles — While the most durable carpet pile you can buy is level-loop, the most camouflaging is short shag (3/4-inch yarn), sometimes called cabled plush. Both are good for use in rentals. Short shag in solid colors, and especially in tweeds, will camouflage anything tweeds will by themselves, and what's more, it will camouflage cigarette burns as well, but it shows traffic wear more than level-loops do. A 20-ounce (face weight measures the weight of the yarn in one square yard and determines a carpet's price) level-loop will actually outwear a 50-ounce shag. Use shag in living rooms and bedrooms which have a moderate amount of traffic and avoid using it in heavy traffic areas like hallways. Those are best covered with sheet goods in shag installations (mixing carpet piles or colors within a single dwelling looks too tacky). Because they are so tightly woven, level-loop carpets wear well and should be installed in heavy traffic areas, but they will definitely show burns. If traffic wear is your primary concern, then choose either level-loop carpeting by itself or short shag combined with sheet goods. If burns are your primary concern, choose short shag.

Pads — Remember that the pad you select is every bit as important as the carpet itself because it is the pad which gives carpeting that luxurious, substantial feeling underfoot and extends a carpet's life. Use a half-inch rebonded polyurethane pad or else a polymeric pad, and avoid jute, rubber, and light polyurethane pads. Rebonded and polymeric pads are in the lower, not the lowest, price range and are well worth the money. They will last through many changes of carpet.

Prices — Don't buy expensive carpet for rentals, no matter how much more wear the salesperson says you'll get from it because it will look just as shabby as an inexpensive carpet after tenants have used and abused it for five or six years. When combined with a good pad, nylon carpeting which sells in the lowest third of the price range will give at least as good service as expensive carpeting.

Suppliers — Carpet peddling is a very competitive business, and you can take advantage of this competition by shopping around for bids on your job. The biggest, most advertised retail supplier for the home market isn't necessarily the cheapest or the best source of carpets suitable for the rental market. Usually you will find better buys by trying small contract carpet firms who supply contractors with lots of yardage and will deal fairly with you as a landlord or landlady because they consider you a businessperson and a source of repeat business. Ask several building contractors for the names of their carpet suppliers and then check the ads in publications from your rental property owners' association.

Installers — If you can, get an itemized bid on your carpeting, at least for materials and labor, so you may hire your own installer if you wish. Many carpet installers moonlight, and you should be able to find a good one through "services offered" classified ads, one who will install your carpet for less than the price of the so-called "free installation" included in a package deal. Be sure you understand who's paying for the tackless strip and the metal threshold pieces, though. Some installers will quote you a price per yard which includes these items and others won't.

Squeaks — Before you have anyone install carpeting for you, tread splayfooted, like Charlie Chaplin playing the little tramp, over every square foot of the installation area to find all the squeaks that have been caused over the years by loosening of the subflooring nails. Then nail the squeaks out with 2½-inch cement-coated screw or ring nails placed strategically alongside the squeaky culprits. Squeaky floors annoy tenants upstairs and downstairs and detract from the image of your building.

HIRING HELP

Having decided to hire help to assist you in your landlording business (see "Should You Do It Yourself?" in Chapter 8), you become a boss, perhaps for the first time in your life.

Suffer no great trepidation over this new role. Just prepare for it. You survived being called a landlord or landlady, didn't you? Surely, then, you will survive being called a boss. The truth is that as a landlord or landlady who hires help, you are more than just a boss supervising people, you're the personnel, accounting, payroll, legal, and executive departments of your business all rolled into one. Sounds impressive and forbidding, doesn't it? It is, but don't worry. If you have shown yourself to be a competent landlord or landlady, you'll be a competent employer as well. It just takes some common sense, some understanding of people, and some acquaintance with several laws, practices, procedures, and forms.

These next few pages are not meant to tell you all you need to know about hiring help, for that is an enormous subject and there are numerous books devoted to it alone. The information here is intended merely to get you started in the right direction and to keep you out of trouble as you face a number of responsibilities and tasks which are altogether different from the usual ones involved in do-it-yourself landlording and probably altogether different from your normal workaday world, too, unless you already happen to be self-employed and have a staff working for you.

Although the information here pertains more to managers than to the other workers you might hire, it is, for the most part, relevant to both. Because residency is generally required for managers and because they have so much responsibility, the hiring process is somewhat more rigorous for them, but it can easily be modified to suit the hiring of other workers as well.

• *Hiring employees or independent contractors* — You have undoubtedly hired help in the past without thinking much about it. You were hiring help when you hired a roofer to repair a leaky roof and when you called a plumber to install a new commode, but that was contractual hiring. In other words, those who did the work were not your employees. They were performing services for you while being either self-employed or employed by somebody else. You agreed to pay them a flat fee or an hourly rate and they gave you a bill for their work. You may have blanched at those bills, but you had no hidden costs, no reports due to governmental agencies, no increased insurance burden, and no extra bookkeeping chores, all of which you would have had if the roofer and plumber, strictly speaking, were your employees.

Because of those benefits inherent in contractual employment and because contractual employees can be expected to do good work without requiring supervision, many landlords and landladies hire only bonded contractual help — commercial gardeners, professional window washers, painting specialists, plumbing contractors, carpet cleaning services, and the like. They may pay more, but they avoid all the hassles and burdens of being an employer, and they get the work done well and quickly.

Some landlords and landladies have tried to avoid the legal obligations and paperwork involved in being employers in another way, by drawing up contracts for those who are their employees and calling the work contractual. Years ago that strategem worked satisfactorily, but it doesn't any longer. "An employee by any other name is still an employee," the government has ruled, especially if the employer controls both what work is to be done and how it is to be done. Other tests to determine whether workers may be considered independent contractors are these — Do the workers have business licenses? Do they pay their own deductions, including self-employment tax? Do they assume legal liability for their work and do they carry appropriate insurance?

If the answers to these questions are in the affirmative, then the workers could be considered independent contractors and your only responsibility would be to pay them. If not, you must consider them your employees and assume all the attendant responsibilities, responsibilities which add approximately 30% to the actual wages you pay them, a heavy burden indeed. In other words, a worker whom you pay $4 a hour will really cost you $5.20. It's no wonder landlords and landladies would like to interpret certain work relationships as contractual, and it's no wonder the government has pursued the matter to recover taxes and protect the welfare of employees.

Keep in mind that apartment managers, the helpers you are most likely to hire, are always considered employees, no matter what ploy you might try for transforming them into independent contractors. Therefore, you might as well resign yourself to having an extra paperwork and expense burden whenever you hire a manager. (Although laws usually require on-site managers only for buildings with sixteen or more units, having someone on the premises of every multiple-family dwelling you own is a worthwhile convenience.) You may get away without assuming this burden if you discount a tenant's rent a few dollars or pay a nominal sum every month to a resident who acts in your stead as, say rent collector and resident keeper of the keys, but even then you should secure both workers' compensation and non-owned auto insurance coverage. The potential liability for not having this minimal insurance when you hire help is too draconian for you to bear.

As for doing the burdensome paperwork involved in hiring employees, that will depend pretty much on whether you are hiring casual helpers or regular helpers and on how much money they are earning over a given period of time. If you wonder whether you should do the paperwork, call the governmental agencies involved with collecting taxes on wages and ask them.

• *Complying with the laws* — As an employer, you must comply with a variety of laws designed to protect employees, collect taxes, and employ countless bureaucratic minions. To find out how these laws apply to you, contact both your federal tax office and your state or provincial department of employment. They will supply you with the proper instructions, employer numbers, tables, timetables, and forms necessary for complying with the laws.

• *Defining the job and setting the pay* — Whenever people consider taking a job, they always have at least two questions in mind — "What's required of me?" and "What's the pay?" You should have the answers at the ready to both those questions and to others as well before you ever begin looking for help, casual or permanent.

If the job involves management, it might include as little as collecting rents when due, showing vacancies, and keeping the keys, or it might include all that plus pursuing late payers, checking applications, selecting tenants, banking, keeping records, doing maintenance and repairs, cleaning, gardening, painting, and reacting to tenants' complaints. List the tasks you expect your managers to perform and also try to establish the amount of time you think they should spend on those tasks during the month. Collecting rents when due, you might figure, would average ten minutes per dwelling per month, and so on. Review your time estimates after the managers have been on the job a while.

Establishing the time which a managerial position should require and keeping records on the time managers actually do spend working at the job became important a few years ago when overtaxed property managers began suing their employers for overtime pay because owners were requiring managers to work and be available long hours, all for a fixed wage. You know who won.

Here are some ideas about pay — Inquire into local practices for compensating full- and part-time managers.

Set the pay for part-time management by multiplying the minimum wage times the anticipated number of hours you expect managers to work, but guarantee to pay a certain salary every month.

Do not agree to pay a manager's utilities. You cannot predict how much they will cost every month.

Pay your helpers after they have done their work, not before. Compensating part-time managers in the form of rent constitutes advance payment. Collect full rent from them, the same as from other tenants, and then pay them a salary at the end of the month. They tend to regard discounted rent after a while as a birthright, not a compensation.

Compensate full-time managers with salary and rent only if that is the accepted practice. Check into the special tax rules which apply to the portion of a manager's income attributable to the residence.

Pay the members of a management team (couple) separately for the work each performs so each of them will receive Social Security credits.

Do not expect your employees to put forth a reasonable effort for unreasonable wages. Raise managers' salaries every time you raise rents.

• *Establishing a worker profile* — Recognizing that careless maintenance workers and bigoted, caustic, timid, or frenetic managers all will cost you time and money and good tenants, too, you should try to establish a profile of the ideal worker your job requires and then identify the categories of people who might be most likely to fit that profile.

Managers for most multiple-family dwellings, for example, should be fair, honest, reliable, used to dealing with people, intelligent, self assured, unflappable, willing to learn, handy, helpful, modest, pleasant, and patient homebodies who can speak with an air of authority and resemble the resident of the property they manage.

Who is most likely to fit a profile like that? Nobody, but those with service-oriented backgrounds would be the most likely. Some owners have identified the clergy and those who do volunteer work as likely managerial candidates.

The chances are you'll have to compromise in your choice, so decide which managerial qualities are most important for the job and which are the least important. Rank them.

• *Finding help* — Just as you will usually inherit tenants when you acquire a multiple-family dwelling, you will also frequently inherit managers, and you will be faced with the decision of whether to keep the managers or find your own. Unless there are obvious reasons to let them go right away, agree to keep them for a month until you become familiar with the place and can make an informed decision whether to keep them or not on a permanent basis. (Because this takeover period is the perfect time for dishonest managers to abscond with funds, be sure to look very carefully through the rental payment records of any property which has a manager and ask questions until you understand precisely who owes what and when it is owed.)

Whenever you're looking for management help, consider your existing tenants first on your list of prospects. They already have a familiarity with the property and its occupants, and they are known to you, so you needn't be particularly apprehensive about their character. Good tenants whom I have approached about becoming managers have invariably become good managers, even, believe it or not, for as many as 113 units. (One good tenant I approached about managing an eightplex, refused the job; he wanted to look after the building all right, but he didn't want tenants banging on his door at all hours. We made a deal that he would keep the keys, show vacancies, and clean around the building but that tenants would send their rent payments to me and call me with their complaints. The arrangement worked beautifully for years.) You might be surprised about the pool of talent that most residential income properties have, and you should not be averse to using it.

If you cannot identify one of your good tenants as a managerial candidate, advertise the position through classified ads, management schools' employment offices, agencies, and your rental property owners' association. You'll likely be besieged with applicants, for there seem to be many people who find the work agreeable.

When you're looking around for maintenance and repair help, consider your tenants second on your list of prospects. Whom would you consider first? Your relatives and friends, of course. Haven't you ever heard of nepotism? After eliminating your relatives and friends as prospects, look to your tenants for this kind of help, and only as a last resort should you have to advertise.

• *Prequalifying* — If you are considering someone you know for a job, you have prequalified them already in your mind before you ever approached them about it, but if perfect strangers are approaching you about a job, you should prequalify them and tell them a little about the position before you arrange for an interview. If the position involves resident management, ask them the same questions you'd ask to prequalify tenant applicants and then ask them about their availability, experience, and salary requirements. If they sound worth pursuing, set up an interview. Otherwise, don't waste your time and theirs.

• *Interviewing* — Arrange employment interviews at the property itself preferably. Outline the job first, including its responsibilities, its advantages, and its drawbacks. Tell applicants whether their living in a certain dwelling is a prerequisite for the position. Explain what the compensation is and when it's paid. Tell them whether there are raises which might be expected after a trial period, and so on.

Employment Application

Name _Charley Goodfolks_   Home Phone **555-0222**   Work Phone **555-1981**

Date of Birth _4/4/36_   Social Security No. _198-83-6509_   Driver's License No. _Z900123_

Own ___ Rent _✓_ at address? _1 yr._

Present Add

How many ye
Present/La
Occupation

Monthly Gross _#13_

Spouse's Name _C_

How many
Present/
Occupati

Monthly Gross

Depende
and age

What s
have

What
spous

What
you

Are
Whe

Sav
Ban

Ch
Ba

Ma
C

Management Agreement

Dated **APRIL 16, 1984**

Agreement between **DUKE & LUCY MILQUETOAST**, Owners, and **CHARLES & AGNES GOODFOLKS**, Managers, for management of property located at **2100 MAIN ST. BIGTOWN**.

Compensation for Managers shall be $ **100.00** per month at a guaranteed minimum and shall be computed at an hourly rate of $ **4.00**. Unless Managers obtain Owners' permission in advance or, in case of emergency, unless they notify Owners within 48 hours afterwards, Managers shall spend no more than **25** hours per month on managerial responsibilities. Managers shall record working hours on time sheets provided by Owners, one time sheet for each person exercising managerial responsibilities, and shall submit those time sheets at least once a month.

Other compensation shall be as follows: **NONE; COMPENSATION ON AN HOURLY OR PER-JOB BASIS FOR ADDITIONAL TASKS.**

Managers shall have days off as follows: **TUESDAY & WEDNESDAY**; vacation time as follows: **ONE DAY PER MONTH (ACCUMULATING)**; sick leave as follows: **ONE DAY PER MONTH (ACCUMULATING)**.

Managers' duties and responsibilities, which will be reviewed jointly in ninety days and annually after that, shall be as follows: **KEEPING THE KEYS, COLLECTING RENTS WHEN DUE, PURSUING LATE PAYERS, SHOWING VACANCIES, MINOR MAINTENANCE (FIX LEAKY FAUCETS; REPLACE LIGHT SWITCHES AND LIGHT BULBS OUTSIDE), CLEAN GROUNDS AS NEEDED.**

Managers shall receipt all monies collected on the Owners' behalf and shall deposit or transfer those monies within **TWO DAYS** of collection as follows: **CALL OWNERS TO REPORT COLLECTIONS; DEPOSIT COLLECTIONS TO MILQUETOAST PROP. TWO.**

Managers shall spend or commit to spend no more than $ **50.00** on the Owners' behalf without first obtaining permission.

Either Managers or Owners may cancel this agreement upon providing **SEVEN** days' written notice.

Managers hereby acknowledge that they have read this agreement, understand it, agree to it, and have been given a copy.

Owner _Duke Milquetoast_

By _____

Manager _Charles Goodfolks_

Manager _Agnes Goodfolks_

Ask them whether the job appears attractive to them and whether they feel capable of handling it. If so, proceed to ask them questions using the employment application as a guide, and transcribe the information yourself so you can measure their responses and let them talk freely. Ask them to go backwards in time and account for all their jobs and schooling over the previous five years. In addition to the questions on the application, you might want to ask such questions as how they feel about living in close proximity with people as manager and not being able to be good friends with anybody, how they would describe themselves to a stranger, what accomplishments they are most proud of, and why they feel they should be considered for the job. Establish eye contact with them during the interview. Be friendly, attentive, and helpful, and encourage them to talk frankly while you take notes.

When you have finished the interview, show them around the place and make a promise to call them back within the next couple of days to inform them of your decision. It's only fair to let them know soon what you have decided so they can make other plans for themselves.

• *Selecting* — Call the employer references and try to verify the information you gathered about the applicants. Ask about the circumstances surrounding their departure from the job and ask quite frankly whether the employer would consider hiring them again.

After calling employers, call one personal reference and maybe run a credit check. Then, if everything appears to be satisfactory and you are interested in hiring the applicants, make an appointment to talk with them where they currently reside.

When you see where they live and how they live, you will be able to decide whether to hire them or not. If you don't like what you see, tell them you have other applicants to visit before you make your decision, and then leave. If you do like what you see, show them a blank copy of your management agreement and go over it with them. Be certain they understand those provisions in the agreement which call for them to submit their hours of work regularly on a time sheet. If the job means that they will be moving into a manager's dwelling, show them a copy of the Rental Agreement, too, and review it. Then complete both forms.

• *Supervising* — If one of your employees were to discriminate against a prospective tenant illegally, give a tenant a black eye, fire another employee improperly, or even cause an automobile accident while on the way to bank your rent receipts, you as their employer would be responsible. You can ill afford those problems. Managers should save you time and worry, not cost you both. Take the time, therefore, to let your managers know how much discretionary authority they have to act on their own, how much money they can spend without asking for your approval, which suppliers and service people you prefer them to patronize, what constitutes an emergency, what necessitates their calling you right away, how they should go about selecting new tenants, how you would like existing tenants to be treated, what your rent collection policy is, and how they should handle time sheets.

After you have told them what you want them to do and how you want them to do it, let them do it. Never undermine your manager's authority either by allowing tenants to approach you behind the manager's back or by making deals without the manager's knowledge. Tenants will try to divide and conquer. Don't let them get away with it. Listen to what they have to say if they take the trouble to contact you directly, but then talk with the manager and either let the manager reply to them or arrange a three-way discussion. Never go to see the tenants by yourself without first consulting the manager.

Time Sheet

Charley Goodfolks
Employee's Name

Charley Goodfolks
Employee's Signature

2100 Main St.
Property

Pay Period **3/1** to **3/15**

DATE	TIMES		HOURS	DESCRIPTION OF WORK PERFORMED	CONTRACT AMOUNT
3/1	5:00 5:30	5:15 7:45	2 ½	groundskeeping; rent collection	
3/2	5	6	1	" "	
3/3	5:20	6:30	1⅙	" "	
3/4	5	5:15	¼	" "	
3/5	12 3	1 5	3	groundskeeping and dump run with my truck	5.00
3/9	5:15	6:00	¾	groundskeeping	
3/10	5	5:30	½	plumbing repair Apt. 4	
3/12	10	11:30	1½	groundskeeping	
3/14	6	7:20	1⅓	"	

Total Hours **12**

Rate **4.00**

Hourly Gross **48.00**

Contract **5.00**

Total Gross **$ 53.00**

Total Contract **5.00**

Approved by _____ **3/16** Date

If your employees are not handling the overall job as you wish it handled, tell them the source of your dissatisfaction and give them an opportunity to improve. If they don't improve, give them the opportunity to quit so they can save face by not being fired.

Since all people like to know that their work is appreciated, show your employees some appreciation. Praise them when they do good work and criticize them as constructively as you can when they err.

• *Doing payroll* — Using both the time sheets which your employees submit at least once a month and the figures for deductions provided by government agencies, calculate your employees' gross earnings and all their necessary deductions. Write those figures in duplicate on a statement of earnings and deductions form (Rediform 4H416 is one of many available for this purpose) for each employee. Tear out the original and give it to the employee along with your check for the employee's net earnings. Leave the copy of the statement attached to the pad as a record of payment and then transfer those figures to the Payroll Record sheet you keep for each employee (see sample in Chapter 11).

Do not deceive yourself into thinking that the employee's deductions are all you need to keep track of and pay to the government. You must contribute, too. Be sure to indicate in the shaded column your own Social Security contribution as an employer. This sum, almost equal to the employee's Social Security contribution, was not reflected in the statement given to the employee, but you must keep track of it nonetheless, and you must forward it, along with the other monies collected, to the various governmental agencies involved at either monthly or quarterly intervals. Failure to do so will result in a response much swifter than any made to the person who fails to file an individual income tax return. For instructions about forwarding these monies, check the employer information provided by the government.

In spite of all the complications involved in hiring help, you will find that your landlording business will prosper so much more with help than without it and that you will feel liberated enough to enjoy some of the advantages of the business. You cannot do all the work yourself. Don't die trying.

INSURANCE & SECURITY

Believe it or not, General Motors' biggest single expense is not steel, aluminum, or even plastic. It's insurance, insurance of all kinds. GM, with its considerable assets, has decided to proceed with caution in a society overrun with attorneys who are quick to place an inflated dollar on stubbed toes and kinked necks and have convinced many people to pursue their fortunes through litigation.

As a rental property owner with assets somewhat less than GM's, you need not follow GM's example by spending more on insurance than anything else, but you should nevertheless be well covered with various kinds of insurance. You become increasingly vulnerable to losses, too, as you build your property assets, assets which look quite attractive to someone contemplating a suit against you. Litigants and their legal counsel don't care how hard or how long you worked to gather those assets. They just want all they can get out of you, and, of course, they know you're wealthy because, after all, you own income property.

Because you do own income property, you have special insurance needs above and beyond those of people who don't. You should know something about the kinds of insurance available to serve those needs and something about the prudence of providing coverage. Here are some important insurance considerations for landlords and landladies.

Fire — Mortgage companies require you to protect their interest in your building with a fire insurance policy at the very least because they figure they cannot afford to risk a loss should the place go up in smoke. You should be even more cautious than they are because your equity in a building represents a much greater proportion of your total assets than what one building represents of a mortgage company's assets. In fact, since your equity in that property keeps increasing while the mortgage company's is decreasing, you should be so cautious that whenever your fire insurance comes due, you should make certain your building is covered with a policy large enough to pay current replacement costs.

Extended Coverage — Fire insurance is great for fires, but what if fire insurance is all the insurance you have and your building is laid waste by flood, earthquake, wind, collapse, explosion, hail, lightning, smoke, hurricane, burst pipes, or rioting? In such calamities you may not be the only one with a loss, but your loss would be yours alone to bear. Be wise. Add water damage coverage to your insurance policy if you're in a flood area. Be cautious. Add earthquake coverage if you're in an earthquake zone (cheap it's not; worthwhile it is). Add other extended coverage, too, if you believe there's any likelihood of other damage occurring to your property. You want to sleep nights.

Vandalism and Malicious Mischief — Should anyone damage your property, say, by driving an uninsured automobile recklessly through an outside wall, tearing your laundry machines apart for the coins, or laying waste a vacant apartment, your vandalism and malicious mischief insurance would pay to repair the damage. Hopefully you'll never have occasion to use such coverage because damage like this is pretty demoralizing to a conscientious owner, but if it should happen, you ought to have the right insurance to pay for the repairs.

Liability — Although you would seldom be held liable for personal accidents which take place on your property so long as the property is kept in good repair, you would have to pay the legal costs necessary to absolve yourself from liability, and those costs could be substantial. Don't take the risk. Buy liability insurance, and while you're at it, buy the highest limits available. You will find that a million dollars' worth of coverage costs little more than a hundred thousand and it could save you from the poorhouse, for the awards people do manage to get in liability cases tend to be high. In addition to regular property liability insurance, you should have non-owned auto liability insurance, too. It protects you in case your employees are driving their own automobiles while on errands for you and become involved in an automobile accident. It's inexpensive insurance and well worth the cost.

Loss of Rents — If a fire or some other mishap should occur and render one of your rentals uninhabitable for a while, your tenants will stop paying you their rent at once, and you will have to pay those continuing bills all by yourself, that is, unless you have loss-of-rents insurance coverage. In that case, your insurance company will compensate you for the loss of rental income over a reasonable period of time while your building is being repaired. With all the other problems you're likely to have if there is a mishap at your property, you don't need financial problems too, not when you can protect yourself for a small premium.

Contents — Your own belongings which you keep at your rental property, belongings such as mowers, tools, laundry machines, furniture, appliances, supplies, and the like, would be covered against loss by a comprehensive rental property owner's insurance policy (check to make sure), but your tenants' belongings would not be covered at all. Because tenants frequently assume erroneously that your insurance does cover their possessions, you should mention when you first rent to them that they should secure their own tenant's insurance policy if they want coverage. You might even remind them of their exposure every so often in a note included with their rent receipt.

Workers' Compensation — Even though you hire only casual help or deduct just a few dollars from a tenant's rent in exchange for minor management services, you are an employer and you must have workers' compensation insurance. If that worker of yours were to require the slightest medical attention or become the least bit incapacitated while in your employ, you would be liable. Don't assume this risk yourself. You know what medical bills can run nowadays and you probably know what awards juries are making to people who become disabled on the job. You cannot afford to pay out such sums. Most states require every employer to have workers' compensation insurance and they control the rates which

February 25, 1984

Dear *Richard and Mary Renter,*

As we do every year, we have been reviewing our insurance policies, and we thought that you might like to know how you are affected by the insurance we carry.

Basically, our policies cover only the building itself where you live. They do not cover any of your own belongings against damage or disappearance, nor do they cover you for negligence should you, for example, leave a burner going under a pan of grease and start a fire which damages the kitchen.

To protect yourself against these calamities, you should get a tenant's insurance policy. Most insurance companies and agents will write such a policy for you, and we would strongly urge that you inquire about getting one.

For the peace of mind that it gives, a tenant's insurance policy is reasonable indeed.

Sincerely,

Lester Landlord

are charged, but you may find that a group coverage available through your rental property owners' association is advantageous.

Mortgage — Homeowners frequently buy mortgage insurance, also known as decreasing term life insurance, to protect themselves in case death puts an end to some or all of the income used to make their house payments. The mortgate would then be paid off in full. You should know that such insurance is available to cover rental property mortgages as well, and it may be just as important for some landlords and landladies to have as it is for homeowners, especially when a rental property is running a negative cash flow and one person is contributing income from a job to sustain it. When determining whether you should get mortgage insurance, consider both the cash (salary) and the time contributions of each person involved with the property because you may find that hired help would be needed to compensate for the work done by one of those involved, and that, of course, would increase the negative cash flow still more. If you do choose to buy mortgage insurance for income property, consult your accountant for advice on whether it is tax-deductible as a business expense in your situation. It may or may not be.

Fidelity — In some businesses where dishonest employees have the opportunity to steal cash and goods, employers buy fidelity insurance, that is, they bond their employees to protect themselves from pilferage and embezzlement. The employees you hire to manage and maintain your rental property have the opportunity to steal from you, but they won't have the opportunity to steal very much if they handle little or no cash, and they won't steal from you at all if you have selected them carefully and if you exercise tight controls. Rather than pay fidelity insurance premiums for a policy which will pay careless employers for their carelessness, save the money and insure yourself by being careful. The premiums for this insurance are really much too high for the limited amount of exposure you have.

Auto — To protect your property assets, you should obtain the highest liability limits available for your own automobiles. Minimum liability insurance may be sufficient for your tenants. If they're hit with a $500,000 judgment, their insurance policy would pay to the limits of the policy, their few assets would be liquidated, and they would simply declare bankruptcy. It's done every day. But what if you get hit with a $500,000 judgment, and you have only $100,000 in coverage? Kiss everything goodbye. Caveat Landlord and Landlady!

Insurance is certainly available for every conceivable risk connected with landlording if you want to pay for it, and there are a great many insurance agents around who would be delighted to sell it to you, but since you surely don't want insurance to become your number-one expense as it is for GM, you should seize the opportunity to save money every time you review your insurance needs. Naturally you might be prudent in trying to save or you might be imprudent.

- Here's how to be prudent:
  Select only the kinds of coverage you need for your situation. (Are there that many hurricanes in Montana?)
  Calculate carefully the amount of coverage you need. (Do I really need $500,000 worth of fire insurance for my $95,000 duplex?)
  Shop around for coverage. ($285? Gerry wants $450 for the same thing!)
  Price package policies. (You mean that fire, vandalism, liability, loss of rents, and contents coverage all together are only $20 more than fire insurance alone?)

Consider policies with deductibles. (Does earthquake insurance with a $1000 deductible clause really have a premium $222 lower?)

- Here's how to be imprudent:

    Buy only the kinds and amounts of coverage your lender and the law require. (The tenant in Apt. 112 wants how much for tripping on that broken step?)

    Buy whatever coverage your agent sells you. (You think I need glacier coverage? OK, if you say so. The winters have been getting colder. Write it up.)

    Buy only from your bridge partner who sells insurance on the side. (Can you get me a deal, Gerry?)

    Buy separate policies. (Is it $85 more for contents and $18 for loss of rents or vice versa?)

    Buy total, non-deductible coverage. (You want to settle my claim about the dent in my commercial washing machine for $12?)

Be prudent whenever you buy insurance affecting your income property business. You'll save on the premiums and you'll protect your assets so someday you'll be able to enjoy them yourself.

FIRE EXTINGUISHERS

Why it is that insurance companies don't require fire extinguishers for all the buildings they insure, I certainly don't know. I do know that no rental building I have ever purchased has had them, and now they all do.

Although you are undoubtedly violating local fire ordinances if you do not have extinguishers available at your rental properties, enforcement of those ordinances is so lax that the chances are good you won't be fined or even warned if you don't have them. But why should you wait for a fire safety inspector to tell you to install extinguishers before you buy them? They are important enough that you should go out and buy them right now, today. Remember that your property and your tenants' lives and their property are all endangered if there's no extinguisher available when needed.

You need witness only one fire in your rentals to become convinced that you need extinguishers, but by then, of course, it's too late. If you haven't witnessed any fires in your rental lately, consider this scenario: Tenants leave a pan of grease on a burner turned inadvertently to high heat. All of a sudden, the grease ignites into flames high enough to burn the kitchen cabinets and set the walls on fire. The tenants rush about looking for an extinguisher nearby, and finding none, they try dousing the flames with water. Naturally, that only feeds the inferno. Finally realizing their plight, they grab their portable color TV, scramble out, and scream "FIRE!" Someone calls the fire department, but by the time they arrive and can put out the blaze, the entire apartment and the one next to it are rendered uninhabitable.

Then what happens? The insurance adjuster surveys the damage. You get estimates for repairs, and sometime later work begins. Three months after the fire you're looking around for new tenants to move into the repaired apartments. You have lost three months' rent on two apartments, spent hours of your own time planning and supervising, and gone through the uncertainties again of selecting more new tenants. In other words, you're out of pocket considerable expenses and you have wasted a considerable amount of time. Even if you do have a rent loss coverage provision in your insurance policy, you still suffer a loss because of all the time you have had to spend on the project, time you cannot be compensated for.

You need fire extinguishers. There's no doubt about it. So the question is what type should you buy?

The extinguisher you buy should be effective in fighting all kinds of fires, it should be easy to carry and use, it should not leave a catastrophe to clean up after, it should be durable, it should be rechargeable, and it should be modestly priced.

There is one type which fits these guidelines fairly well, but first let me warn you about two types of extinguishers which are widely used around rental properties and should be avoided as if they were incendiary bombs. Soda-acid and pressurized water extinguishers they're called. They are easy to recognize because they both come in shiny chrome or brass cylinders about two feet tall and eight inches in diameter. You'll notice them around many apartment houses. I suppose they're still used because grandpa used to use them, and I suppose they're still all right if you happen to have a stationery store, a lumber yard, or a yardage shop because they're great for putting out paper, wood, and textile fires, but they're as messy as untrained quints to clean up after. They're also heavy, and they only aggravate other types of fires because they shoot water, hardly the best extinguishing agent for small fires.

You should use dry chemical fire extinguishers exclusively, ones which are filled with a mono-ammonium-phosphate-base dry chemical or its equivalent as an extinguishing agent and will work on any class of fire. These extinguishers fit the guidelines well. The five pounder, rated 2A, 40B, and C is ideally suited for apartment installations. It's called a five pounder because the fire-fighting chemicals inside weigh just that. Its total weight is around ten pounds, still light enough so almost any tenant could wield it.

Check the letters and numbers on any extinguisher you are considering in order to determine the class and size of fire it can effectively extinguish. The letters stand for classes of fire: A — wood, paper, cloth, rubbish, and some plastics; B — flammable liquids, paint, grease, and cooking oil; and C — electrical (live). The number appearing before each class was assigned by Underwriters' Laboratories (UL) and indicates the size fire in that class which the extinguisher will put out. The larger the number, the larger the fire it will put out, and hence the greater is the extinguisher's effectiveness. A 1A extinguisher, for example, will put out 50 burning pieces of wood, 2″ × 2″ and 20″ long; a 2A extinguisher will put out a fire twice that size, and so on. A 1B extinguisher will put out 3.25 gallons of naphtha blazing away in a 2.5 square foot pan, and, likewise, a 2B extinguisher will extinguish a blaze twice that size. Only the C class has no numerical rating. C means that the chemical in the extinguisher does not conduct electricity and is therefore safe to be used on electrical fires. The big soda-acid and pressured water extinguishers have a 2A rating, and that's all. They're totally worthless on flammable liquids and on electrical fires, whereas the five pounder is just as effective on Class A fires as the water monsters are, besides having a 40B and a C rating, too.

Having selected a suitable type, you will still have to decide where to place your extinguishers, what size to buy, what brand to buy, and whether or not to house them in glass-fronted boxes. Generally speaking, one five pounder is enough for four to five single-story apartments if their doors are within thirty feet of the extinguisher's location. If you have a fourplex with entrances on two levels, install two extinguishers, one on each level, and be safe. If you can't decide where to place them outside, try mounting one two pounder in every kitchen. Sometimes this course is more economical anyway because you don't then have to buy glass-fronted boxes (around $20 apiece), something I always do when mounting extinguishers outside. Two pounders with a rating of 1A:10BC run between $12 and $30 each, while the five pounders with a rating of 2A:40BC are $25 to $40. Shop around and compare prices because extinguishers are often discounted.

The cautions which follow all resulted from costly or painful experiences I have had with extinguishers myself. I hope you may learn the lessons involved without having to repeat the experiences.

• Caution One — You would think that extinguishers which are labeled "rechargeable" are, in fact, rechargeable. Well, technically they may be, but in a practical sense they may not be rechargeable at all because they may be able to hold only their original factory charge and not one they get in the field. When their contents have been spent on a fire or they have lost their pressure spontaneously over time, you might try to have them recharged at an extinguisher service shop only to learn that what you purchased are disposable extinguishers rather than rechargeable ones. If you expect your extinguishers to last a long time and take recharging, then before you buy, ask the advice of someone trustworthy who recharges extinguishers for a living, preferable someone who does not also sell extinguishers.

• Caution Two — If you do buy the smaller extinguishers, be wary about placing them in any exposed areas, including shared laundry facilities. They're the perfect size for use in cars, trucks, boats, and recreational vehicles, and they sometimes develop legs. Engrave them with your name and a distinguishing number, such as the address of your rental building, so you can identify them positively when necessary.

• Caution Three — Heads, bare fists, and feet were not made to break glass, TV barroom brawls notwithstanding. Instruct your tenants to use a shod foot or any hard object that doesn't bleed when they have to break the glass in an emergency to get an extinguisher.

• Caution Four — No extinguisher lasts very long. Nine to twelve seconds is all a five pounder will last in a sustained blast. It's made to be used in short two-second bursts rather than all at once, and though it certainly will not extinguish a burning house, it will extinguish any small fire your tenants are apt to have.

SMOKE DETECTORS

Some landlord or landlady must have invented paint rollers and smoke detectors because both of these devices are so tailor-made for use in rental properties — the one to minimize endless painting work, the other to minimize exposure to fire damage.

Even if you do hang fire extinguishers on every wall, you're still exposed to fire damage, for someone has to act fast and use those extinguishers when they're needed. If no one acts fast enough, a whole building could quickly become a midden of ashes with some brand-new, unused extinguishers down near the bottom.

Along with your carefully selected fire extinguishers, therefore, you should provide carefully selected smoke detectors, passive devices to warn tenants of any impending fire danger which they can act upon before it gets out of control. Because tenants tend to be a little more careless about handling fire-causing agents than you would be and because you can't possibly keep watch over them constantly, smoke detectors are ideal watchdogs to protect life, limb, and property.

Now that so many manufacturers make them, perfectly adequate smoke detectors are available for as little as $10. These are battery-operated ionization detectors which can be mounted anywhere since they need no electrical outlet. Select a detector which uses a readily available battery like the standard 9 volt battery used in transistor radios and make sure you check the functioning of each detector periodically.

THE PIN-TUMBLER LOCK MECHANISM

The type of lock mechanism used to secure most residential property, both houses and apartments, in the United States and Canada is called the pin-tumbler mechanism. It seems complicated enough with its strange inner works, its numerous pin chambers, its key varieties, and its 36,000 different key combinations, but it's not.

Basically, it consists of only two pieces, a revolving plug and a cylinder surrounding the plug, and it works on a simple principle. Running vertically through the plug and the cylinder are pin chambers, each of which has at least two pins (sometimes called tumblers) and a spring. When a wrong key is inserted into the plug, the pins act like dowels holding the plug and cylinder in place together and preventing the plug from turning. (See illustration). When the correct key is inserted into the plug, the key cuts push up all the lower pins to

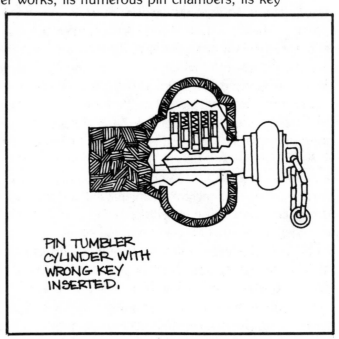

PIN TUMBLER CYLINDER WITH WRONG KEY INSERTED.

form a shear line level with the surface of the plug, and they, in turn, force all the upper pins up inside the cylinder's pin chambers. The plug can then revolve and move the various parts which open the lock. (See illustration showing plug follower.)

Like most products, locks with pin-tumbler mechanisms vary considerably in quality and price. They may all look shiny and similar on the outside, but on the inside you'd notice a big difference in their complexity and in the materials used. Some plugs and cylinders are made of plastic, some of pot metal, some of steel and others of solid brass. These differences are generally reflected in lock prices which range from less than $10 to more than $50. Strangely enough, however, prices do not necessarily determine the strength, reliability, or useful life of a lock.

All things considered, Kwiksets, largest selling of all key-in-the-knob and deadbolt locks for domestic applications and among the least expensive locks available, are the best buy I have found for residential income properties. Kwiksets have few moving parts and are so reliable that even those I have encountered which have been used daily for twenty-five years have worked perfectly. Their key duplicates always work, and their key blanks and parts are readily available. In addition, because the top of the pin chambers is removeable, you can rekey a Kwikset lock even if you don't have the original keys, without first having to pick it open, something important to amateur locksmiths.

Because key-in-the-knob locks have all their pin-tumblers in the outside knob and are therefore quite vulnerable to a forceable assault with simple tools, you should combine a doorknob lock with a one-inch deadbolt to provide something more than minimum security for your tenants. Remember, of course, that no matter how many or what kind of locks you provide, you'll never be able to deter for very long someone who is determined to break in.

KEYING LOCKS ALIKE

In these crime-crazy times, you have to provide more locks than ever. Some cities are enacting ordinances requiring landlords and landladies to install one-inch deadbolts as well as spring latches on every outside entry door where they can be installed, and some tenants are asking for even a third or fourth lock. You have to make your rentals secure, certainly, but more locks mean more keys, and more keys mean more complications. How can you keep things simple and check this proliferation of keys?

One thing you can do is key all the locks in a dwelling alike so that one key will fit every lock. Ordinarily each dwelling in an apartment house requires a different key for every door lock, plus one for the mailbox and one for the common laundry room. Since you probably provide two copies of each key for your tenants, give one to a manager on the premises, and keep one for yourself, you need, all together, four identical keys for each lock. That translates into a lot of keys, especially when you multiply your total number of locks by four. By keying locks alike, you can reduce the number of different keys for each dwelling to only two, one for the mailbox and one for all the other locks, no matter how many there are. Added deadbolt locks on outer doors and additional locks on inner doors can be keyed to the original doorknob lock, and the laundry room lock can be specially keyed by using pins in only one or two pin chambers so that any key in the building will fit.

You might think that for any two locks to be keyed alike, they must have keys that look alike, but surprisingly enough, that is not the case. Even though you may have locks from two, three, or even four different manufacturers and even though the keys may look completely different, you still may be able to key those locks alike. The most important consideration is whether the key fits the keyway, not what the key itself looks like. Kwikset, Weiser, Dexter, and ILCO locks all can be keyed alike even though the keys that come with them look very dissimilar. To see what I mean for yourself, take any Kwikset key and insert it into the keyway of any

Weiser, Dexter, or ILCO lock. You'll find that it slips in easily. It won't open the lock, to be sure, but it could open the lock if it were keyed to do so. (Because Weiser keys are slightly

thicker than those for other locks and fit other keyways rather snugly, always key, say, a Weiser lock and a Kwikset lock, both to a Kwikset key.)

Locksmiths will key your locks any way you like, but you might be wise to learn how to do it yourself if you have more than a dozen rentals, do your own maintenance, are somewhat nimble fingered, and are interested. It's easy to learn, and all you need for parts is a master pin-assortment kit which your local hardware store can special-order for you.

To change a key combination, a procedure commonly called rekeying, you merely release the cylinder from the lock body (for the releasing method appropriate to each kind of lock, either watch a locksmith do it or consult instructions in any detailed locksmithing book) and insert the proper key in the keyway. Using a plug follower (buy one ready-made or use a short length of wooden dowel the same diameter as the plug), push the plug out the front of the cylinder case. (See illustration.) Remove the old key and insert the key you now want to fit the lock. Change the pins which are not level with the body of the plug for sizes that are (before reaching for new

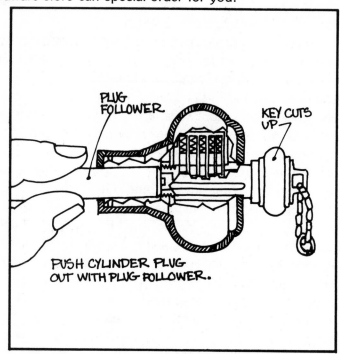

pins, try switching the old ones around to see whether they will fit in any other pin chambers and also try filing down those pins that protrude from the plug; remember that you are merely trying to make the pins level with the plug when a key is inserted; whether you make them level by switching them around, dropping in new pins, or filing down the old ones doesn't matter in the least), reinsert the plug, and reassemble the lock. It's easy. Really it is.

KEEPING KEYS AND KEEPING THEM STRAIGHT

A jailer fumbling with a huge ring of keys is almost a cliche, and so is a landlord or landlady who keeps a big board full of keys on hooks. The jailer's system of keeping keys on a ring has the advantage of portability but it lacks positive identification of each key. The landlord and landlady's board method has the advantage of positive identification but it lacks portability.

I know of one landlord who used the jailer's method and was forever trying each of his fifty keys before he could find the right one. One day when he noticed smoke coming from an apartment while the tenants were gone, he called the fire department and rushed over with a fire extinguisher to see what he could do. When the firemen arrived, they found the landlord fumbling with his keys trying to open the door. How much extra fire damage do you think that delay cost?

The best method for keeping keys and keeping them straight should combine portability with positive identification of each key. You have to be able to take your keys with you when you make your rounds, and you have to be able to select the right key quickly when you need it. The method should also allow for lock changes, and it should keep the keys unobtrusive enough so that a burglary of the owner's or manager's dwelling wouldn't result in the keys being found easily and wouldn't necessitate frantic lock changes as a consequence. Engraving each key is out because it's too permanent and so is keeping the keys all arranged neatly on a board.

The one method that satisfies every condition is keeping the keys for a building on a ring of some sort, preferably one much smaller than a jailer's ring, and keeping them identified with small adhesive labels which can be changed whenever the locks are changed. You may then keep the keys with you or keep them hidden away somewhere, and you'll know when you need them just exactly which one is which.

CHANGING LOCKS

Give your new tenants the assurance that the locks on their dwellings have been changed so that previous tenants couldn't possibly use their old keys for access. The simplest way to make this change if you lack the expertise and equipment to rekey the lock cylinders is to keep several spare locksets on hand and circulate them from place to place (some call it "musical locks"). For ease of installation, buy spares just like the ones you already have so you won't have to take the time to change the latches or worry about adjusting cutout sizes.

You can change locks quite simply by zipping out two screws with your Yankee screwdriver, removing the old lock, putting the new one in its place, and securing it by zipping the two screws back in again. (To keep dust and water from settling inside the pin chambers and gumming up the works, always install locks so the flat edge of the keyway is on the bottom. In other words, the key cuts should point up whenever a key is inserted. To reverse their keyways, Kwikset locks require a special cylinder removing tool, an inexpensive item available from your hardware store or locksmith shop.) That's all there is to it, and for this meager effort on your part, your new tenants will feel considerably more secure.

PADLOCKS

To gain access with just one key to all the padlocked garages and storage enclosures where you keep your landlording equipment and supplies, buy padlocks which are keyed alike. All padlock manufacturers make them and most regular hardware stores carry them in stock. Just ask.

Don't use keyed-alike padlocks for those applications at multi-family dwellings where every tenant needs access, applications such as gates and common storage areas. You don't want to have to issue still another key to each of your tenants. For those applications, use a special kind of combination padlock called the Sesamee Keyless Padlock. It can be set to any of 10,000 combinations and can be reset very simply at any time. Set it to an easily remembered number like a building address or the current year, and your tenants will all have access when they need it without having to fumble for keys.

Any padlock which is used by more than one tenant will soon disappear, however, unless you attach a chain to its shackle. Ask at your hardware store for a special padlock chain restraint made by the Master Lock Company which fits most padlocks and eliminates this lost-lock problem.

PEEPSCOPES

Some entrances to dwellings are blind, that is, there's no way for the occupants to see who's at the door. Occupants have to either talk through the door or open it a crack to answer. Sometimes people attach security chains to their doors and door jambs to limit the door's movement and hence restrict access, but these chains provide more psychological than physical security because they pull loose from their mountings in response to the slightest blow and expose the occupants immediately to outside danger.

A far better way to solve this problem is to install a peepscope right in the door itself so that occupants can see who's out there knocking on the door without jeopardizing their own safety. Peepscopes cost less than $5 each and take less than five minutes to install. Tenants appreciate them.

PREVENTING BURGLARIES

You will want to try what you can to prevent burglaries from occurring at your rental property because every burglary reflects negatively on the property itself and scares off better tenants, but you hardly have unlimited funds to spend for prevention and you must recognize that no measure you take will be 100% effective, no matter what it costs. Before you go out and spend the big bucks to hire a guard service or install decorative iron grillwork around your building, therefore, you should first try taking other much less expensive measures which your tenants would surely appreciate: strategically located outside lighting, "Operation Identification," and the closet safe.

• Outside lighting deters burglars by increasing the chances of their being seen lurking around doors and windows after dark. They much prefer to keep to the shadows and out of sight so they cannot be identified. Light as much outside area as you can with energy-efficient fluorescent or mercury vapor lamps, and you'll be marking your building as a poor target for nighttime burglars, as well as assisting your tenants in their nocturnal peregrinations.

• "Operation Identification" involves engraving every item of value with the owner's name and driver's license number to prevent burglars from fencing it easily. Burglars might be able to keep this marked booty for their own use and have no problems, but whenever they try to convert it into cash, they encounter difficulties. Fences certainly don't want stuff which is plainly identified because it is just too easy to trace. Burglars can try to eradicate the engraved marks by grinding them off, but that's too much like work and it leaves marks which diminish the item's value. Whenever they come upon engraved goods, then, burglars tend to leave them behind because there's plenty of other stuff around for the taking that won't cause them a bit of trouble.

Many urban police departments lend engravers and supply warning decals which can be placed near every likely burglary access to strike the fear of "Operation Identification" into any burglar who's casing the joint. You might consider buying an engraver yourself (they're less than $15), identifying all of your own tools and valuables, and then lending it to your tenants. They'll appreciate it, and you'll all find that it works. By the way, for less laborious, better-looking engraving, try using cursive script rather than printing each letter separately.

• The other burglary prevention measure is one designed more to lessen the impact of burglaries than to prevent them from happening altogether. It involves creating a closet safe where tenants can secure their valuables right at home. A closet safe is merely a closet with a lock on it which is intended to delay burglars, forcing them to spend more time and make more noise than they would like to, many times frustrating them completely and causing

them to leave with far less than what they came for. The lock on a closet safe might be a doorknob or dead-bolt lock keyed like the entrance locks or it might be a padlock which the tenants supply themselves. Having tenants supply their own padlocks is preferable, of course, because it relieves you of the responsibility of looking after still another lock and key. The usual padlock hardware is unsightly, I know, and you might shake your head at the thought of installing it on an inside door, but Master No. 60 Padlock Eyes, which are designed to be used on any ordinary household door, are almost un-noticeable. Yet they, together with a

good door and a strong padlock, make a fairly invulnerable closet safe and provide excellent protection for valuables.

Whatever else you can do to thwart burglars and give your tenants a sense of security will help you keep good tenants longer, and that's good business.

TAKING SAFETY PRECAUTIONS FOR HANDLING RENT

You are a wise landlord or landlady to insist on cash, a money order, or a cashier's check for a tenant's initial rental payment. You have to be absolutely certain that you're not giving a new tenant the keys to a $50,000 dwelling in exchange for a bum check or some worthless collateral. After that, however, you should be more concerned about the risk involved in handling cash, for you could lose your property's entire monthly income all too easily by misplacing it or getting robbed, and since there's no commercially available and affordable insurance policy to protect you from the loss, it would be yours alone to bear. Take the precaution, therefore, of refusing to accept cash.

Some tenants will want to pay you their rent in cash, and since cash is legal tender for all money transactions, you will have to take it unless you stipulate with adequate notice in advance that you won't. State in your rental agreement or takeover letter that rent must be paid by check or money order and insist on it! Some contrary tenants who deal strictly in cash may wave a fistful of greenbacks in your face and say, "Take it or leave it," and you'll have to weigh all the factors of the situation before deciding what to do. If you accept it, they will probably continue trying to pay you in cash month after month, and if you decline it, you may never collect their rent at all. I usually accept their cash and patiently explain each time why I prefer rents to be paid by check or money order, until they finally tire of hearing my repeated explanations and give in.

Even though you are resolute about not accepting cash, you may face a loss if someone robs you and gets away with your rent checks and money orders, because even stolen checks and money orders can be negotiated by a thief who knows how. Add one extra safety precaution — the Little Old Rubber Stamp Trick.

Invest a few dollars in deposit stamps for yourself and any manager who handles rent for you so that stolen checks and money orders cannot be negotiated easily, if at all. As soon as a tenant hands you a check or money order, stamp the back with a rubber stamp which might read like one of these:

FOR DEPOSIT ONLY
to the account of
Lester Landlord

or

PAY TO THE ORDER OF
BIG BANK
Lester Landlord
011-123456
FOR-DEPOSIT ONLY

Such a deposit stamp marked on the back of your checks and money orders, renders them virtually worthless except as deposits to your own bank account. No one can cash them by trying to impersonate you at the corner liquor store or delicatessen. They can only be put into your account.

These same deposit stamps are also handy for marking the coin wrappers you use for rolling all those quarters, dimes, and nickels generated by your coin-operated laundry machines. Banks usually insist that rolls of coins be identifed in case they are found wanting.

If using the Little Old Rubber Stamp Trick saves you just one unauthorized check cashing, it's well worth the small cost.

KEEPING RECORDS

For some people the most onerous chore of landlording is keeping records. They'll look after their properties with great vigor and delight, but speak to them about keeping records and they'll laugh nervously, perhaps they'll point to a dog-eared, old rent receipt book and a stack of shoeboxes stuffed with miscellaneous slips of paper, and they'll say they just haven't got the time to sit down and shuffle papers. They have much more important work to do. Besides, they have an accountant who does it all for them. Sound familiar? Have any more excuses to add?

Unfortunately those people who neglect recordkeeping don't recognize what's truly important in this business. Since they keep their records haphazardly, they don't really know what's happening at all and they can't make good decisions. They don't know whether their rents are covering their expenses, so they haven't a clue whether a rent raise is warranted. They don't know how much they're now spending on utilities compared to previous periods, so they have yet to consider conserving utilities as a cost-saving measure. They don't keep any figures on their washer and dryer, so they're still charging 25 cents to wash and 10 cents to dry. They don't even know when they'll be making the final payment on a second mortgage, and consequently they can't know when to expect an increase in cash flow. When can they plan to buy their new Rolls? They can't say.

Those things are truly important in this business. Sure, you have to do a great many other important things, but few are ever more important than recordkeeping, and none will assist you in both managing your property day by day and satisfying the requirements of the tax collector. You cannot afford to neglect it.

Landlording without recordkeeping is like baseball without a scorekeeper. Some business, some game!

To do recordkeeping right, you must have a system. The one outlined in this chapter might be considered rudimentary by some standards, but it is wholly sufficient for landlords and landladies who do their recordkeeping themselves. Some people have used it for just a rental house and others have used it for more than three hundred rentals. It's a flexible system, simple to follow, easy to crosscheck, and exhaustive enough to lead into tax prepara-

tions. It's based on forms which are designed to be read vertically and to fit into a standard 8½″ × 11″ binder, and best of all, it's all right here in your hands. You can get started using it right away by making copies of the forms included in the back of the book.

Before we get to the forms themselves, though, let's consider a way to keep those miscellaneous slips of paper out of your old shoeboxes.

FILING

You handle so many important written records in your landlording business that you have to organize them so they are readily accessible when needed or you will become hopelessly

bogged down in unnecessary hunts for lost records now and then. A simple filing system will help.

For each property, make up three file folders (you might want to use folders of a different color for each property). Label each folder with the property's address or some other designation and "RECORDS," "TENANT RECORDS," or "RECEIPTS."

• In the RECORDS file folder, keep the property's insurance policies, title papers, termite reports, tax information, deeds, notes, loan records, and anything else pertaining to the property as a whole that you're not already keeping in a safe deposit box.

• In the TENANT RECORDS file folder, keep rental applications, rental agreements, leases, condition and inventory checksheets, and any other papers pertaining to the tenants of the property, including those tenants who have moved out.

• In the RECEIPTS file folder, keep the paid receipts for expenses related to the property.

As soon as you get a receipt, circle the amount paid and mark it with the date of payment, the method of payment ($ or ✓), and the property's address, so you'll be able to identify it easily if it happens to be misland. If the receipt does not include a description of the item or service paid for, write a description on it.

Prorate on an itemized or percentage basis those receipts which cover expenses for more than one property so that each property pays its own share. If two properties are involved, make a duplicate receipt for one property's share and reference it to the original bill, which should be adjusted and then inserted into the other property's file. For unreceipted expenses, such as casual labor, make up your own receipt with the important information, get a signature if you can, and file it with the other expense receipts.

Arrange all receipts chronolog-ically in the file folder so they will be easier to post. Arranging them is easy to do unless you get very far behind and your receipts become mixed up. Just put the most recent receipt face up and in the back of the folder, and you won't have to bother about sorting them later. All the receipts for one month should be kept together and slipped into a folded sheet of paper which is identi-fied with the month and year. When you finish recording the receipts for the month, staple them together in-side the folded sheet and leave them in the folder.

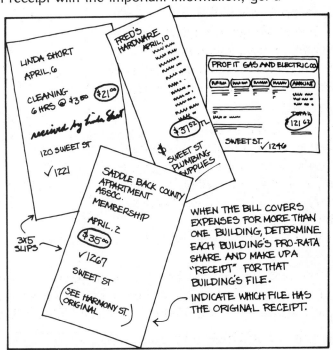

At the end of the year, empty the RECEIPTS folder of that year's receipts and put them, along with the year's income and expense sheets referred to later, into a large envelope for storage. Because you never can tell when the tax collector will demand a reckoning, you would be wise to keep them forever.

If you begin accumulating more and more properties, you will probably want to add more folders to your filing system to accommodate the greater volume of paperwork. The following might prove useful: INCOMING, UNPAID BILLS, BANKING, LOANS, and PAYROLL. You'll find plenty of stray items to keep safely tucked away in these folders, too.

That's all there is to keeping your written records organized. Read on to learn how to use those records in doing your bookkeeping.

BOOKKEEPING

Basically, the loose-leaf book kept for recording purposes has five sections: TENANTS, INCOME, EXPENSES, SUMMARIES, and LOANS/INSURANCE. Properly filled out and kept up to date, the forms in these sections will give you quick access to most of the infor-mation you need to operate income-producing property.

Blanks for every sheet used in these sections appear in the back of the book. Use the blanks as originals and copy them for your own loose-leaf book. Do not write on the original forms themselves. Write only on the copies.

- TENANTS — Tenant Record

The first section, the one for tenant information, has only one form, the Tenant Record. Record information on it which you'll need to refer to occasionally, information such as tenants' telephone numbers (nowadays many people have unlisted phones), which will save you lots of fumbling and wasted trips.

Although you hope you won't have to use such information, you may use the Tenant Record to keep track of each tenant's current checking and savings account numbers so you'll know what there is to attach if you have to collect a court judgment. The savings account number should be on the Rental Application, and the checking account number will be written in those funny-looking magnetic numbers at the bottom of the tenant's rent check. Be prepared!

Because you will refer to the Tenant Record repeatedly and because these sheets should last for years, you may wish to keep them clean with a transparent sheet protector that slips

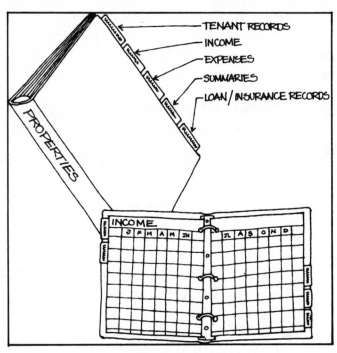

on and off easily and is available in most stationary stores. When tenants move, cross them off the Tenant Record using a yellow or pink highlighter felt pen which does a neat job and still gives you access to the old information if you need it.

Add new tenants to the bottom of the list. Even though they won't be in order according to the dwelling number or letter designation, they will be readily accessible.

Use a separate Tenant Record sheet for each multiple-family property.

Tenant Record

Location 456 SWEET ST.

	Unit	Tenant	Phone	Moved In	Moved Out	Rent Date Gross	Deposit/ Rent Less	Bank/Ck. Acct. Nos.
1	456	RICHARD & MARY RENTER	555-1280	1/84		1ST 228	275	BIG BANK ✓04039586
2	458	AMELIA BILTRONG	555-1362	3/80		✓ 197	263	CENTRAL BANK ✓1074372
3	460	CHESTER & CATHY CAREFREE	555-1441	4/81	3/84	✓ 186	250	BIG BANK ✓04040853 SAV 04040853
4	462	ERNIE PEABODY	555-1862	10/83		✓ 210	272	
5	464	SONDRA FREELY	555-1940	6/76		✓ 192	248	1ST NATL BANK ✓11803532
6	460	HENRY & GLADYS ANGEL	555-1812	7/84		✓ 244	285	MECHANICAL BANK ✓12011790
7								

- INCOME — Monthly Rental Income Record

The second bookkeeping section, income, includes three different forms: Monthly Rental Income Record, Laundry Income, and Other Receipts and Income.

Unless you have quite a few properties, one of each form should suffice. For example, if you are Lester Landlord and you have one duplex, half of which you occupy yourself, and one fiveplex, you can easily list both properties on a single Monthly Rental Income Record.

If you do enter more than one property on a form, use a highlighter pen to mark the "TOTAL" lines all the way across both sheets, and you'll find that the totals are easier to see.

If you have room, you can even use the same record sheets for subsequent years by listing the properties again further down the sheets and indicating on each "TOTAL" line which year you are recording. One advantage in recording your rental income this way is that you have instant access to past years' rental income for comparison purposes. You'll know when you last raised rents and how much of a vacancy factor you created by doing so, and you can use this information to help you prepare for the next increase.

After using these sheets to record rental income for a full year, calculate the total year's income for each dwelling and enter it in the "Year's Totals" column. Total that column so you can crosscheck the monthly totals for all buildings on the sheets. If your figures don't match, find out why they don't and correct your error.

This kind of crosschecking is no work for a pocket calculator. Get yourself an adder or a calculator which can produce a paper tape record of its entries. Sometimes just one slightly incorrect entry will cause an error and you can find it without painstakingly adding each item again merely by comparing the adder's tape, item for item, with the Income Record figures.

MONTHLY RENTAL INCOME RECORD

Page __1__

Location(s) SWEET ST. & NEAT ST.

Period __1984__

	Unit	Jan.	Feb.	Mar.	Apr.	May	
1	456 SWEET ST.	355 —	164 50	255 —	255 —	255 —	1
2	458 ″ ″	243 —	243 —	243 —	243 —	243 —	2
3	460 ″ ″	230 —	365 —	153 90	265 —	265 —	3
4	462 ″ ″	252 —	252 —	252 —	252 —	252 —	4
5	464 ″ ″	228 —	228 —	228 —	228 —	228 —	5
6	TOTAL	1308 —	1252 50	1131 90	1243 —	1243 —	6
7							7
8							8
9	125 NEAT ST.	275 —	275 —	293 —	293 —	293 —	9
10							10
11	TOTAL BOTH BLDGS.	1583 —	1527 50	1424 90	1536 —	1536 —	11
12							12
13							13
14							14
15							15

• INCOME — Other Receipts & Income

The last of the income forms, called Other Receipts & Income, uses two sheets to span a full year and is used to record whatever income cannot be classified as rental income.

Income items which may be included here are these: added appliances or furniture, deposit forfeits, interest on deposits, late charges (unless you use the discounted rent policy, in which case both gross and net rents could be recorded as rental income), laundry collections, laundry commissions, garages, etc. Those income items which are normally included in the rent should be recorded as rental income and not here. Rents for furnished apartments, for example, need not be itemized separately, nor should garage rental be recorded separately if it's normally included in the rent. If, however, you bill tenants separately for their garage, air conditioner, or anything else, then you may wish to include those separate amounts here. Still, don't worry yourself much about where to include an item. Worry instead about whether you have inadvertently recorded any income on both the Monthly Rental Income Record and the Other Receipts & Income record. Do avoid that! Only the laundry income should be recorded in two places — the Laundry Income sheet and the Other Receipts sheets.

Although tenants' deposits may be treated as income when received and may be recorded here as other income, you're wise not to do so. Instead of handling them that way and being taxed on them just as if they were rent, do not record them anywhere as income. Record them on the Tenant Record and list as income only what you do not return to the tenants after they move. That, after all, is when deposits become income.

Advance rents are another story. The tax collector tells us that they have to be recorded as income when received. There's no choice.

One Other Receipts & Income form may last you a year or it may last you several, depending on the number of properties you have. Fill it out pretty much the same way you do the Monthly Rental Income Record, grouping all the items for one building together.

OTHER RECEIPTS & INCOME

Added Appliances or Furniture,
Deposits, Interest on Deposits,
Late Charges, Laundry, Garages, etc.

Page ___1___

Location(s) __SWEET ST. & NEAT ST.__

Period ___1984___

	Description of Income	Jan.	Feb.	Mar.	Apr.	May	
1	SWEET ST.						1
2	Laundry	86 75	86 75	92 25	78 75	92 25	2
3	Late Rents			20 —			3
4	Interest on Deposits				18 86		4
5							5
6	TOTAL	86 75	86 75	112 25	97 61	92 25	6
7							7
8	NEAT ST.						8
9	Late Rents						9
10	Interest on Deposits				3 90		10
11	TOTAL	0	0	0	3 90	0	11
12							12
13	TOTAL — BOTH BLDGS	86 75	86 75	112 25	101 51	92 25	13
14							14

- INCOME — Laundry Income

If you own coin-operated laundry machines, use the Laundry Income sheet to record each collection before you post the monthly totals to the Other Receipts & Income sheets. Otherwise you'll be saving little scraps of paper which represent each collection until you have a full month's collections and can make the monthly entry, and those scraps may very well get lost in the wash.

There are seven columns on the Laundry Income sheet, but you need not use every one. If you don't wish to compare washer and dryer receipts and you're not interested in cumulative totals, don't bother with them. Use only the columns you want, the bare minimum being a "Date" entry and a "Both" entry. The "Both" entry, of course, would be your total for each collection.

The other columns provide quite useful information to those who take a little time to complete them, though. The separate washer-dryer columns tell you how much use each machine is getting, and from these figures you can determine each machine's exact number of loads. Use this information to check on a machine's reliability whenever it needs repair. Perhaps, because of this information, you'll want to change makes of machines when they need replacement or when you purchase a set for another location. The separate washer-dryer columns also provide a revealing ratio of use for the machines. If a tenant claims that the dryer is requiring twice as many coins to dry each load as it used to, you can calculate whether it is or not by checking for a change in the income ratio between the machines. You'll find out whether the machine does need repair or whether the tenant is testing your gullibility.

The "Cumulative Totals" column tells you at a glance whether your investment is paying off. Let's say your machines cost you $900 and you take in $170 in the first six months. At that rate, just recouping your investment would take two and a half years, and that's not including the utilities it takes to run them or the cost of repairs. But if the machines last ten years and on a projected basis take in $7,200, $2,000 of which goes for utilities and $1,000 for repairs, you'll make a return on your investment of 37% per year simple interest. That's not bad! The "Cumulative Totals" column will also help you decide whether to increase or decrease the amount you're charging per load.

The "Monthly Totals" column is a convenience expressly for the purpose of entering the necessary figures on the Other Receipts & Income sheets, but these figures will also let you compare month-by-month laundry receipts if your collection dates are fairly consistent and frequent. Remember that not every line requires a monthly entry, only those which represent the last collection for the month.

Laundry Income

location 456 SWEET ST.
period 1984

	Date	Washer	Dryer	Both	Cumulative Totals	Monthly Totals	
1	1/5	22 50	21 25	43 25	43 25		1
2	1/24	21 —	22 —	43 —	86 75	86 75	2
3	2/5	18 25	16 —	34 25	121 —		3
4	2/20	21 —	24 50	52 50	173 50	86 75	4

• EXPENSES — Expense and Payment Record

There are three forms in the expense section of the loose-leaf record book: Expense and Payment Record, Payroll Record, and Depreciation Record.

The first one, the Expense and Payment Record, is probably the most used of all the forms in the book. Remember all those receipts you moved from your shoeboxes and shopping bags into a neat file folder labeled "RECEIPTS," which you then organized by date of payment? Well, here's where you record them all.

The entries are made chronologically and should include all the expense receipts in the RECEIPTS folder, plus the payroll expenses from the Payroll Record and the loan payments which are recorded on the Loan & Note Record sheets.

Besides being chronological, the entries are separated into eleven categories which enable you to refer easily to certain kinds of expenses whenever you want to find out where all your money's going. You may find some surprises when you examine the categories, surprises that appear only when you examine a series of similar expenditures rather than just one bill. Might you, for example, have inadvertently paid your property taxes or your insurance twice? Don't laugh. It happens. Here's where you can check on your own absentmindedness.

If it weren't for the loan payments, filling out expense sheets would be idiot's play. What makes the loan payment entries a little tricky are those portions of the payments that aren't actually expenses. Column 2, which is the amount you pay on the principal of your loan, represents an investment rather than an expense. Yet, since it is money paid out, it should be recorded as such. Likewise, Column 9, your impounds account, is a savings account, forced savings, to be sure, but still a savings account. It's used by the mortgagor to pay taxes and insurance when required, and it's not an expense, strictly speaking, until it's used to pay the taxes or insurance.

EXPENSE AND PAYMENT RECORD   Page __2__

Location(s) __SWEET ST.__

Period __1984__

	Date	How Paid	To Whom Paid	For	1 Total Paid Out	2 Mortgage Principal	3 Interest	4 Taxes, Licenses	
1			BAL BROT FWD		2516 05	696 09	732 75	Ø	1
2	4/2	267	Big Bank	1st mort.	589 —	185 03	179 37		2
3	4/2	268	S. Moneybags	2d ✓	122 —	68 66	53 34		3
4	4/6	269	LTWN. Hdwr.	misc hdw acc't	43 39				4
5	4/9	IMP	Saddleback Cnty	prop taxes	674 31			674 31	5
6	4/10	270	Monopoly Gas & El.	gas & lts.	37 12				6
7	4/11	#	K-Mart	shades	12 26				7
8	4/12	271	Water of Ltwn	water	41 30				8
9	4/12	272	Monopoly Garbage	garbage	22 50				9
10	4/15	273	Phoenix Pts.	pet supplies	32 64				10
11	4/19	274	Lester Landlord	personal draw	280 —				11
12	4/20	imp	USA Insurance	ins.	254 00				12
13	4/31	#	Ltwn Stationery	envelopes	3 18				13
14	5/1	275	Searson's	water heater	443 64				14
15	5/2	276	Big Bank	1st mort.	589 —	186 17	178 23		15
16	5/2	277	S. Moneybags	2d ✓	122 —	69 03	52 97		16

When the mortgagor uses your impounds to pay taxes or insurance, record the payment like any other and stipulate in the "How Paid" column that funds for payment came out of the impounds account. I know, I know, this means that the amount in the "Total Paid Out" column is actually more than what you will have paid out. Trust me, though, and I'll show you on the Summary of Business and Statement of Income how everything evens out again. Just don't worry about it now, and don't worry about the matter at all if you're not even paying into an impounds account with your mortgage payment. That's just fine.

Now let's take a look at the procedure for normal entries. After you fill in the information called for in the first five columns, you come to the columns with the eleven different headings. Choose whichever one best fits each expense and put the amount in that column. Be sure, however, that it's all on the same horizontal line. Even though the lines are numbered four times on the two sheets, sometimes your eyes will play tricks on you and you may use the wrong line. Use a ruler as a guide if you have to.

Don't deliberate too much about the proper categories for ambiguous expenses. If you can't easily decide whether something should be called a "service" or not, then it can't matter too much, and since you identify each item in the "For" column anyway, you always have backup information in case you want to change categories later for some reason or other.

If you find that you have no use for a certain column heading, if, for example, you have no payroll to enter, change the heading to something more useful to you. Other possibilities are travel/telephone, advertising/rental fees, and non-employee labor.

Now look again at the sample Expense and Payment Record for Lester Landlord's fiveplex. Note that the distribution of the mortgage payments is broken into three categories: mortgage principal, interest, and impounds. Note also that the first line of these sample sheets has the

DISTRIBUTION OF EXPENSES AND PAYMENTS

Page **2**

	5 Insurance	6 Utilities	7 Services, Repairs, Maint.	8 Merch., Supplies	9 Impounds	10 Payroll	11 Misc.	12 Non-deductible	
1	Ø	176 12	67 63	138 48	673 80	Ø	31 18	225 -	1
2					224 60				2
3									3
4				43 39					4
5									5
6		37 12							6
7				12 36					7
8		41 30							8
9			22 50						9
10				32 64					10
11								280 -	11
12	254 88								12
13				3 18					13
14								443 64	14
15					224 60				15
16									16

154

totals brought forward from the previous sheets. You must do this on every page except the first one for the year (corresponding left and right sheets should have the same page numbers).

After you have entered your last expenditure for the year, total the last sheet and you'll have your annual expenditures for the property.

Let me caution you about two taboos related to your Expense and Payment Record sheets. Never include as a regular, deductible expense either the money you pay yourself or those items which you have to depreciate.

Money which you pay yourself from your property's income is called a personal draw, which is definitely not an expense. Therefore, it is not tax-deductible. Enter it on the Expense and Payment Record if you wish to keep track of the money you pay yourself, but be sure to list it as a non-deductible item in column 12.

Handle depreciation items the same way. You may think that a new roof is an expense which you should be able to charge off against this year's income. After all, you had to pay for the whole thing this year, didn't you? You should be able to write it off. Sorry, scrupulous landlord and landlady, but you can't write it off as an expense all at once. You have to depreciate it, so you'll have to enter it in column 12 and record it on a separate "Depreciation Record" sheet as well. Actually, it's not something to be too glum about. Think of it this way. If you had to buy a new roof one year and you charged it to expenses, and then you decided to sell, you'd probably have expenses that greatly exceed income, and your prospective buyers would be skeptical about the place. But if you take approximately 7% of the roof as an expense each year for fifteen years, then your buyers will have a truer picture of the ordinary expenses you incur in operating the building.

• EXPENSES — Depreciation Record

Items which have to be depreciated over a number of years rather than be considered expenses during the year of purchase, generally cost more than a hundred dollars, as a rule of thumb, and have an extended useful life of more than two years. Here are some examples:

1) Appliances
2) Carpeting
3) Laundry Machines
4) Major Equipment
5) New Linoleum
6) New Wiring
7) Roof Replacement
8) Swimming Pool

Each of these items should be depreciated on a separate Depreciation Record sheet unless they were purchased about the same time as other depreciable items with a similar useful life, in which case they may be combined on one sheet. You might have as many as a dozen or more sheets for a single building, depending on the number of capital improvements you've made, but the very minimum for each building is, of course, the one Depreciation Record sheet for the building itself.

Before you can even begin filling out a Depreciation Record, you must determine which method of depreciation is best suited to your financial circumstances. The various methods available are called "straight line," "declining balance" (125%, 150%, or 200% of straight line), and "sum of the years digits." You will find lucid explanations of all these methods in *Your Income Tax* and the *Realty Bluebook,* together with comparisons of the effects which each method has on one depreciable sum over a period of years. Study the examples carefully.

Once you pick a method, you can calculate the amount of depreciation available for each and every year on one Depreciation Record form.

DEPRECIATION RECORD

Property or Capital Improvement Location and Description _456-464 SWEET ST.,_
A FIVEPLEX APARTMENT BUILDING

Date Acquired or Converted to Business _SEPTEMBER, 1968_
New or Used _USED_
Cost or Other Basis _$55,000_
Land Value (Not Applicable to Capital Improvements) _$13,750_
Salvage Value _Ø_
Special 20% First Year Depreciation _Ø_
Depreciable Basis _$41,250_
Method of Depreciation _125% DECLINING BALANCE_
Useful Life _20 YEARS_

Tax Year	Prior Deprec.	Deprec. Balance	% Year* Held	% Bus. Use	Deprec. This Year		Special 20%		Total First Year Deprec.
1st 68		41,250–	33.3	100	868.51	+	Ø	=	858.51
2nd 69	858.51	40,391.49	100	✓	2524.46				
3rd 70	3382.97	37,867.03	✓	✓	2316.68				
4th 71	5749.65	35,500.35	✓	✓	2218.77				
5th 72	7968.42	33,281.58	✓	✓	2080.10				
6th 73	10,048.52	31,201.48	✓	✓	1950.09				
7th 74	11,998.69	29,251.31	✓	✓	1828.20				
8th 75	13,826.89	27,423.11	✓	✓	1713.95				
9th 76	15,540.84	25,709.16	✓	✓	1606.82				
10th 77	17				1506.40				
11th 78	18								
12th 79	2								
13th 80	2								
14th 81	2								
15th 82	2								
16th 83	2								
17th 84									
18th									
19th									
20th									
21st									
22nd									
23rd									
24th									
25th									

*Conversion: Months to % of Year

DEPRECIATION RECORD

Property or Capital Improvement Location and Description _SWEET ST._
COIN-OPERATED WASHER & DRYER

Date Acquired or Converted to Business _JUNE, 1981_
New or Used _NEW_
Cost or Other Basis _$876_
Land Value (Not Applicable to Capital Improvements) _Ø_
Salvage Value _$50_
Special 20% First Year Depreciation _$175_
Depreciable Basis _$651_
Method of Depreciation _STRAIGHT LINE_
Useful Life _6 years_

Tax Year	Prior Deprec.	Deprec. Balance	% Year* Held	% Bus. Use	Deprec. This Year		Special 20%		Total First Year Deprec.
1st 81		651	58.3	100	63.25	+	175–	=	238.25
2nd 82	63.25	587.75	100	✓	108.50				
3rd 83	171.75	479.25	✓	✓	✓				
4th 84	280.25	370.75	✓	✓	✓				
5th 85	388.75	262.25	✓	✓	✓				
6th 86	497.25	153.75	✓	✓	✓				
7th 87	605.75	45.25	✓	✓	45.25				

156

Straight line, the method used in the laundry machines' sample given here, is perhaps the simplest. Here's the way it works. First, if you wish, you may subtract 20% of the cost of the machines as your special first year depreciation (see *Your Income Tax* for an explanation of what qualifies for the special 20% allowance). Then subtract a presumed salvage value. The result will be the depreciable basis. Divide that figure by the length of the machines' useful life, and you will have the amount of depreciation allowable for each year.

If you happened to own the machines for less than twelve months during the first year, multiply the annual depreciation figure by the percentage of the year you did own them and you will get the depreciation for the first year, to which, of course, you should add the special allowance.

Depreciation for all succeeding years except the last one is simply the annual figure which you have already determined. The very last year picks up the balance for those months you didn't own the machines during the first year.

For ordinary real estate depreciation (land may not be depreciated, of course), you may use this same Depreciation Record form, using a method consistent with current tax laws and appropriate to your situation. The sample shows how to record the depreciation on Lester Landlord's fiveplex using the declining balance method at a 125% rate for twenty years. Notice that each year he must figure the straight line depreciation on the depreciable balance first and then multiply that amount by 125% to arrive at the depreciation for a particular year.

Look at 1975, for example, which has a depreciable balance of $27,423.11. Straight line depreciation for twenty years on this amount is $1,371.16. He arrived at this figure by dividing 20 into $27,423.11, remember? After that calculation, he multiplied $1,371.16 by 125% and got the depreciation for 1975, $1,713.95. That's all there is to it.

Remember that you may use one method of depreciation on one building and another method on another building or on your capital improvements, whichever is best suited to your needs. You need not use a single method throughout.

Try your best to understand how depreciation works and try to make the calculations yourself, but do seek out a tax oracle for advice when you have to make depreciation decisions.

• EXPENSES — Payroll Record

For each employee you hire, you will have to keep a Payroll Record. It's absolutely essential. Fortunately it's a relatively simple form to use. Once you have calculated the employee's various payroll deductions and have prepared the statement of earnings and deductions form to accompany each payroll check (see Chapter 9), you merely post those figures onto the Payroll Record, and then to all that you add the employer's contribution to Social Security (shaded column).

Refer to this form whenever you have to prepare monthly, quarterly, or annual reports for the governmental agencies involved.

• SUMMARIES — Annual Summary of Expenses and Payments

The summaries section includes two different forms. The first one closely parallels the Expense and Payment Record and is solely for the purpose of gathering together the expenditures for several properties. If you have only one property, you would already have figured your expenditures for the year on the final Expense and Payment Record page, and you would not need to use this form.

PAYROLL RECORD

Property: **2100 MAIN ST.**
Employee: **CHARLES GOOD FOLKS**
Social Security No.: **198-83-6509**
Pay Rate: **$4.00**
Exemptions: **2**
☒ Married
☐ Single

	Period	Gross	Federal Withholding Tax	State Disability	Employee FICA	Employer FICA	State Withhding Tax	Other	Net	Ck No.	
1	3/01-3/15	57.00	⊖	.57	3.19		⊖		47.36	1318	1
2	3/16-3/31	44.00	⊖	.44	2.70		⊖		40.86	1321	2
3	3/01-3/31	95.00	⊖		5.83	5.82		QTR TTLS	11.65	1330	3
4	4/01-4/15	46.00	⊖	.46	2.82		⊖		42.72	1346	4
5	4/16-4/30	49.00	⊖	.49	3.00		⊖		45.51	1352	5
6	5/01-5/15	46.00	⊖	.46	2.82		⊖		42.72	1367	6
7	5/16-5/31	41.00	⊖	.41	2.51		⊖		38.08	1372	7
8	6/01-6/15	42.50	⊖	.43	2.60		⊖		39.47	1387	8
9	6/16-6/30	45.00	⊖	.45	2.76		⊖		41.79	1392	9
10	4/01-6/30	2,695.00	⊖		16.51	16.52		QTR TTLS	39.03	1397	10

The only difference between the regular Expense and Payment Record form and this Annual Summary of Expenses and Payments form is that "Unit(s)" takes the place of the first four columns, "Date," "How Paid," "To Whom Paid," and "For," and there's a thirteenth column for recording both regular and supplemental depreciation.

List each property's location on the form first and then record the total expenses just as you calculated them on the final Expense and Payment Record sheets for each property. That accomplished, you will be prepared with the figures needed for the next form.

EXPENSE AND PAYMENT RECORD
Annual Summary

Location(s): **SWEET ST. & NEAT ST.**
Year: **1984**

	Units	1 Total Paid Out(2-12)	2 Mortgage Principal	3 Interest	4 Taxes, Licenses	5 Insurance	
1	456 SWEET ST.	12576 75	2896 72	2930 71	1348 62	541 86	1
2	123 NEAT ST.	4025 68	1158 69	1172 28	539 45	216 74	2
3							3
4	TOTAL	16529 34	4055 41	4102 99	1888 07	758 60	4
5							5
6							6
7							7
8							8
9							9
10							10
11							11
12							12
13							13

• SUMMARIES — Summary of Business and Statement of Income

The Summary of Business and Statement of Income form brings together all income and all expenses for a final reckoning. Use them monthly if you want to and you'll be very well informed about the financial status of your property. We do this for each of our larger properties. Though desirable, monthly summaries are hardly indispensible, however, and most landlords and landladies use them just once a year.

Whether you use it on an annual or a monthly basis, you will make some important calculations using this form. Here's where you subtract from your expense totals the following: payments on loan principals, impounds, and sundry non-deductibles. Here's where you add your depreciation allowances to your expenses, too. And if you haven't done so already, here's where you have the opportunity to deduct as business expenses your telephone, the office space used in your house (use great discretion with this one; be prepared with proof), and your mileage (log your landlording trips for substantiation). When you have completed all these calculations, you'll have a profit or loss figure ready to give the tax collector.

Summary of Business and Statement of Income

Location(s) __SWEET ST. & NEAT ST.__

Year/Month __1984__

		Totals	
1			1
2			2
3	INCOME:		3
4	Rental	18432 40	4
5	Other	1104 25	5
6	TOTAL INCOME	19536 65	6
7			7
8			8
9			9
10			10
11	EXPENSES:		11
12	Mortgage Principal	4055 41	12
13	Interest	4102 99	13
14	Taxes, Licenses	1889 07	14
15	Insurance	758 60	15
16	Utilities	591 77	16
17	Services, Repairs, Maintenance	2272 21	17
18	Merchandise, Supplies	775 49	18
19	Impounds	2695 20	19
20	Payroll	0	20
21	Miscellaneous Expenses	174 60	21
22	Non-deductible	1260 —	22
23	_Telephone_	144 48	23
24	_Travel_	169 70	24
25			25
26	TOTAL EXPENSES (GROSS)	16843 52	26
27	less mortgage principal and Non-deductible	5315 41	27
28	TOTAL	11528 11	28
29	less impounds & 50% non-business	9122 65	29

...ES (NET) 4te of ...

• LOANS/INSURANCE — Loan & Note Record

The Loan & Note Record enables you to keep tabs on your loans, an activity some might say is akin to the miser's counting his stacks of Krugerrands. It ain't necessarily so. Actually this form provides you with information which is very useful when you're renegotiating a loan, when you're checking a lender's interest calculations, or when your payment book is lost in the mail. Everything's here, the original amount of the loan, the interest rate, payment, principal balance, etc., and filling it out takes just a moment after you receive your payment book back from the lender.

Come to think of it, filling out this record is kind of fun, too, because you can see the equity in your property gradually build up each time you fill another line with figures. Maybe misers do know how to have fun. Well, in this business you'd better take your fun when and where you can get it.

LOAN & NOTE RECORD   Page 3

Property: 456-464 SWEET ST. LITTLETOWN
Noteholder & Address: BIG BANK, P.O. BOX 678, LITTLETOWN
Loan Number: 01-4321   Original Loan: $38,500
Interest: 7 1/2 %   Payment: $589   Due Date: 8/01/88

#	Payment Date Paid / If Changed	Principal	Interest	Impounds & (Imp. Disb.)	Impound Balance	Principal Balance	#
1	BAL BROT FWD				929 17	28701 12	1
2	4/2	185 03	179 37	224 60	1153 77	28516 09	2
3	4/7 (taxes)			(674 31)	479 46		3
4	4/25 (ins)			(254 86)	224 60		4
5	5/01	186 17	178 23	224 60	449 20	28329 92	5
6							6
7							7
8							8
9							9
10							10
11							11
12							12
13							13
14							14
15							15
16							16
17							17
18							18
19							19
20							20
21							21
22							22
23							23
24							24
25							25
26							26
27							27
28							28
29							29

- LOANS/INSURANCE — Insurance Record

This last form may be used to keep track of your insurance policies. It's not an essential part of your records, and you won't get any jollies out of it, but you will find that having all your insurance information in one place is surely convenient when you begin wondering how soon a policy's due or what kind of coverage you have on a certain property. Insurance policies are not written to yield that kind of information quickly.

Insurance Record

Property 456 SWEET ST.

Company / Agent	Type of Policy	Policy Number	Limits	Premium	Expiration Date
USA INSURANCE	FIRE	FI-778-1101	175,000	$254.86	4-30-85
(AMOS BEER BARREL 555-1068)					
UMBRELLA MUTUAL	EARTHQUAKE	099837	125,000	$287.00	12-2-85
(JOE ROGER 555-6620)					

Do your recordkeeping regularly at least once every month, and you'll find that it's practically tolerable.

DOING TAXES

During the first two weeks of April every year, most adults seem to suffer from the same malady, the dreaded DT's. They wobble a little and complain a lot, and their eyes grow bug-eyed and red. They start imagining all kinds of devils and demons and beastly beasties, and it isn't until after the fifteenth of the month that the symptoms finally disappear, because not until then do they finish DOING TAXES.

Landlord and landlady, if you're among those seasonal sufferers, you should be ashamed of yourself! Income tax time is an especially good time for you, and you should enjoy the opportunity to snicker a little over your good fortune. Don't wait until April 15th to file your return. Do it as soon as you can, so you'll have your income tax refund check in hand when everyone else is suffering those dreaded DT's. Anyway, you need that check by April to help pay property taxes.

You get to snicker over your income taxes because at tax time you may take advantage of two of the four ways to make money in landlording (see Chapter 2 for all four) — depreciation and capital gains.

Every year, little by little, you get to depreciate the value of the capital improvements on your property, and then you get to deduct this amount from your income. After you have enjoyed this depreciation deduction for a few years and you decide to sell the property, you'll have to pay income taxes all right, but you'll have to pay them on only a portion of the difference between the selling price and the depreciated value. This amount is known as a "capital gain" and much of it is tax free or subject to only a minimum tax.

For example, if you bought a used fourplex ten years ago for $40,000 and you depreciated it down to $31,250 over ten years, (using the straight line method and a useful life of 20 years), that means you saved paying income taxes on an average of $1875 of your income every year, a total of $18,750. If you now sell the property for $100,000, (to learn about the impending tax consequences every time you plan to acquire or dispose of income property, spend a few bucks and consult with an accountant or tax attorney), you have a capital gain of $68,750, but you have to pay income tax on only 40% of the difference between the selling price and the depreciated value, or $27,500. In other words, you keep all of $41,250 out of the tax collector's hands. Pretty neat, huh?

It's even better if you trade your property for a bigger property. In most cases you pay no income taxes on your capital gains at all when you trade. You may not only defer the payment of taxes until you finally sell out, but you may also keep trading properties and keep postponing the payment of taxes until you die. It's mindboggling to think that you might be increasing your net worth by leaps and bounds year after year and yet be liable for minimal income taxes, if any! Don't you wish you could retrieve all you've ever paid in income taxes and could use it for property acquisitions? By making the right investments, some people have been doing that all along, paying no taxes year after year. That's how they become millionaires.

Ah, but you say, "I've only got a fourplex, and I just want to know how to prepare the tax forms I need to submit with my income tax return. I can't be wasting my time dreaming about owning more property and becoming a millionaire. I have all I can handle right now. One place is plenty."

Okay, okay. Here's how to do your return, and here are some sample tax form sheets completed for Lester Landlord (he's no millionaire either), who has a duplex, half of which he occupies himself, and a fiveplex. (Note that Lester in these examples is using his two buildings more for cash flow than for tax write-offs. He's retired and doesn't need tax shelter to protect any wages. If he were working and did need greater depreciation to protect his wages, he'd be wise to trade his properties into a larger building.)

Begin preparing your taxes by completing a "Depreciation Record" sheet (see Chapter 11) for each of your capital improvements: the building (check with an accountant about the advisability of your using component depreciation as a means to increase the depreciation available to you during the early years that you own a particular property; using component depreciation, you would separate those items, like appliances and carpets, which have a useful life shorter than the building's but were included in the original acquisition, and you would depreciate them apart from the building itself), a new roof, and appliances. Use the same form for all of them, but use a separate sheet for each one or for those which might be combined because they were acquired at the same time and have an identical useful life. For example, carpets and drapes which were purchased at about the same time of year and could be considered to have useful lives of, say, five years, might be depreciated together on one sheet. All of these depreciation sheets should remain in your three-hole recordkeeping binder

FORM E-3	RENTAL INCOME AND EXPENSE		YEAR 19 _84_

NAME(S) OF TAXPAYERS: _LESTER LANDLORD_   SOC. SEC. NUMBER: _123_ | _45_ | _6789_

PROPERTY LOCATION & DESCRIPTION | GROSS INCOME

- PROPERTY A ___123 NEAT ST.___ — _3,495.60_
- PROPERTY B ___456-464 SWEET ST___ — _16,040.45_
- PROPERTY C ___
- PROPERTY D ___
- PROPERTY E ___
- PROPERTY F ___
- PROPERTY G ___

Total Income (to Schedule E, Part II, Column B) _19,536 65_

EXPENSES

	A	B	C	D	E	F	G	TOTALS
Interest	1172.28	2930.71						
Taxes, Licenses	539.45	1348.62						
Insurance	216.74	541.86						
Utilities	169.08	422.69						
Service, Repairs, Maintenance	64.90	162.31						
Merchandise, Supplies	221.57	553.92						
Payroll	θ	θ						
Miscellaneous Expenses	49.88	124.72						
Other: _Tel_	θ	144.48						
Travel	θ	169.70						
Subtotal	2433.90							
% Bus. Use	50%							
Subtotals (to Schedule E, Part II, Column E)	1216.95	6399.01						7615.96
Depreciation (Form D-1)	553.12	958.82						1511.94
Supp. Depreciation (Form SD)	48.33	150.81						199.14
Totals	1818.40	7508.64						9327.04

*Sum of depreciation and supplemental depreciation totals (to Schedule E, Part II, Column D) _1711.08_

FORM D-1	DEPRECIATION WORKSHEET	YEAR 19 84

NAME(S) OF TAXPAYERS: *LESTER LANDLORD*   SOC. SEC. NUMBER: 123 | 45 | 6789

PROPERTY LOCATION & DESCRIPTION

PROPERTY A _123 NEAT ST._

PROPERTY B _456-464 SWEET ST._

PROPERTY C _____

PROPERTY D _____

PROPERTY E _____

PROPERTY F _____

PROPERTY G _____

	A	B	C	D	E	F	G	TOTALS
Date Acq'd or Conv. to Bus.	3/67	9/68						
New or Used	USED	USED						
Cost or Other Basis	29,500	55,000						
Land Value	7375	13750						
Salvage Value	0	0						
20% 1st Year Deprec.	0	0						
Deprec. Basis	22125	41250						
Prior Deprec.	18,621.89	25,908.84						
Deprec. Balance	3503.13	15341.16						
Method of Deprec.	S.L.	125%db						
Useful Life	20	20						
Full Year Deprec.	1106.25	958.82						
% Year Held	100	100						
% Bus. Use	50	✓						
Deprec. This Year	553.12	958.82						1511.94

PAGE TOTAL 1511.94

for reference every time you do taxes and should be increased by one more sheet whenever you add another capital improvement.

Next comes the biggest job of all for procrastinators, completion of the annual summary sheets for all rental property held. Once you have completed these summaries, keep them close at hand. Together with the depreciation sheets, they comprise the primary source of data essential from here on.

Now, make blank copies of tax forms E-3, D-1, and SD in the forms section of this book, and using applicable information from your "Depreciation Records," fill out D-1 and SD. Use D-1 for buildings only and SD for anything else depreciable, from furnaces to roofs.

Enter the appropriate property location and description information on form E-3 and post each building's depreciation for the year from form D-1 to E-3. Add all the supplemental depreciation as noted on SD for each property and post these figures onto E-3 in the space marked "Supp. Depreciation." Remember that all the supplemental depreciation for each building must be lumped together before it is posted.

After you post both regular and supplemental depreciation for your properties onto E-3, enter the gross income as calculated on the "Expense and Payment Record Annual Summary." Then post all the expenses from the summary sheet to E-3 and calculate the totals. Remember to add the two asterisked boxes and post their sum in the bottommost box on the form.

Using all this information, you can easily fill out your Form 1040, Schedule E. In Part II of Schedule E, simply write "see attached form E-3" across the columns. Check the notes in parenthesis on E-3 for posting locations and then post the totals from E-3 to the corresponding "Totals" lines of columns "b," "d," and "e." Now, depending on whether you show an income or a loss for the year, combine the totals for Part II on line 8 under either "f" or "g," and post this figure in line 9 as well. It should correspond to the figure on line 35 of the "Annual Summary of Business and Statement of Income" in your recordkeeping book. If it doesn't, check your figures once again.

Next, write "see form E-3" in Part VII as your explanation for column e, Part II, and write "see forms D-1 and SD" on any line in Part VI as your explanation for column d, Part II.

Finally, total Parts I, II, and III as indicated in Schedule E. Enter that figure in Part IV and on Form 1040. From this point on, just go ahead and finish your tax computation as you normally do, snickering as you go, and remember to attach forms E-3, D-1, and SD to your Schedule E when you mail it in.

SHOULD YOU DO YOUR OWN?

There are those naysayers you'll encounter in this world who will say you're a pig-headed fool for doing your own taxes. They'll say you should have a sorcerer in money matters do them for you, someone who's thoroughly experienced in doing income taxes for propertied folk, someone who knows all the latest loopholes applicable to your situation, and those naysayers may be right. It all depends on your ability and your inclination. Some people have the good sense to invest in rental property, but they lack the capacity to deal with numerical data and complicated instructions. People like that should leave their taxes to experts.

If you happen to be a landlord or landlady who possesses the ability and inclination to prepare your own taxes, however, do them yourself, by all means, but once you have finished with them, get a second opinion from a specialist by buying an hour or two of professional advice. You cannot possibly keep abreast of the volumes of current tax laws, and

FORM SD	SUPPLEMENTAL DEPRECIATION	YEAR 19 *84*

NAME(S) OF TAXPAYERS	*LESTER LANDLORD*	SOC. SEC. NUMBER	*123*	*45*	*6789*

CAPITAL IMPROVEMENT LOCATION & DESCRIPTION

1. *123 NEAT ST. — ROOFING*
2. *456-464 SWEET ST. — WASHER/DRYER*
3. *" " " " — WATER HEATER*
4. _____
5. _____
6. _____
7. _____

	1	2	3	4	5	6	7	TOTALS
Date Acq'd or Conv. to Bus.	6/83	6/81	5/84					
New or Used	NEW	NEW	NEW					
Cost or Other Basis	1450.00	876.00	444.00					
Salvage Value	-0-	50.00	-0-					
20% 1st Year Deprec.	-0-	175.00	-0-					N.A.
Deprec. Basis	1450	651.00	444.00					
Prior Deprec.	24.16	280.25	-0-					
Deprec. Balance	2142589	370.75	444.00					
Method of Deprec.	SL	SL	SL					
Useful Life	15	6	7					
Full Year Deprec.	96.67	108.50	63.43					
% Year Held	100	100	66.7					
% Bus. Use	50	100	100					
Deprec. This Year	48.33	108.50	42.31					199.14

PAGE TOTAL   199.14

you could unknowingly be throwing money away by overlooking perfectly legitimate tax angles.

Whether you have your taxes prepared for you or whether you do them yourself, try to get a feel for the tax principles which affect your landlording business. Read about taxes in periodicals and jot down questions for your consultant. A capable professional will save you money and give you a tax education at the same time.

Whereas you may not be foolish for preparing your tax return yourself, you certainly would be foolish for submitting it to the tax collector without first reviewing it with someone who knows the subject intimately.

TOOLS & EQUIPMENT

Whether you do your own maintenance and repair work or have a trusty handyperson do it for you, you need tools, and you need good ones. That delightful book, *Know How, A Fix-it Book For The Clumsy But Pure of Heart,* states as the "First Principle of Fixing":

A good tool does work for you.

A bad tool makes work for you.

Since you already have tenants who are making work for you, you hardly need tools which will only make more. Buy good tools.

Although even well known companies manufacture tools which are designed for light, occasional use and are priced accordingly, you cannot afford them. They cost too much. They may be cheap to buy initially, but when they malfunction at inopportune moments and you have to call a professional to complete a job, you'll learn how much bad tools really cost. You're not a homeowner do-it-yourselfer, remember, and you're not just buying tools to use them once and then display them on the walls of your garage. You'll use them over and over again. Besides, the tools you buy and use on your rental properties are every bit as tax-deductible as any of your other property expenses, and in that context, the difference between the price of a poor tool and the price of a good one is trivial.

Buy middle-of-the-line and top-of-the-line tools with brand names like Channellock, Craftsman, Ridgid, Rockwell, Skil, and Stanley. They won't fail you when you're called out of bed at 3:30 A.M. to mend a broken water pipe or shore up a floor joist that just collapsed beneath a tenant's busy bed.

When you have good tools, you certainly don't want to lose them. Ah, but unfortunately you will. No matter how vigilant you are, your tools will simply disappear now and then. You might misplace a tool and lose it or inadvertently leave it behind. Tenants' children might play with one and carry it off. Tenants might borrow a tool and forget to return it. Your tools might get mixed up with those of someone who's working for you, or they might actually be stolen. However they disappear, once they leave your possession, you have no way to identify them as yours unless you have them individually marked. Because your exposure to the mysterious disappearance of tools is far greater than normal, you are wise to engrave every one with your name and your driver's license number, or some other traceable number, so that when they do reappear in someone else's possession, you will have a case for proving they are yours.

LANDLORDING TOOLKIT

Every item in the kit was selected because it meets at least one of the following criteria: light, small, useful, or versatile. Heft a 14-inch steel pipe wrench in one hand and a 14-inch aluminum one in the other, and you'll get the idea about lightness. Compare the measurements of a standard hacksaw with those of the Stanley mini hacksaw, and you'll get the idea about smallness. Leave one of these tools out of the kit for a month and you'll get the idea about usefulness. Try using diagonals for crimping solderless connectors and cutting small diameter bolts and stripping wire and cutting wire and holding small objects. Then try the same tasks with the handy-dandy electrician's tool and you'll get the idea about versatility.

In addition to the tools and supplies illustrated here, you might want to include in your toolkit these five rather mundane items which also fit the selection criteria.

BLOCK OF WOOD (½" plywood about 4" x 6" is best because it won't split) — for taking your hammer's beating when you want to tap, but not mar, a surface; also useful for backing up your drill work.

OLD TOOTHBRUSH — for general-purpose cleaning and brushing.

RAG OR PAPERTOWEL — for wiping and drying everything, especially your hands.

SMALL PIECE OF SOAP — for lubricating sticking drawers and doors and for washing up between the dirty and the clean jobs.

WOODEN MATCHES — for lighting pilot lights and packing loose wood screw holes so the screws will hold more tightly.

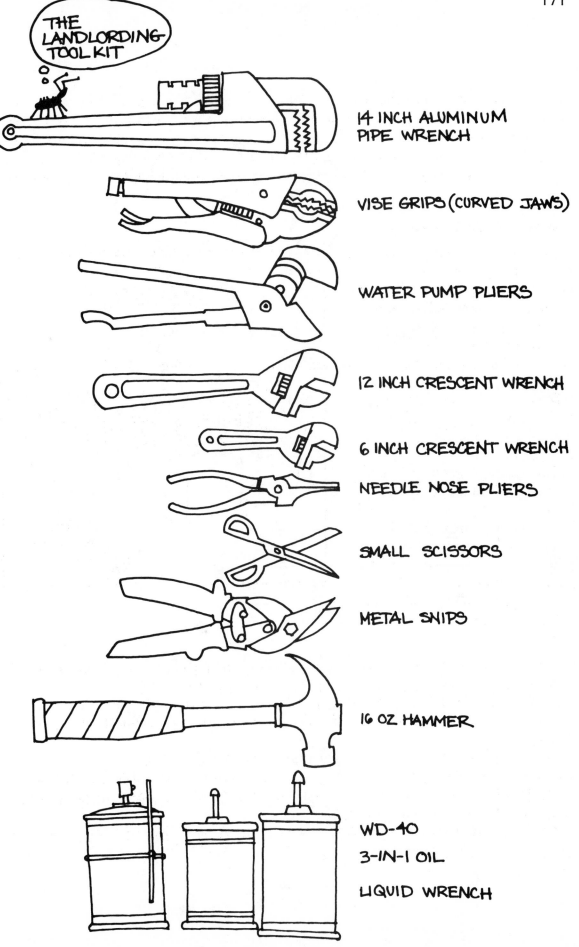

THE LANDLORDING TOOL KIT

14 INCH ALUMINUM PIPE WRENCH

VISE GRIPS (CURVED JAWS)

WATER PUMP PLIERS

12 INCH CRESCENT WRENCH

6 INCH CRESCENT WRENCH

NEEDLE NOSE PLIERS

SMALL SCISSORS

METAL SNIPS

16 OZ HAMMER

WD-40

3-IN-1 OIL

LIQUID WRENCH

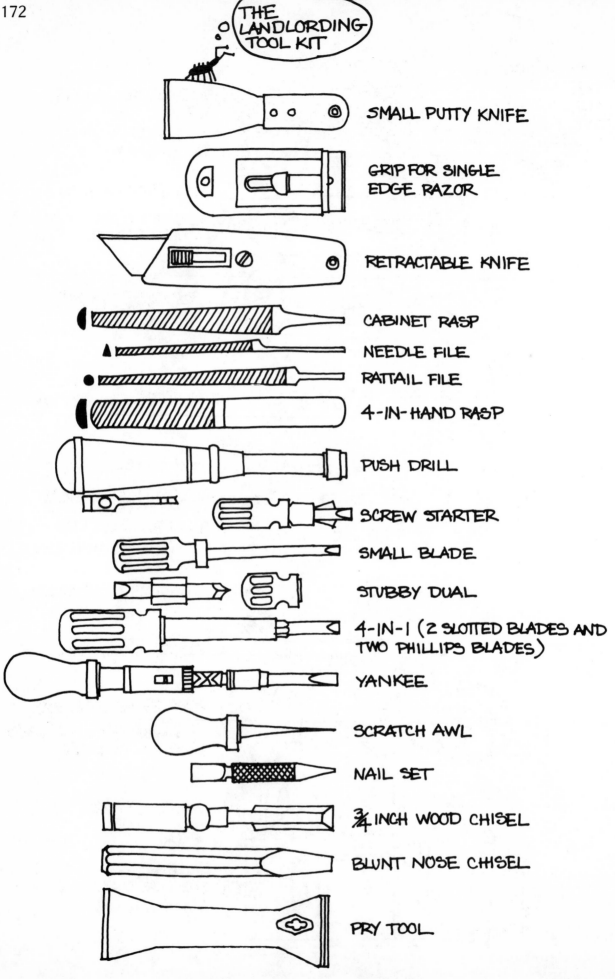

THE LANDLORDING TOOL KIT

SMALL PUTTY KNIFE

GRIP FOR SINGLE EDGE RAZOR

RETRACTABLE KNIFE

CABINET RASP

NEEDLE FILE

RATTAIL FILE

4-IN-HAND RASP

PUSH DRILL

SCREW STARTER

SMALL BLADE

STUBBY DUAL

4-IN-1 (2 SLOTTED BLADES AND TWO PHILLIPS BLADES)

YANKEE

SCRATCH AWL

NAIL SET

¾ INCH WOOD CHISEL

BLUNT NOSE CHISEL

PRY TOOL

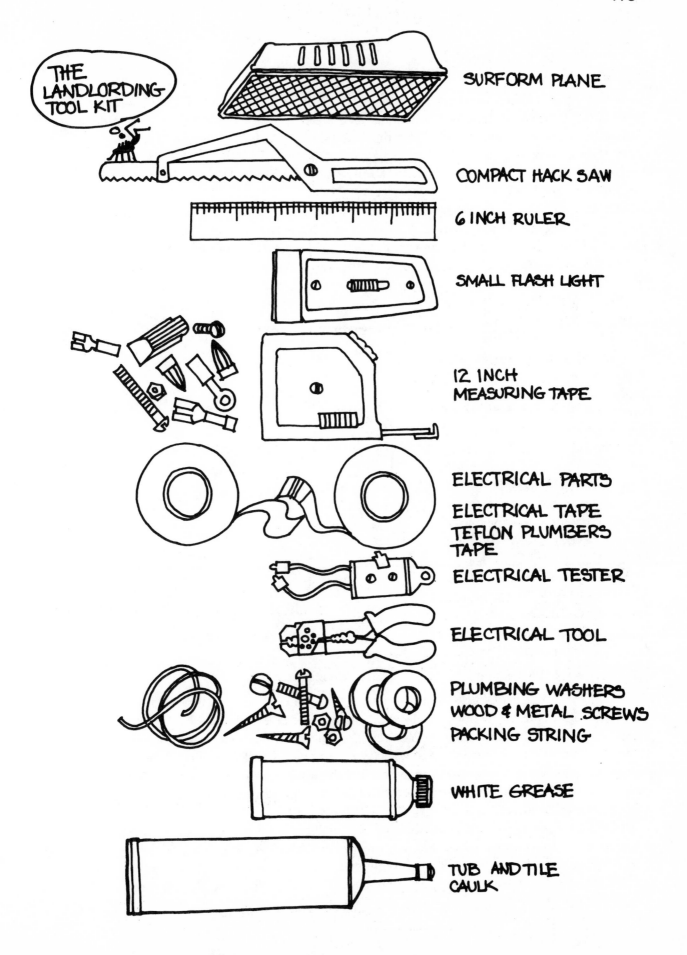

PLUMBING TOOLS

Some of the landlord's and landlady's plumbing jobs require certain bulky or specialized tools which you may want to acquire as the need arises, but which you won't want to carry around with you on every fixit visit. The most useful tools for the landlord and landlady plumber are these —

BASIN WRENCH — for wrenching sink nuts way up in those inaccessible spaces when you are removing or installing sink faucets.

CLOSET AUGER (sometimes called a toilet snake) — for unclogging toilets of sanitary napkins, disposable diapers, sunken toys, and tough turds. It's a surer curer than a plunger. Spend $15-25 for one that will work more than once without kinking. *Definitely a must!*

DRAIN JET — for clearing troublesome drains with a garden hose and water pressure. They come in various sizes and are especially useful on exterior cleanouts.

DRUM AUGER — for interior uses, clearing sink and tub drains with little muss 'n' fuss. Buy one with a drop head if you can because it always seeks lower levels in the pipes just as water does. If two basins on opposite sides of a wall are connected into a tee within the wall, the rigid spring bore head will go right through the tee into the other basin next door. It will not seek the path of the sewer water unless it has no other route to follow. My own 25 foot drop-head drum auger (Sears Craftsman 9-55356; same thing, drill-assisted, Craftsman 9-55472) has *never* failed to clear a backed-up drain which could be cleared from the inside of a building. *Another must!*

A DROP HEAD DRUM AUGER!

FAUCET HANDLE PULLER — for removing stuck faucet handles without damaging the valve stem itself, the faucet body, or the escutcheon. Few faucet washers can be changed unless the faucet handle is removed. Yet how do you remove a faucet handle which has been "welded" to its shaft by an accumulation of mineral deposits and dirt? Wiggle the handle too much and you'll break the stem off at the neck. Then you'll have to replace the entire assembly. This puller applies pressure at exactly the right point to remove the handle without damage. *A must!*

PLUMBER'S DEEP SOCKET WRENCHES — for removing bathtub and shower faucet stems without breaking the whole wall down. The most used single size in 31/32".

STRAP WRENCH — for installing chrome fittings without leaving teeth marks.

TUBING CUTTER — for cutting any copper water supply tubing neatly in a trice.

VALVE SEAT REMOVER — for replacing seats in washer-type faucets. Faucets which use washers nowadays have brass seats that can be unscrewed with this tool. When you have to replace a faucet washer, inspect the seat as well for nicks and pits. If it's not reasonably smooth, replace it. Otherwise even a new washer will fail to shut off the water flow entirely. *Also a must!*

ELECTRIC TOOLS

Besides all of these various hand tools, the intrepid landlord or landlady do-it-yourselfer also needs a few electric tools — a drill, an engraver, a sabre saw, and a sander, for sure, and maybe a circular saw, too. A drill, engraver, and a sabre saw are essential electric tools for obvious reasons, but a sander fits into that same category as well because it saves so much time in tedious preparation for painting, and you know how frequently you paint.

When you have to repair holes that tenants have kicked in walls and doors, something that most homeowner do-it-yourselfers never have to face, you need a sander to take the roughness out of your repair work.

The one sander above all sanders is the Rockwell Speed-Bloc. It's light, it's comfortable in the hand, it's fast, and it uses exactly one quarter of a standard sheet of sandpaper, so you won't have to buy any special size of sandpaper. Its motor turns at a speedy 12,000 RPM, and it sands wood or plaster many times faster than you could ever do it by hand. There are sanders sold for $15, and there are sanders sold for $29, and those are cheap prices, I'll

grant you, but the Speed-Bloc is mighty cheap at $74.50. There's nothing like it.

A circular saw is essential if you have to do any structural work, like repairing porches, stairs, or floor joists, and it's equally useful if you have to build or mend wooden fences, but you can get along without one otherwise.

A suitable electric tool isn't all that you need for a job, however. You must have electricity, too. To accommodate your electric tools anywhere you have need of them, make certain you have an adequate extension cord, and be sure you keep a three-prong plug adapter handy also.

OTHER USEFUL TOOLS AND EQUIPMENT

Almost any size landlording operation will find the following tools and equipment either quite useful or absolutely indispensable:

APPLIANCE DOLLY — for preventing hernias when you're carting in a "loaner" refrigerator or carting out an evicted tenant's worldly goods. Some dollies are much better stair climbers than others. If you have any choices, try them out. I paid $25 for a used one at an equipment rental yard which was upgrading its equipment. Sears lists a good one in its tool catalog.

BLACK AND DECKER WORKMATE — for clamping or holding any bulky work at a reasonable working height.

DYMO LABELER — for making neat mailbox name labels.

FLUORESCENT CAMP LIGHT — for showing prospective tenants through empty units at night when the electricity's turned off.

LADDERS GREAT AND SMALL — for getting you to the top safely. They should be light, compact, and sturdy enough even for acrophobes. For indoor work, use a four-foot stepladder, all the height you're likely to need to reach any ordinary ceiling. Six footers are much too unwieldy indoors. Write the Little Giant Ladder Company, American Fork, Utah 84003, for information and prices on the unique ladder they manufacture. It has a wide stance, which makes it quite stable. It can be either an extension ladder or an adjustable stepladder, and because of its unique telescoping legs, it even works as a stepladder on stairs.

PARTS CARRIER — for carrying those frequently used fixit parts right with you to the job. I use one called a Partfolio. When closed, it's an eight-inch plastic cube with a handle; opened, it's a ten-tray parts chest with adjustable bins. Order one from the Partfolio Company, 1281 Anderson Drive, San Rafael, CA 94901 It's $15, postpaid.

PROPANE TORCH — for loosening old floor tile, sweating copper pipe fittings, and doing a host of other tasks which require plenty of concentrated heat.

SAW HORSES — for supporting large work projects, such as doors, which must be shortened to clear those new carpets you had installed. Stanley makes a sturdy metal sawhorse which folds to a compact 4" x 36". U.S. General Supply carries them.

STAPLE GUN — for tacking down unruly floorcoverings and installing insulation.

TROUBLE LIGHT — for snooping out trouble beneath buildings and working late at night in units which lack ceiling fixtures.

UTILITY BOX TRAILER — for hauling trash, cash, furniture, and appliances. Once you master backing up your car with a trailer hitched to it, you'll find that a trailer with a box about 4' wide by 6' long by 3' high is extremely useful and even has certain advantages over a pickup truck. For example, it can be unhitched and left for a time fully loaded so you don't have to lug its contents around with you all the time. It can be left for the tenants to fill with their seasonal trash and then hauled off to the dump. It can be unhitched and dumped like a dump truck to empty its contents quickly. It likely has a low bed which makes loading heavy appliances relatively easy. I treasure mine.

Naturally, you may want to rent some of these items if you feel you wouldn't use them often enough to justify their purchase. Be certain you are familiar with the purchase prices of those items you rent, though, because some may be purchased for little more than their rental fees, while others have a wide spread between purchase prices and rental fees.

CATALOGS

No treatment of tools and equipment for the landlord and landlady would be complete without mention of those mail-order companies which specialize in selling tools. Two companies especially should be mentioned: U.S. General Supply, Jericho, NY 11753, and Brookstone Company, Peterborough, NH 03458.

U.S. General publishes what they claim is America's largest catalog of brand-name tools and hardware. Send them a dollar and they will send you three of their latest full-sized catalogs and numerous small catalogs over a twelve-month period, whether you buy anything from them or not. They will also send you a one-dollar credit certificate which you may apply to your very first order. U.S. General lists a complete range of tools, from homeowner quality (useful life—minutes) to industrial quality tools (useful life—years), and they discount all their tools from list prices. The Rockwell Speed-Bloc sander is discounted at approximately 25% off the list price.

Brookstone, on the other hand, lists only top-quality tools and hardware, all sold at regular prices. They fill orders quickly and carry unusual tools which are hard to find elsewhere. Brookside has, for example, a completely enclosed electric extension-cord reel, which will hold up to one hundred feet of 12-gauge, 3-wire cord; virtually indestructible 100-year screwdrivers, which will take any physical or verbal abuse; and an assortment of 200 O-rings which will save any landlord or landlady plumber many trips to the hardware store.

Although it's by no means strictly a mail-order company, Sears does publish a special tool catalog which lists items of interest to landlords and landladies, items such as an appliance dolly, aluminum pipe wrenches, and drum augers. Ask for this catalog at your nearest Sears catalog store or write your nearest catalog distribution center, and while you're at it, get a copy of the Sears Business Equipment & Supply Catalog to peruse, too. You're in business, remember.

If nothing else, you will find these catalogs ideal to use for comparison shopping at home.

MAINTENANCE & REPAIR HINTS

Rentals take more of a beating than owner-occupied dwellings, and consequently they require better maintenance and more repairs. In general, the best way to approach this work is to assume that the many components of a rental dwelling will get dirty, wear out, fall apart, break down, crack, leak, or otherwise deteriorate sooner than they would in your own home and to handle the maintenance and repairs as if you had the brothers of a disreputable fraternity as your tenants. The hints in this chapter suggest some ways to mend, improve, and foolproof your rentals so they will take less time, effort, and money to look after, no matter what kind of tenants you have.

Although this is a landlord and landlady do-it-yourselfer's book, you'll notice that there's a lot of landlord and landlady do-it-yourselfing which doesn't appear here, like unclogging a toilet with a closet auger, replacing defective light switches, laying floor tile, and so forth. Such information is readily available in a variety of general-purpose homeowner do-it-yourself books, like the *Reader's Digest Complete Do-It-Yourself Manual*, the *Whole House Catalog*, and Time-Life's *How Things Work in Your Home*, which you should have available to consult when needed. The maintenance and repair hints in this chapter cover problems which are specifically related to landlording and which are seldom mentioned in general-purpose do-it-yourself books.

FIXING BROKEN WINDOWS

Windows seem to break all by themselves in rental units. Nobody ever seems to know how they break. They just break somehow. That's reason enough to have a clause in your rental agreement making your tenants financially responsible for any windows broken in their dwellings while they live there, regardless of who actually does the breaking.

Although this may relieve you of the expense, it does not necessarily relieve you of the task of arranging for the replacement, since broken windows reflect negatively on your rental building. See that the work gets done promptly yourself and collect from the tenant later.

Here are some handy hints about fixing those broken windows —

• When you learn of a broken window at your rentals, the first thing you have to do, after swearing softly, is to take its measurements. That necessitates making a special trip with your tape measure and ladder before you can even order the replacement. You can avoid having to make two trips every time there's a broken window by preparing for that inevitable breaking of glass before it ever happens. Take the time to measure all your windows in advance. The chances are good that you won't even have to measure them all individually once you notice how the sizes are repeated from room to room. With these measurements on hand when windows do break, you will save yourself aggravation, time, and fuel. When informed of a broken window over the telephone, you only have to inquire which window pane it was that broke, refer to your measurements for that window, and then secure a replacement. If you don't keep track, you may wind up measuring the same window individually many times.

• Sometimes, for one reason or other, broken windows cannot be repaired immediately, so until you can either hire the work done or do it yourself, make a temporary repair. Cover both sides of the hole or crack with transparent Contact Paper. This expedient reduces the danger of cuts from glass shards, eliminates drafts entirely, and still lets the sun shine through. What more can tenants ask of a window?

• When replacing glass in aluminum windows held together by a screw at each corner, remove only the screws at two opposite corners and then pull the frame apart carefully. You'll have two L-shaped aluminum pieces which are much easier to align when they're being reassembled with a new pane. If you can't get the frame to come apart in two pieces and you have to disassemble it completely, mark the corners plainly with letters or numbers to assist you in reassembling the frame exactly as it was.

• Consider replacing those frequently broken windows with clear acrylic, commonly known as plexiglass. It is every bit as transparent as ordinary glass, but it has the advantage of being less breakable, a most important advantage for rentals. It does have the disadvantage of being quite a bit more flexible than glass, however. Plexiglass replacements, therefore, should be thicker than original glass so they won't blow out of their frames under pressure. Unfortunately, some frames will not accept a thicker pane, and you may have to use glass anyway, whether you want to or not, unless you care to try using 3/32″ plexiglass. Plexiglass this thin is the thickness of ordinary window glass and is satisfactory only for panes that are narrow or have an area of four square feet, more or less, but it should be avoided otherwise.

• Plexiglass that can be used for window replacements comes in a variety of thicknesses and qualities. Buy the thickest second-quality grade (industrial seconds, they're sometimes called) that will fit your frame and application (normally 1/8″ to 3/16″ is thick enough), and you'll find that it costs about the same as glass.

• If you have aluminum windows with a plastic bead holding the glass pane in place, you should be able to use a thick enough plexiglass replacement merely by discarding the plastic bead. Absence of the bead leaves room for a pane considerably thicker than the original glass. Puttied window frames and frames with wooden retaining strips will accommodate the thicker plexiglass, too, and so will most doors. In doors, plexiglass provides greater security than glass panes because burglars can't easily break through, reach in, and open the door locks from the inside.

• Plexiglass does have the disadvantage of showing scratches, of course, but there are polishes on the market which were originally formulated for airplane windshields and do a good job of making the scratches disappear as if by magic.

• Besides resisting breakage during use and providing good security, plexiglass does have one other big advantage over glass. A replacement pane won't break while it's being manhandled during the replacement process, something that happens all too frequently to us amateur glaziers as we struggle to install large pieces of fragile glass.

• Whenever a window pane has broken in a wooden casement window and you notice that the casement is deteriorated, consider replacing the entire casement right then with an aluminum-framed window. The window itself will cost approximately twice what the pane would cost, but you will save that much and more later on when you are painting the building because you'll be able to skip the laborious task of painting the casement both inside and out.

INSTALLING WINDOW COVERINGS

Installing drapery rods, curtain rods, and shade brackets can be distressing work unless you know what's behind that sheet rock or plaster you're blindly poking holes into. You

should know that every window has at least 3½ inches of wood concealed around its frame. You will always hit wood within this 3½-inch limit, and you can nail or screw to your big heart's content knowing full well that there is wood behind that wall for secure support. If you have to go beyond 3½ inches with your bracket fasteners, test for the presence of wood by hammering in a thin nail first, but be prepared to use some sort of anchoring device.

The best anchors for strength and ease of installation are made of nylon (plastic ones are the next best if nylon is unavailable), cost a nickel each in quantities, hold fast, and may be used in sheet rock or plaster

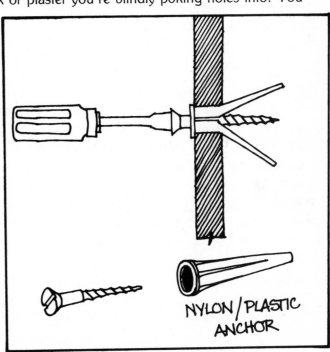

NYLON/PLASTIC ANCHOR

walls. The key to using them is to drill a hole which will grasp the anchor firmly enough to keep it from revolving at the turn of a screw.

PICKING PROPER SHADE BRACKETS

Window shades may be mounted inside window casings or on wall surfaces. Each of these installations requires a different type of bracket. The one used for shades mounted on wall surfaces can be bent back or forth to compensate for inaccurately measured or inaccurately cut shades, and it can also be moved if need be, but the ordinary bracket which mounts inside the casing cannot be bent or moved to compensate for a shade that's too long or short. If a shade is too short, you can only shim the brackets to make it fit, a laborious job which involves removing the brackets and renailing them.

While there never could be a bracket to compensate for shades that are too long to fit inside a window casing, at last someone's invented one that works for those that are a wee bit

too short. Basically it's just a flat piece of metal with a tongue that can be bent to fit the length of the shade. Presto, the shade fits perfectly. No shimming, no renailing, and no cussing. It has saved me countless hours. K-Mart handles them.

Unless the exposed casing around your window is wood, discard those puny nails that come with all shade brackets. They just won't extend far enough through the sheetrock which lines most window casings to pierce the wooden framing underneath. Nailed only into sheetrock, they will hold for a time, but they will surely be the cause of a repair call later, after the stresses of raising and lowering the shade have taken their toll. Use galvanized 4- or 5-penny common nails in their place. They hold well.

MEASURING FOR CONTRACT DRAPERIES

Ignorance of the correct method of measuring for new draperies once cost me several wasted hours, a little humiliation, lots of aggravation, and fifteen wasted dollars for a remake. Unless you know the few simple directions for measuring draperies, the whole business seems hopelessly confusing, for drapery sizes, strange as it seems, are not actual drapery measurements. To avoid frustration when ordering draperies, follow these three simple steps —

• First, measure the distance across the front (face) of the installed rod. This measurement is called the drapery width and is always expressed first.

• Second, measure the distance from the top of the rod to one inch above the floor for floor-length draperies, or measure from the top of the rod to four inches below the window sill for apron-length draperies. This measurement is the drapery length and is always expressed second.

• Third, indicate whether the drapery is to be a panel (one-way draw opens from one side) or a pair (two-way draw opens from the middle).

Do not measure and include in your total measurements either the rod projections (distance at each end between rod and wall) or the center overlap. Contract drapery shops make allowances for these.

Do not measure an old drapery's exact dimensions and submit them for duplication.

Do not add any height above the top of the rod up to that point where you think the drapery will extend.

Do not be afraid to inquire whether this is the very method used by your drapery supplier.

Whereas contract drapery suppliers do use this method, suppliers who deal with the general public may use another. To find a contract drapery supplier, look under "Draperies — Whsle & Mfrs" in the Yellow Pages. Yes, they will sell to you. Give them your business card and they will probably even set you up with a billing account.

If there's no drapery rod in place and you have to install one, install it so you can take advantage of the standard sizes which contract drapery shops keep in stock. Standard sizes will cost you much less and will not require you to wait those precious days while custom draperies are being made up to your specifications, something that is especially important when you have just finished redecorating a dwelling, have advertised it for rent, and then you learn that the draperies won't be ready for another two weeks. The sheets, old draperies, bedspreads, or drop cloths you'll then have to put on the windows detract noticeably from that rental's appearance.

These are the standard contract sizes generally available (width × length), together with the common window openings they fit.

Window Opening	Drapery Size	Window Opening	Drapery Size
Two-Way Draw		*Two-Way Draw*	
3' × 3'	42 × 44	8' × 4'	102 × 56
4' × 3'	52 × 44	8' × 5'	102 × 68
4' × 4'	54 × 56	8' × 6' 8"	102 × 84
4' × 6' 8"	54 × 84	10' × 4'	126 × 56
5' × 4'	64 × 56	10' × 6' 8"	126 × 84
6' × 3'	78 × 44		
6' × 4'	78 × 56	*One-Way Draw*	
6' × 5'	78 × 68	5' × 6' 8"	64 × 84
6' × 6' 8"	78 × 84	6' × 6' 8"	78 × 84
8' × 3'	102 × 44	8' × 6' 8"	102 × 84

As you can calculate from this table, the ends of the rod should normally extend three inches on either side of the window opening, and the top of the rod should be three and a half inches above the window opening. Such a rod installation will be firmly anchored in the wood of the window framing. If, because of an odd-sized window opening, you have to fudge a little to create a standard size, by all means, fudge, using nylon anchors for mounting the rod brackets so you can avoid having to order a custom size.

Likewise, if there is a drapery rod already installed and it isn't exactly standard in length, don't despair. You can usually fit a drapery size which is an inch too big or too little without having to move the brackets. If, however, a standard-size drapery varies too much to fit your existing rod installation, just move the rod brackets so the standard size will fit and use anchors as necessary.

MENDING TORN WINDOW SHADES

Very often the bottoms of window shades will tear and become unsightly. If they're long enough, cut off the ragged bottoms and sew a new slot for the wooden grab stick. If they're not long enough, apply a clear Contact Paper patch to both sides of the tear. It's not as good as cutting off the old bottom, but it beats buying a new shade.

184

CLEANING VENETIANS

Unless you consider your own time worth about a dollar an hour or you can get good cleaning help for such wages, cleaning dirty Venetian blinds is best done professionally. A professional has special hanging devices and washing tanks which do the job far better and more cheaply than you ever could. I have had what might best be termed "tenement Venetians" cleaned and retaped for less than what cleaning alone would have cost if I had had my usual housecleaning helper attempt the task.

If you do try a professional Venetian blind cleaners, call around for the best price and then take your Venetians in for service rather than calling for pickup and delivery. You'll find that they're easy to take down and put up again, and you'll save still more.

CLEANING CARPETS

Shampooing used to be the only way to clean carpets, but shampooing merely relocates the dirt, much like a ragamuffin's spit bath. The dirt lies buried somewhere in the carpet, for shampooing simply does not remove it. Fortunately shampooing is not the only way to clean carpets any longer. In the past few years there have been significant improvements in carpet cleaning machines, chemicals, and techniques, most of which involve carpet steam cleaning.

Don't let the term "steam" mislead you. Carpet steam cleaners all use hot water under pressure, not steam. True steam might boost cleaning efficiency, but it would turn a Karastan into a cat tree in no time.

The basic carpet cleaning process consists of only two primary steps, spraying a hot solution of special detergent deep into the carpet fibers and vacuuming that solution up with the dirt. That's all. Beforehand, the carpet should be vacuumed thoroughly with a good conventional vacuum cleaner, preferably an upright, and the noticeable spots and traffic lanes should be preconditioned with an appropriate remedy.

The results of this process are impressive, even downright astounding at times. Carpets so dirty that you couldn't tell what color they once had been, are revealed in their true colors, or close to them. Naturally, steam cleaned carpets are not restored to new condition by the process. They are no less threadbare or tattered than they were before, but they look clean, they smell clean, they are clean, and they last a whole lot longer.

Whether you hire a professional with steam cleaning equipment to do the job, rent a machine and do it yourself, or rent a machine and hire a helper to do it, matters more in terms of costs than in results. Few landlords and landladies can justify purchasing a steam cleaner, because good ones with sufficiently powerful vacuum motors to extract a high percentage of the solution (a good machine at sea level will extract at least 80%) cost around $1000. Renting a machine, though, is good economics. They generally rent for $5 – $15, depending on the time required. If you hire an operator at $5 an hour and the job takes three hours, you'll save approximately half the cost of a professional carpet cleaning service. If you want to do it yourself, of course, you can save even more.

What really costs, if you purchase them where you rent the machine, are those special cleaners, conditioners, deodorants, stain removers, and defoamers used in carpet steam cleaning. It's not uncommon for people to spend $15 for the chemicals to clean the carpets in a one-bedroom dwelling, but if you buy them right, those chemicals will cost you mere pennies, and since you will likely clean many carpets in your landlording days, the savings could be significant.

Years ago I bought a keg of soil extraction powder from Century Chemical, 22924 Sutro Street, Hayward, CA 94541, after a professional told me about the place. That powder is the only steam cleaning detergent I use, and that 25-pound keg is the only one I have ever bought. The powder is a high-alkaline (12.5 pH) industrial-strength cleaner which surpasses the cleaning power of every low-alkaline (8.5 pH) home-market cleaner I've ever tried, and it costs substantially less. Depending on the size, condition, and pile of the wall-to-wall carpet in a one-bedroom dwelling, the soil extraction powder to clean it will cost somewhere between 8 cents and 40 cents. Yes, you read that right. Those figures are not misprints. Between 8 cents and 40 cents! One 25-pound keg, the smallest quantity sold, costs around $25, plus shipping (send for Century's latest price list and catalog). It's so highly concentrated that you dissolve only a half-ounce of the powder into each gallon of hot water.

On the retail market, that keg is worth somewhere between one and two thousand dollars! What other legitimate business has such a markup? That's 5000%! If you weren't so involved in your properties, you could deal in the stuff. Repackage it in little half-ounce plastic bags for about 4 cents each, including the bags, and sell them for $2. Think of it, 5000%!

If you take my advice, though, don't sell Century's soil extraction powder, use it, but before you use it, read the instructions on the label carefully. This is a powerful, professional carpet cleaning product. Do not use it on natural fiber carpets or on any white or pastel carpets with jute backing. They may turn brownish. Since rental dwellings rarely have such impractical carpets, however, you should be able to use the powder on all of your carpets safely. I have used it on all of mine.

Century also markets other good carpet-care products which are useful to landlords and landladies and are not readily available elsewhere, products such as a gum and candle wax remover aerosol, a pet urine deodorizer, a rust remover, a clean and tint solution which any novice can use, and a large syringe for injecting deodorant directly into carpet pads (useful in eliminating especially stubborn pet odors).

You do have carpets to clean. You are in business to make a profit. So you might as well buy right.

WISKING GREASE AWAY

Its label modestly claims that it cleans soiled laundry, but that's not all Wisk does. It cuts the cooking grease in kitchens, the body grease in baths, and the elbow grease in cleaning more than anything else I have ever tried.

You know how greasy those areas around stoves can be in some rentals which tenants have "cleaned" on their way out. Range hoods and filters, especially, are missed more often than they're hit. You can clean range hoods well and quickly with Wisk, and you can unclog those hood filters by soaking them in a solution of Wisk and water or, as an alternative, by running them through a regular dishwasher washing cycle. Either way, they'll come clean.

Bathtubs, showers, and sinks which have accumulations of body oils also come clean if they're first wet with Wisk and left to soak for a few minutes before they're washed down.

These otherwise laborious cleaning chores become quick work, easy work, tolerable work when you use the right cleaning agent. Wisk is just that. Try it yourself.

BEAUTIFYING NATURAL WOODWORK WITH LIQUID GOLD

Sometimes varnished cabinets will develop bleached spots where the finish has worn away, and they'll make an untenanted kitchen look grim indeed. If you don't have the time or the inclination to varnish the cabinets again, rub them with Liquid Gold and they'll look quite presentable.

REPAIRING THE BURNED KITCHEN COUNTER

A burned Formica counter makes any kitchen look unappetizing and even downright dirty, but you can't easily justify spending a hundred dollars to replace a 2,400 square-inch counter just because of a 16 square-inch burn spot.

Don't replace the whole counter. That's a lot of work and expense, and there's no guarantee you won't have another burn spot there in the future. Cover the burn spot instead!

Remember that some tenant at some time past needed a stand for a hot pot. That's how the burn got there in the first place. If you cover the spot with four bullnose ceramic tiles (bullnose tiles are the ones with two finished sides and one rounded corner), you create a hot pot stand, and you can't possibly have another burn spot there in the future.

To do the job, arrange four bullnose tiles in a square so there are finished sides and rounded corners all around the big square. Cement the tiles in place with white caulk, allowing a little to ooze up between the tiles so you won't have to grout later. That's all.

Your bullnose tile coverup caper covers the burn spot that's already there, creates a great place to set a hot pot, and absolutely guarantees that there won't be any more burns there ever again. Honest it does.

Oh yes, if your tenants are cutters rather than burners, do the cutting board coverup caper. Cement a thin cutting board in place over the damaged counter area and let your tenants cut contentedly away.

SAVING TIME WHEN LAYING FLOOR TILE

At one time or another you will probably try laying floor tile in a kitchen, bath, or laundry area, and hopefully you will read about how to do the job properly before you attempt it. There are some procedures you should definitely know about before you begin, and you will find them carefully outlined in the *Reader's Digest Do-It-Yourself Manual.*

One simple, timesaving technique you won't find there is this —

  • Fit the floor tile *underneath* wooden doorway moldings instead of around them. Cutting straight across the bottom of a wooden molding with a compact hacksaw is much easier than trying to cut the floor tile itself with a scissors or knife to make it fit around the molding's contours. You will produce a neater, more professional-looking installation and you won't waste tiles making inaccurate cuts.

REPAIRING HOLLOW-CORE DOOR DAMAGE

Hollow-core doors are nothing but two thin layers of plywood sandwiching a few wooden boards and battens which give the doors their thickness and rigidity. For the most part, there's just a lot of air inside.

As doors go, they're perfectly sufficient, except when they have to offer firm resistance. When your tenant wants to free his hysterical three-year-old who's locked in the bathroom, he doesn't waste time looking for a way to open the lock. He kicks or punches the door in.

What a mess! You survey the damage and you notice that the striker plate has splintered the jamb, and the door has a gaping hole. Repairing the jamb is something of a job but not a big one. You cut out the broken section, square it off, nail a new piece into place, paint it to match, and presto, few people could tell the difference.

The hole in the door is another story, however, because you cannot fit a new piece into the hole if there's nothing to attach it to. You could replace the door entirely, but that's expensive and needn't be done unless the wooden pieces inside have broken and can no longer provide support for the lock and hinges. So you have two choices — cover the hole with something more substantial than Contact Paper or fill it.

Thin plywood paneling or "doorskin," as it's called in carpentry jargon, works great for covering large holes. You simply cut an eye-pleasing geometrical shape and screw or glue the patch over the hole. Paint or stain the patch to make it contrast with the rest of the door and it will look almost as good as any decorator design.

A mirror tile or a self-adhesive floor tile may be used to cover holes as large as a fist, but not much larger, because the tile's adhesive must have enough flat door surface to grip and support the weight of the tile or else it will keep falling off. Again, you may turn this repair of a mishap into a decorator design by selecting a tile that will look like a medallion on the door. Try positioning it in various ways to achieve this effect all the more.

Repairs with a quick-setting patching compound work well to fill small holes where the door is only dented or the broken piece is still firmly attached by one edge and can provide some support, but they will also work on larger holes. As in the repair of good-sized sheetrock holes with these compounds, you must first stuff the hollow cavity behind the hole with crushed newspapers to create a backing for the putty mixture before you begin filling. Remember that these compounds dry to a tan color which will most likely broadcast the repair instead of hiding it. To hide the repair, either paint the whole side of the door with one color of paint or apply a Contact Paper cutout or blend the patch into the rest of the door using an antiquing paint kit.

USING CONTACT PAPER

Contact paper is, of course, not paper at all. It's paper-thin plastic with one sticky side, and it comes in many patterns and colors. As such, it has numerous creative uses in landlording. Here are but two —

• Besides being great for temporary repairs of broken windows and torn window shades, Contact Paper works well for covering paint chips in enameled walls and appliance surfaces that you don't want to repaint. Cut out a shape, such as a heart, club, spade, or diamond, from opaque Contact Paper and stick it over the chip. No one notices the chipped paint, but everyone notices the cute applique.

• For extra protection and colorful decor, select an appropriate Contact Paper pattern and use it to cover those kitchen and bathroom wall areas which get splattered constantly with water or grease. I've even used Contact Paper to protect the three walls around a tub when a shower was added. Amazingly enough, it held up well for three full years. Take special care when applying Contact Paper. Clean and dry the wall surfaces thoroughly first, and then remove the paper backing as you go, little by little, so you don't get all wrapped up in your work.

USING THE BIG BLADED STRIPPER

High on the list of wretched landlording jobs is the exceedingly tedious task of stripping old wallpaper. You never know just how weak any wallpaper glue is until you try painting over a papered wall and find that sheets of the paper, when saturated with paint, begin to curl and peal off by themselves. Ah, but as soon as you decide to take the initiative yourself and strip the paper off completely, the glue seems to gather up all of its strength, and it grips as tenaciously as any contact cement, grudgingly releasing the old wallpaper inch by inch. Happily there is a pretty good solution to this problem in the form of a nifty tool.

You're already familiar with the virtues of the single-edged razor blade. Think how much more useful would be that blade which is just as sharp, thicker so it won't break, three times wide, but set in a long, comfortable holder. The Warner Big Bladed Stripper is such a tool. Its handle is about twelve inches long, and it has a replaceable blade four inches wide, which is thick enough so it won't break, yet sharp enough to shave even a peach fuzz beard.

For stripping wallpaper and Contact Paper or for scraping windows, this tool has no equal. Before you slash away with abandon, however, experiment in an area where your mistakes won't show. The broad, stiff blade will not normally gouge into flat surfaces, but it definitely will gouge unless you keep it at a proper angle of attack.

REMOVING CEILING HOOKS

Many swag lamps, plants, and bird cages have hung from the hooks which tenants have attached to the ceilings in my rental units, and though I have sometimes winced upon seeing an enormous Zebra basket vine dangling from one of these hooks, amazingly enough, not one hook has ever yielded under the weight of its burden.

Even though I don't particularly like the hooks, I have never prohibited my tenants from using them because I have always felt that such a prohibition would be too restrictive to tenants' interior decorating practices. Even if a hook did pull out, the damage would be relatively insignificant and could be repaired cheaply.

Instead of prohibiting them outright, I used to remove the hooks every time a vacant unit was being redecorated. Two years and about fifty hooks later, I discontinued the practice for I had erroneously assumed that new tenants would not wish to look at or use ceiling hooks installed in places selected by previous tenants. I had also assumed erroneously that removing the hooks would discourage new tenants from using them at all. I might just as well have been trying to remove the towel bars in the bathroom. New tenants would have their hooks in the ceiling before the milk was in the refrigerator.

Don't waste the time necessary to remove those ceiling hooks. You are not preparing your rental units to be vacant. You are preparing them to be occupied, occupied by people who will certainly want those hooks right where they are.

FILLING CRACKS AND HOLES

To fill cracks and holes before painting, you need either a plastic spackling compound like Spackle or a quick-setting plastic patching compound like Fixall. Buy the spackling compound premixed in a one-pound can to save yourself the time and trouble of mixing it. Fixall and its generic equivalents don't come premixed because they harden so quickly that they have to be used up within ten minutes after being mixed. They come only in powdered form and must be mixed in small batches.

Fill small cracks and tack holes with a spackling compound, but remember that it dries slowly and tends to sag when spanning any but tiny gaps. If these problems occur, either apply a second dab of your spackling compound or switch to a quick-setting compound.

Try to fill every hole. Nothing looks worse than a newly painted wall with holes showing. Eccch! Holes apear unsightly in walls you aren't going to repaint, too, but you can fill them so they won't show by using a finger for a putty knife. Your finger will conform better to the wall surface than a putty knife and you'll be able to fill just the hole itself, leaving no excess. You can also skip the sanding if you use your putty finger on any walls to be painted with flat paint. Walls to be painted with a satin or semi-gloss enamel should have their puttied holes sanded, if only superficially, because any roughness always seems to shine through glaringly.

The center of a half-inch lump of spackling compound takes hours to dry, whereas quick-setting compounds will fill fairly large holes and dry in minutes. Use them for doorknob-sized and larger holes, but be aware of the following:

1. Quick-setting compounds require backing for support. Use whatever's handy for backing, steel wool, window screening, wads of newspaper, cardboard, rags, or what have you.
2. Quick-setting compounds are hard to sand, so leave no excess if possible. If you have to sand at all, try "sanding" with a moist rag.
3. Sometimes a water stain will bleed through paint applied over a repair made with a quick-setting compound. You can prevent or kill such stains by spraying or brushing them with titinated shellac.

There is still another alternative for repairing holes in walls, one suggested by a painter who redecorates rental dwellings for a living and is so proficient that he can prepare and paint every room in a normal two-bedroom apartment in only four hours. For this whirlwind of activity he charges $400!

Here's his method for repairing holes up to a foot in diameter. He stuffs the wall cavity with crushed newspapers, mixes a batch of plaster-of-Paris, trowels this mixture to within a sixteenth inch of the wall surface, lets it dry, and fills the remaining depression until it's flush with the wall by applying a good spackling compound. His final touch before applying paint is to sand the surface lightly if necessary.

This layering technique makes the finished repair blend better with the rest of the wall than does a repair made entirely of plaster-of-Paris or a quick-setting compound. By itself, this technique won't cut your time for repairing and painting a two-bedroom dwelling to four hours (this professional painter's real speed secret, by the way, is airless spraying), but it might cut your time by four hours.

REPAIRING LARGE SHEETROCK HOLES

If a sheetrock hole is too big to stuff and patch, and you may come across one now and then in your rentals, you'll have to use another method. Here are two —

• The first method requires enlarging the hole horizontally to reach studs for under-pinning the patch. You cut a squared-off rectangular hole so its vertical sides are on the centers of the nearest studs. Remember that studs are sixteen inches apart. Allowing for some clearance around the edges, measure the hole and then cut a piece of sheetrock the same thickness as the old one. Fit it into the opening, nail it to the studs, and tape the seams as follows: Using a four-inch putty knife, lay a bed of paper-taping compound about three inches on either side of the seams; cut the paper tape to fit; lay it on the bed and push it down firmly with the putty knife, adding more compound as necessary. This kind of compound dries slowly and should be spread thinly in two coats about 24 hours apart. You'll know it has dried by the change in color from gray to white. If you're in a hurry, forget the taping procedure, and instead, fill the gaps around the edges of the patch with a quick-setting compound, then spread a thin coating of spackling compound on top of that, and sand to suit.

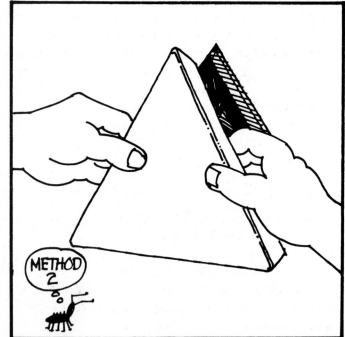

• The second method is similar, except that the sheetrock around the damaged area is cut in such a way that it provides its own support and doesn't have to be cut back to the studs. I call this method the "pyramid patch" because the plug itself resembles a slice of pyramid base. First, cut a triangular hole, holding your retractable knife or sabre saw at a 45-degree angle with the tip pointing toward the center of the hole. Second, cut your pryamid plug to fit so its edges will seat on the edges of the newly cut hole and be held there flush with the wall. Third, spread spackling or quick-setting compound on the edges of the plug, press it into place, and spread more compound to conceal the seams. If you want to finish the job better still, follow the taping procedure above, and you'll have a perfect "pyramid patch" invisible to the naked eye once it's painted.

TILING WINDOW SILLS

When you're preparing to paint window sills made of sheetrock (most often found with metal windows), you'll sometimes notice that they have disintegrated so badly that they just cannot be painted over. This condition is caused by condensation from the windows dripping onto the sills and eventually causing them to rot.

To repair the sill and prevent this from happening again, remove the decayed material completely first. Then cut a new sill out of wood or sheetrock and shim it with pieces of wood until it is slightly below the window frame. Top off your repair sill with pieces of ceramic tile (use tiles with one finished edge) cut so they protrude slightly beyond the surface of the wall.

Once you seal your repair with caulk and putty, You can rest assured that the sill will neither disintegrate nor require painting ever again.

GETTING YOUR PAINTING STUFF TOGETHER

The proper and swift application of paint, that interminable landlording chore, requires good equipment. Here are some painting equipment hints –

• Use the best four-inch brushes money can buy. They hold more, drag less, clean well, and last through many miles of use. Buy one polyester brush for water-base (latex) paints and one natural-bristle brush for oil-base paints. Polyester brushes will work satisfactorily with any kind of paint, and you may wish to use them for both water-base and oil- base paints because they're easier to care for and retain their resilience better, but if you do, use one polyester brush only for water-base paints and another one only for oil-base paints. Residues left from these completely different paints in a single brush which is used for both, tend to gum it up after a while even though it's cleaned well.

• If you can find one, buy a thick sheepskin roller for applying flat latex paint. The best size is about four inches in diameter, outside diameter (o.d.), that is, and nine inches wide, attached sturdily on both ends to a four-foot extension pole. You can load this big roller with lots of paint, apply pressure to the handle, and cover a room in a hurry.

• Rather than using a regular paint tray with this roller, use a five gallon paint bucket outfitted with a grid which hooks onto the rim of the bucket, hangs down inside, and helps to distribute the paint evenly on the roller. You can then dump in a gallon or more of paint at a time and you won't have to fiddle with cans and stirring so frequently.

• Latex enamels and oil-base enamels are both best applied with a medium-nap roller but never, never, with the same one. Remember that latex and oil-base paints do not mix. They can be in the same can, on the same brush, or on the same roller, but they still will not mix. Keep them apart. For each of these enamels, use a 2 inch diameter (o.d.) roller, 9 inches wide, with a short handle threaded for taking extensions.

• Use plastic throwaway paint-tray liners, particularly if you're using oil-base paints, and you'll find that cleanup is almost bearable.

• Before you ever paint again, hasten to a good paint store and buy yourself the professional brush and roller cleaner (Model MSS) which is made by the Shur-Line Manufacturing Company, 80 Drullard, Lancaster, NY 14086, (send for a catalog) and sells for around $13. It may have the mechanism of the musical toy top you remember playing with when you were younger, but I assure you it is no toy. The centrifugal force you generate by pumping the cleaner's ramrod literally throws all the paint and thinner

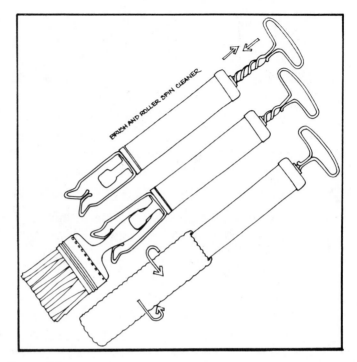

out of your brushes and rollers that will possibly come out.

How many times have you dunked your brushes and rollers in thinner or water after you sleepily put that final paint stroke on some rental's wall at 3 A.M. and then have left them immersed for days before cleaning up? Be honest now. More than once, I'll bet. Well, I used to do it too until the professional brush and roller cleaner entered my life. It has made child's play of a chore every bit as messy and distasteful as changing dirty diapers. It has saved my good brushes from being discarded before their time, and it has actually made my regular rollers reusable after they've been used with oil-base paints.

To keep from splattering yourself and anything else within twenty feet while you use this cleaning tool, suspend the mounted brush or roller vertically inside a sturdy paper bag or plastic-lined garbage can before you start them spinning.

• After bathing and spinning your brushes and rollers, wash them with soap and warm water, comb the brushes using a metal-toothed brush comb, and put them all out to dry. You'll then be all set for your next paint job, and you won't need to buy any new brushes or rollers either.

• By the way, since paint thinner is becoming more and more expensive, try recycling it. Save used thinner in see-through jugs until you notice that the paint pigments have settled to the bottom (usually a couple of weeks), decant it, and you'll have 80-90 percent of the original amount to use over again.

• Unless your units have very high ceilings, use a four-foot ladder for inside painting. It's far more maneuverable than anything taller and still it makes you tall enough to reach every bit of the ceiling.

• Buy one (12' x 15') or two (9' x 12') fabric drop cloths big enough to cover an entire room at a time. Plastic cheapies may be useful for certain jobs, especially when you need to cover delicate furnishings, but don't expect to reuse them and don't use them on floors where they will be stepped on, for they will split and tear at the slightest provocation.

PAINTING THE INTERIOR

Painting really makes a big difference in a rental's appearance and in the rent it will bring in, and the good thing is that you can hire friends, relatives, tenants, or teenagers to paint for you. Be sure you work along with your painting crew to get them trained, though, for careless painters cost money. They paint around pictures and over electrical plates. They get paint on windows, and they splatter paint on the floors. They paint only as far as they can reach and not one inch further. They paint over whatever's sticking to the kitchen walls and whatever's crawling on the bathroom walls. They mix latex paint with oil-base enamel, and then they "clean" the mess with lacquer thinner. Sometime during this whole process, they manage to paint themselves, and they do do a good job of that.

Be careful whom you trust with that loaded paintbrush or roller, dear landlord and landlady, for a careless painter can do as much damage to a rental as a loaded, cuckolded sailor returning home after six months high on the seas! A sloppy paint job means days of cleaning and sanding, a dreadful experience.

The interior of almost any vacant rental may be painted to your standards in a day by two or three amateur painters who are well supervised, but because preparation is so important, you should plan to spend some time before they arrive in getting things ready for the job — buying paint and supplies, washing walls and woodwork, filling cracks and holes, removing fixtures and electrical plates, and covering everything that shouldn't be freshly speckled.

If you paint all your rentals the same color, you won't waste money or space accumulating stacks of paint cans partially filled with many colors of paints which deteriorate before you find a need for them, and you'll find that touching up is simple, too, because the right color will always be handy. An off-white paint works well. Whites make rooms appear larger and fit in nicely with any furniture color scheme.

The quality of interior paints is only important so long as you can find one that covers in one coat. There's no reason to pick a so-called "twelve-year" over an "eight-year" paint because the chances are good that the place will have to be painted within a couple of years anyway. Usually when tenants or a succession of tenants move after several years, painting is necessary no matter how good the old paint was, for the surface fades and you can easily identify the shapes of all the previous tenant's pictures. The surface just can't be cleaned like new.

With paint prices soaring, however, those "necessary" paint jobs can often be postponed if you paint just the one wall that really needs it and you spot-clean the others well with a TSP (trisodium phosphate) solution. *Do* rinse off the TSP and *do* wear rubber gloves while washing those dirty walls and woodwork. TSP may be a great cleaner, but it's also a voracious skin eater.

Whereas flat latex has long been the traditional choice for painting bedrooms, living rooms, and hallways, and semi-gloss enamel has been the choice for kitchens, baths, and woodwork, many landlords and landladies are now using satin latex enamel throughout their units. It has some of the virtues of flat latex during application and cleanup, is easy to care for, and has a finish that seems dull enough for the bedroom, yet bright enough for the kitchen. Tenants like it because it's scrubbable, and landlords and landladies like it because it's durable and needs repainting less frequently.

I tried using satin latex in every room for a while myself, but I returned to using the flat and semi-gloss combination of paints for these four reasons: First, flat latex requires less preparation than enamels because it doesn't reflect imperfections in the surfaces it covers. Second, it takes much less time to brush or roll on flat latex because it applies more easily in one coat than enamels. Third, flat latex blends better when spot painted. And fourth, just as important, new tenants prefer freshly painted walls over freshly scrubbed walls. Using flat latex, I can afford to paint some walls almost every time there's a vacancy and I scrub down the others.

Before applying any enamel paint, be certain you prepare the surface well by washing with TSP and rinsing with clean water. After that, apply an undercoat so the top coat will cover better and will adhere well without sagging. Because of the drying interval required between coats, undercoating does extend the time required for a total paint job, but you can circumvent this problem by applying a thin first coat of enamel (the same enamel used as the top coat) swiftly to all four walls and then continuing on around the room again with a second more careful coat.

Another problem you'll likely encounter painting the interiors of rental dwellings is staining, primarily mildew and water staining. These stains cannot be covered at all with a regular undercoat or with regular paint either, for that matter. They'll just bleed right through and ruin your beautiful new paint job. To prevent bleeding, seal the surfaces with titinated shellac. Before you apply the shellac, however, wash those meldewed areas with either undiluted white vinegar (works much better than commercial preparations) or a solution of 2/3 cup TSP, one quart bleach, one tablespoon detergent, and three quarts of water. Wash water-stained areas first with just TSP and water. Next, rinse the stained areas, let them dry, and finally spread on the titinated shellac.

Titinated shellac also prevents paint bleeding from crayons, and ball-point pen inks. It is white when dry and may be used as a regular undercoat, too. You can paint right over it with any paint in an hour or two, and you'll have a paint job which will hide most any sin. Professional painters usually carry a 16-ounce spray can of titinated shellac so they can avoid fussing with cleanup, but I've always been so unlucky with the plumbing of those aerosol paint cans that I apply mine by brush out of a quart container. The gallon size is cheaper per ounce than the quart size, but since the shellac dries up in the can before it's all used up, the gallon size actually winds up costing more.

PAINTING THE EXTERIOR

If anything, the exterior of a rental building is more important than its interior because prospective tenants see the exterior first and decide from its appearance whether they will even bother looking inside.

Here are some hints you might use the next time you must paint the exterior of your rental building —

• Since exterior painting is such a labor-intensive operation and since the durability of exterior paints is so important in determining when the job will next have to be repeated, use the very best exterior paint available. Check the latest *Consumer Reports Buying Guide Issue* for impartial ratings of widely distributed brands, talk with profesionals about the various brands they use, and test several yourself.

• Remove all loose paint by chipping, scraping, heating, or wire brushing, or, better still, consider using these more modern labor-saving methods for preparing exterior surfaces — waterblasting (rent a waterblaster for small jobs) and sandblasting (get several bids from independent contractors who use bigger equipment than what you could rent). Not every building can be blasted, of course, but those that can be, should be because blasting is more thorough than handwork, is much more quickly accomplished, and actually costs far less.

• Remember that wooden window sashes require painting both inside and out. It's tedious work, must be done all too frequently, and always increases the total cost of a paint job. If your wooden sashes are beginning to rot or jam, consider replacing them with aluminum windows (the job takes only about twenty minutes to do yourself) just before you paint. You'll pay more for new windows than what you'll save on that first paint job, but you'll never have to paint window sashes again, either inside or out, and you'll begin noticing the savings the very next time you have to paint.

• Unless they are cracking, porous, or very unsightly, avoid painting stucco walls which have never been painted before. Their color is blended right into the stucco itself; it's not painted on. Once coated with paint, stucco walls will have to be repainted at regular intervals. Spruce the place up with a coat of trim paint instead.

INSURING UNINTERRUPTED UTILITY SERVICE

Normally when tenants move out of dwellings which have individually metered utilities, they contact each utility company to discontinue service. Yet you require use of those utilities during the period of vacancy to test the light fixtures and appliances, run the vacuum and steam cleaners, see whether the paint is covering well, get hot water for cleaning, power your electric tools and radio, show the dwelling to prospective tenants, and warm or cool the place as necessary.

How do you assure yourself of uninterrupted utility service during this time when you really need it? You may, of course, hope that the tenants forget to contact the utility companies or, if they do, that the companies will be too busy to send anyone out for a while. That way you'd get to enjoy some free gas and electricity. Someone else would be paying the bill. Don't be tempted.

Instead, call the utility companies in advance and arrange for the utilities to be transferred to your name if you can expect any interim period between tenants. You never know how much you rely on those utilities until they're denied to you. You have too many things to do in a vacant rental unit which requires utilities. Be certain you'll have them available when you need them.

There's another reason to consider when you are deliberating about ordering uninterrupted utility service for a vacant rental unit, whether you have to do any work there or not, a reason which applies only to the gas, not the electricity. Shutting off the pilot lights in gas appliances, I have found, frequently causes malfunctions in thermostats, thermocouples, pilot generators, regulators, flame switches, and ignition assemblies. When denied the gas that sustains them, these parts will fail mysteriously far more often than at any other time. Besides being expensive to purchase, these parts are often hard to find, requiring many hours to unearth.

Keep the gas on in the first place and avoid such problems.

SAVING WITH FLUORESCENTS

Multiple-family dwellings usually have common areas, such as stairways, stairwells, halls, landings, carports, breezeways, laundries, porches, and vestibules, many of which are lighted at the owner's expense. Unless the areas are vast, like parking or yard areas, which are generally lit by more-efficient mercury-vapor lamps, these common areas are ordinarily kept lighted by incandescent fixtures. Incandescent lighting, however, is hardly the best kind of lighting for these applications.

Fluorescent lighting is much better. Compared to incandescent light bulbs, fluorescents produce five times the illumination for every watt of electricity consumed. Such energy efficiency enables you to keep common areas lit all night long with the same amount of electricity necessary to burn a light bulb for a couple of hours. That's one advantage, but there are others just as important to the landlord or landlady conscious of costs.

Fluorescent tubes have considerably longer lives when burned for hours at a time. In continuous lighting applications, they will last 20 times longer than incandescents. When switched on and off as they would be in laundry rooms, they still last at least seven times longer, and because they last so long, you spend less time changing bulbs.

You might be surprised to learn how inexpensive standard-sized fluorescent tubes are, too, if you have never purchased them before. Probably the most standard is the 4-foot 40-watt tube which sells most everywhere for less than two dollars and can be found for less than a dollar when on sale at discount stores. With its long useful life, the fluorescent tube itself actually costs far less than equivalent short-lived incandescent light bulbs.

Still another reason favoring the use of fluorescents by landlords and landladies is, strangely enough, its lack of use in the home. Tenants snatch incandescent lightbulbs and use them in their lamps and fixtures at home, but they won't snatch your fluorescent tubes. Why should they? They have no use for them.

There is only one drawback in converting to fluorescents, the initial capital outlay. Each single-tube strip fixture costs around $13 and takes about ten minutes to install. That's $13 and ten minutes more than you need to spend on those incandescent fixtures you already have, but because you can expect one forty-watt strip light to take the place of two sixty-watt incandescent bulbs, you will find that fluorescents will soon cut your electrical bills and your bulb replacement bills in half.

If only it were possible to cut other bills so dramatically and so easily!

CONSERVING WATER

Since they seldom pay water bills directly themselves, most tenants are unaware of any need to conserve water. Water is free, isn't it?

You can do little to change climbing water rates, and you can do even less to change your tenants' habits. You can't expect them to shower less, wash less, drink less, flush less, or skip the ice in their gin and tonics, but you can do a few things to help conserve water by making your plumbing more efficient. Here are four things you can do—

- Let's start with the biggest water consumer in any household, the toilet. This one plumbing fixture alone accounts for a whopping 45 percent of all household consumption. Designed way back when clean water was as plentiful as clean air, it flushed 5-6 gallons down the drain whenever its chain was pulled. Most toilets nowadays still flush 5-6 gallons down the drain. Yet a toilet using only 3½ gallons has been shown to be perfectly adequate, even for a diarrhea ward.

To save the 1½-2½ gallons wasted in each flush, which could amount to 20 percent of your total water bill, you could try jamming bricks in the tank or squeezing in plastic jugs filled with rocks or bending the float rod or fitting the tank with a plastic damming device. Any one of them would help, but the damming device seems to work best because it neither deteriorates nor interferes with a toilet's normal operaton.

Although manufacturers of these clever devices recommend using two per tank, I have had great success using only one, placing it on the side opposite the inlet valve and hence away from all the moving parts and rushing water. If your hardware store or plumbing supplier doesn't carry the dams and you can't locate any elsewhere locally, call your rental property owners' association and inquire. Someone there should know where they may be found.

• The price is right for this next water saver. The Vulcan Company, P.O. Box 33, Grand Valley, CO 81635, will give two of them away to scrupulous landlords and landladies as a demonstration. Additional ones cost little more than a buck apiece. What are they? Stainless steel faucet seats mated with Delrin washers.

The bane of every landlord and landlady is the leaky faucet, and unless tenants are bothered enough by the dripping to complain, you never know whether your units have leaky faucets or not. The problem is further compounded if it's hot water that's leaking and you're paying to heat the wasted hot water as well. That's more of your money down the drain.

A new washer will often solve the conventional faucet's leakage problem, but many times it's a corroded or pitted valve seat which is at the bottom of the trouble and a new washer will provide only a temporary repair. Many faucets have replaceable brass seats which can be unscrewed from the faucet body, but you may have to look hard to find an exact replacement.

The Vulcan universal reseating kit, which sells for around $10, can be used with any conventional faucet and is fully guaranteed to end your leaky faucet problems. Before you buy a kit, though, you might want to see how they work. Send along two seats from an old faucet and Vulcan will mount new stainless steel seats on them free just so you can give them a try.

• This next water saver costs anywhere from five cents to five bucks, depending on whether you can fit one into your present shower head or whether you have to buy a whole new shower head with one already installed.

Essentially this water saver is just a plastic washer with a rather small (1/8") orifice. Installed in a shower head, this washer reduces the flow of water by almost half, from a normal 6½ gallons per minute all the way down to 3½. That's all the water that can possibly fit through the little hole in one minute. Because most people time their showers by the clock or by the shriveling of their fingers, this water saver succeeds quite well, and nobody knows the difference. It fails only when used by those who stay in the shower until they have used up all the available hot water.

• The fourth water saver doesn't apply to every rental property situation as do the previous three. It applies only to those rental properties which have a single water heater for a number of units. It's a solution to the problem of hot water lag.

How long do you have to wait for hot water in most homes when you haven't used any for hours? Twenty seconds? Sixty seconds? Well, in one of my eightplexes, tenants have had to wait at least two minutes with the tap on full blast before getting any hot water. So what happens to all the water that pours from the faucet as they wait? It goes directly down the drain and onto the building's water bill. It's entirely wasted.

There are two possible remedies that I know of. Install additional heaters closer to the taps, something the Europeans and Japanese do as a matter of course with their small geyser water heaters, or install a hot water return pipe and recirculating pump so there would be hot water coursing through the pipes all the time, always ready for a twist of any tap in the system.

This might sound complicated and expensive. It's neither in most cases. It requires only one pipe to be tapped into the hot water system at a point furthest from the water heater (even a simple, inexpensive tap-on saddle fitting will do). The other end is connected to the water heater itself, usually with a "T" fitting at the heater tank drain valve. Somewhere in this line there needs to be a small pump to keep the water moving. This pump and the return pipe together allow the water to recirculate through the water heater and thus to remain hot constantly instead of cooling at rest in the hot water pipes until a tap opens. The Teel Model 1P760 hot water booster pump, which costs around $60 and uses but 30 watts of electricity, works well in this application.

For such a job on an eightplex, figure about $120 for parts and eight hours of your time or four hours of your plumber's time. While you're at it, you might as well do the job right and insulate the hot water lines to reduce heat loss. Have a plumber eyeball the job for you to get a better rough estimate, get the work done, and then check your utility bills to see what you have saved.

A two-year comparison study of my own utility bills on two almost identical eightplexes showed that this return line and pump installation saved one-third on the water bill, and incredibly, one-fourth on the gas bill. The installation paid for itself within ten months and at the same time made the tenants happier because they could always draw instant hot water.

PRESERVING THE BATHROOM FLOOR – ONE

So long as their toilet flushes properly, tenants won't notice whether anything else is amiss with the toilet even though the flooring may be rotting away underneath. You must check the toilets in your rentals yourself.

Most toilets are held in place with only two slim bolts which aren't even attached to the floor. They're attached to a flange on the drain pipe. Somehow, though, the two bolts usually manage to keep the toilet from traveling about the room, and the contraption works more or less the way Thomas Crapper designed it. But over time and with constant use, the nuts tend to loosen up, and the toilet will move, especially when someone chubby sits down on it.

This movement of the toilet eventually breaks the seal between the drain pipe flange and the toilet bowl horn, and with every flush, some water seeps out to puddle on the floor or dampen the subflooring and floor joists below. After awhile, the flooring begins to sag from decay in the wooden structural members, and you have to make an expensive repair.

What can you do? Check every toilet in your rentals periodically for looseness. If one is loose, try tightening the hold-down nuts. Careful, not too tight or the ceramic stool will crack. Once that's done, check for water leakage both from above and, if possible, from below. At the first sign of leakage, pull the toilet (I must caution you that there are those who believe that removing a toilet is akin to a religious experience, but I must admit that I have yet to have one while being so engaged), and replace the old wax seal with an urethane wax seal (only pennies more). This new seal will bond the flange and the horn together twenty times more powerfully than a regular wax seal because it's impregnated with urethane and will expand and contract as necessary in response to weight on the seat. A regular wax seal, on the other hand, will only contract and will begin leaking as soon as the first air gap forms.

Use a little preventive maintenance to preserve your bathroom floors.

PRESERVING THE BATHROOM FLOOR - TWO

Leaky toilets aren't the only destroyers of bathroom floors. Leaky shower tubs rank a close second. The leakage I refer to comes not from the deterioration of the tub overflow gasket or the caulking around the rim of the tub. Those are problems of another sort. I am referring strictly to the water which manages to dodge the shower curtain and winds up on the bathroom floor, especially at the end by the shower head. Tubs with sliding doors avoid this problem. If kept shut during a shower, sliding doors block off the water completely so that little or none reaches the floor outside the tub.

Unfortunately, most rental units have shower curtains rather than sliding doors, and whereas shower curtains do prevent flooding of the bathroom floor, they do not prevent puddling. A shower curtain invariably leaves two triangular openings for water to spray through at each end of the tub where the tub rim abuts the wall. The inside curvature of the tub keeps the shower curtain from hanging straight down, so that unless it is carefully arranged, the curtain will not hang flush with the wall, and out splashes the water.

Where do you find conscientious tenants who, before showering will arrange the curtain, and after showering will mop up the puddles? You don't. Instead of pursuing that impossible task, you can solve the problem another way. Fill those triangular openings with a barrier so the water will never leave the tub. You could spend the time to design and craft

200

such a barrier yourself, but fortunately someone has already done it. The device is called Splash-ender, and it is designed to nestle neatly into that opening. It is made of white plastic, and it attaches to the tub and wall with adhesive caulk. The shape blends almost unobtrusively into its surroundings, and, best of all, it works. If you can't find Splash-ender locally, write the manufacturer, Waterguide, 8700 Southwest 26th, Portland, OR 97219.

KEEPING A PLUMBING PARTS INVENTORY

If you maintain your rental property yourself, you ought to keep a small inventory of parts which need replacing regularly. The more versatile the part is, the better. Four versatile plumbing parts you should consider keeping on hand are a universal drain trap, a Fillpro toilet fill valve, a Fluidmaster flusher fixer kit, and a flexible water supply pipe. With these four parts, you can repair virtually any leaky sink and any temperamental toilet.

• The universal plastic drain trap fits 1¼" × 1¼", 1½" × 1½", or 1½" × 1¼" installations, the three most common applications for drain traps, not quite "universal," but close. The only applications it will not fit are those requring high-neck or metal traps. Any common 1½" × 1½" metal trap, by the way, can become "universal" if used with commonly available adapter slip nuts and washers made to fit smaller diameter drain pipes.

• The Fillpro toilet-tank fill valve, a compact plastic device which resembles a set of castinets, fits most any toilet and, believe it or not, replaces that entire Rube Goldberg ballcock contraption with all its tubes and wires and its bulbous float. It's fully adjustable for various tank sizes and water levels, too.

• The Fluidmaster Flusher Fixer kit also fits most toilets, and it solves the two distinct causes of leaks at tank drains — worn tank balls or flappers and corroded drain seats. The whole kit consists of a flapper valve mated to a stainless steel seat and a ribbon of epoxy putty for sealing the new seat to the old. With this kit installed, the tank cannot possibly leak its reservoir of water into the bowl.

• The fourth versatile plumbing part you should keep on hand is an 18 inch long, 3/8 inch diameter, flexible water supply pipe. This tubing, corrugated in the middle to facilitate bending without kinking, can be coiled easily to fit short-pipe applications or kept straight for long-pipe applications. It ordinarly comes with a variety of washers to fit several different sizes of supply valves, but if it doesn't, you can still purchase the washers separately. Be prepared, you landlord and landlady plumbers. Remember, stores aren't always open when you need parts for those plumbing emergencies.

SAVING FAUCET PARTS

Plumbing supply houses cannot possibly keep parts for all the thousands upon thousands of different faucets that have been and still are being sold, and you might find yourself replacing an otherwise perfectly good faucet for lack of only one part.

If you must change a faucet because it needs a part which is unavailable or because it is otherwise inoperable, don't throw the whole faucet away. You may later need a handle, stem, escutcheon, spout, or body for an identical faucet, and you may be able to salvage those replacements from the junker.

JOINING PLASTIC AND METAL DRAIN PIPES

The correct compression fittings aren't always readily available for those plastic and metal drain pipes you're trying to join together under a sink, and you certainly can't solder them together. Try this alternative — slip one inside the other in the direction of the water flow and bond them together with liberal amounts of caulk (silicone caulk works especially well for this purpose). Give the caulk time to set up and you'll have a good, durable, dry joint.

USING THE CEILING ACCESS PLATE

If you own any building with two or more stories, you're probably already familiar with how a plumbing problem in an upper unit will cause damage to the unit below. Most often the culprit is a tub or shower drain trap which is completely inaccessible except through the ceiling of the lower unit. You or your trustworthy plumber open the ceiling and repair the problem, and then the plumber leaves. Either way, doing the plumbing yourself or having it done, you're still stuck with a gaping hole in the ceiling and the task of covering it up.

Your first impulse is to plaster or sheetrock the hole, restoring the ceiling to its original condition, but doing such work above your head makes you even more awestruck by Moses' feat of holding his arms aloft for one whole day. Fitting, nailing, puttying, taping, sanding, and painting all have to be done overhead to complete the job. In all, it would take about four hours to complete and three separate trips to allow for drying time, but it could be an admirable job when finished. No one could ever tell where it was that you had opened the ceiling.

Unfortunately, eight months later, after you have tapered off on the chiropractic treatments, the same drain again springs a leak and you hit your own ceiling.

There is a better solution to the problem. Instead of attempting to restore the ceiling to its original condition by laboriously fitting a flush patch into place, cut a piece of 1/4" plywood big enough to cover the hole and also big enough to reach to the next ceiling beam so the plywood's edges can be nailed down. Next, round off the corners and edges of the plywood and nail it into place. Paint your new access plate to match the ceiling or, better still, paint the whole ceiling. The completed job will look great, take far less time than a restoration job, and provide ready access should the problem later recur.

BATTLING ROOF LEAKS

Flat roofs may save on construction costs, but they sure do develop leakage problems sooner than other roofs. Water collects on them and stays for days after a storm, all the while seeking to penetrate the tiniest weaknesses in the roof, and if any water does get through to the inside, it leaks not only during the storm and as long as puddles stay on top, but also until water pockets within the roofing felts have evaporated.

Even though you find where a leak is coming from (which isn't easy on a flat roof because water "travels," that is, it seeps into the roof at one point and may travel ten feet horizontally before it finds a choice spot in the ceiling to leak from) and even though you patch the roof properly on the outside, the leak inside may not stop completely for days. When this happens, you may appear like an unscrupulous landlord or landlady to your tenants and you may feel like one as well, but all you can do is explain the situation as best you can and keep a close eye on the problem.

All roofs, especially flat tar-and-gravel roofs so common on multiple-family dwellings, are best repaired when dry. Brush off the suspect area and moisten it with paint thinner or some other solvent before you apply any patching compound, and the solvent will act as a binder,

202

blending all the remaining dirt right into the patch. Otherwise the patching compound will not adhere well.

If you have to patch a wet roof, you'll need a special wet-patch compound designed specifically to adhere to wet or damp surfaces. The best around is made by the Celotex Corporation of Tampa, Florida, and goes by the quaint name of Noah's Pitch. Its label shows an old bearded Noah painstakingly daubing pitch onto the sides of a very big ark bulging with his menagerie. Since that ark survived a deluge for forty days and forty nights, the pitch he used must have been pretty effective. I cannot tell you for sure whether the pitch that Noah used and the pitch that Celotex makes have the same formula, but I can tell

you that the Noah's Pitch that I use is an outstanding quick-patch pitch, and it has easily sealed every leak I could ever find in my wet roofs.

Any wide gaps or breaks you might encounter in your roof patching may be bridged by fabric coated on both sides with an appropriate patching compound. Instead of fabric, professional roofers used a tough plastic gauze they call a "membrane" which helps to keep the compound in place and gives lateral strength to the repair, but any reasonably strong fabric will do for such repairs.

Whether you're fixing leaks with a wet-patch compound in a pouring rain or with an ordinary roof patching compound on a dry roof, be careful how you spread the compound around. Spread on too thickly or too widely, it may actually conceal leakage problems and not really fix them at all.

KNOWING WHEN TO QUIT PATCHING THAT LEAKY ROOF

Sometimes, rather than repeatedly patching a rental building's old roof when it is near or past the end of its useful life, and always risking further leakage anyway, you would be wise to spend the money for a whole new roof. By doing so, you spare yourself the nuisance of worrying about the roof every time it rains, patching the roof every time it rains, and repairing the interior damage every time the roof leaks.

Consider also the effect a worn-out roof would likely have on any sale of the building. The roof inspection your buyers will probably insist upon will state indisputably that the building needs a new roof, and your buyers will make every effort to deduct the entire cost of a new roof from the agreed-upon sales price for the building. In other words, you would likely wind up paying for the new owners' new roof.

Why should you endure all that worry and patching and repairing while you own the building only to pay the new owners for a new roof so that they will not have to suffer the same aggravations? If your roof needs to be replaced, replace it now, and enjoy it yourself for a few years before you sell. It won't cost you any more.

EXTERMINATING PESTS & ABOMINABLE PESTS

No good tenants will long remain in your units if they have to share their homes with ants, roaches, or rodents, so regardless of how responsible you feel for the intruders, exterminate them promptly if you wish to keep the tenants.

Seldom will tenants blame the landlord or landlady for an invasion of ants, but there are times when only an all-out attack covering the entire building will be effective. Ant stakes placed every six feet around the outside of a building are a most effective attack. Tenants can do their own spraying inside for the malingerers.

Roaches are different. They are so tough to exterminate that they deserve to be called "abominable pests," and they are so smart that they have to be attacked on a building basis. Individual tenants spraying their own units with a pesticide only cause their roaches to move next door, and that's bad for you.

Tenants naturally want a dramatic solution to a roach infestation. They want you or a professional to spray a liquid pesticide that kills roaches on contact so the little corpses can be swept up like dead locusts and the tenants can go on with other things. If you can, resist this kind of chemical magic show and settle for a more effective, if less dramatic, solution.

We have UCLA Professor Walter Ebeling, author of *URBAN ENTOMOLOGY,* to thank for this one because he persisted in some novel experiments which proved the effectiveness of boric acid as a roach killer. That's right, boric acid, the selfsame stuff widely used as an eyewash before all those patent medicines came along. The only difference is that for killing roaches it must be in powdered form.

Boric acid is not new as a roach killer. It's been around since the turn of the century, but few people really knew how it worked and recognized its effectiveness. Curiously, the standard method for determining the effectiveness of roach killers was to place both insects and insecticide together in a container, pop the lid on, and time how quickly they died. In such an experiment there was no way a roach could avoid certain death. It was trapped. But such is not the situation out in the greater roach world. There a roach can choose where it wants to go. It can avoid those sprayed areas which it recognizes as lethal, and it does.

Boric acid fared poorly in the closed container experiments. Calendars, not stop watches, had to be used to time how quickly the roaches died.

So Ebeling tried an experiment using "choice boxes," one which more closely approx- imated the situation in the macrocasm, and he learned that roaches will avoid a dark area that has been sprayed with a lethal insecticide, much as they love darkness, choosing instead to remain in a lighted area which hasn't been treated, but that they will cavort in a dark area that has been dusted with boric acid just as if nothing were there. They simply do not sense the danger to them in the odorless powder.

Boric acid works on roaches both as a contact poison and as a stomach poison, but it works slowly. In seven to ten days after application, you shouldn't see any of the little critters about. If there are any, they'll seem to have aged a great deal and in fact be quite moribund. Though it is slow-acting, boric acid continues to be an effective killer indefinitely so long as it stays dry and powdery, and roaches have shown no signs of building an immunity to it as they have to each successive new insecticide that modern chemistry has provided us.

You might want to combine a boric acid dusting with an application of liquid insecticide to avoid having trails of white powder all over the place, say, insecticide in the bedrooms and living room and boric acid in the bathroom and kitchen, but you shouldn't use both in the same area if you want to take advantage of the best qualities of each. Remember the "choice boxes." Boric acid is quite nontoxic to adults, but for safety's sake it should be kept away from children and pets.

Boric acid powder is available in drug stores, and the latest, most potent liquid insecticide may be purchased through hardware stores or from pest control operators directly. Be sure the boric acid is powdery. Screen the lumps out if you have to, and then apply it with a plastic squeeze bottle or a spoon. Use a strong hand-pumped stream sprayer for the liquid insecticide and think like a roach as you scout out all those warm, dark hiding places to spray.

No tenant of mine has ever reported seeing a mouse. They all see rats, and when they've seen one, they phone me to shriek out the bad news that they'd always suspected and to lament that their children are going to be devoured, or at the very least permanently disfigured, by the detestable rodent. A rat, I try to ex- plain to them, looks very much like a mouse except that it's bigger. Oh yes, I'm told, this rat is no little thing. It is monstrous.

Not one to treat any rat sighting lightly or to argue with hysterical mothers whose children are about to be eaten alive, I hurriedly set out some anticoagulant such as d-Con and a couple of mouse traps baited with peanut butter. Then I wait.

I wait and I wait, but I never do hear from the tenants again about the rat problem. Finally when I do inquire, they tell me they caught him

in the rat trap that I brought over and threw him in the garbage and haven't seen
any more since.

Peanut butter is very good bait for the traps.

Whether you act to exterminate your tenants' pests and how soon you act will depend on
the kind of rental unit, the kind of tenants, and the kind of pest, to be sure. Tenants in a
single-family dwelling should be expected to get rid of their own pests unless they were there
when the tenants moved in. In multiples, though, one tenant can battle the pests, but usually
the landlord or landlady must declare war on them before they all leave or die.

FIXING IT OVER THE PHONE AND KEEPING SANE

Don't expect spontaneous remission to remedy many of your tenants' complaints for
repairs, but do give it a try sometime by prescribing the tardy treatment for certain piddlin'
problems. Since no one has yet found a way to clear a clogged toilet over the telephone,
you must make a visit for that kind of thing, but if the problem's of a lesser magnitude, you
should reassure the tenant with a gentle voice that everything will be taken care of in due
time and then jot down the job on a priority list. Don't rush over to your properties for every
little thing. You'll soon need a new spouse and a shrink if you do. Accumulate the little
repair jobs until they warrant a fixit visit themselves or until you need to go there for some
other reason. You'll be surprised how often the little problems will have taken care of
themselves in the interim.

Just because you don't leap up immediately to respond to every tenant's complaint doesn't
mean you should discourage your tenants from reporting the little repair problems they
notice. On the contrary, you should be encouraging them to report these problems because
you will pay dearly for postponing repairs on your rental property too long.

Linoleum which is just beginning to pull loose at a seam is so much easier and cheaper to
fix than when a piece has torn away and been lost. A water leak under a kitchen sink will
eventually cause wood decay in the cabinetry if it's neglected, decay which certainly won't be
overlooked by the termite inspector.

Use your good common sense to determine when you should make a visit to your
property and when you should stay away.

KEEPING STORE HOURS

Your spare time, more specifically that portion of your spare time given over to maintaining your rental property, hardly coincides with normal business hours. You likely work at
your properties in the evening, late at night, in the morning, and on weekends. Because
these times are all on the fringes of most stores' normal hours, you have undoubtedly experienced the frustration of scurrying off to the paint store at 6:15 on a Sunday evening to buy
that last can of paint needed to complete redecorating a dwelling which a new tenant wants
to move into the next day, and when you arrive, you find that the paint store closed at 6.

How can you avoid a repetition of this frustration? The next time you go on your buying
errands, write down the hours for each store you visit. Keep these times in that wallet, purse,
or glove compartment which usually accompanies you on your landlording tours of duty.
One quick glance at this information will tell you which store is still open at 9:12 on a Tuesday night when you need to buy the parts to replace an old toilet valve that came apart in
your hands. You can spare yourself more spare time for plotting rent raises and smoking

noxious-smelling cigars if you aren't waiting around for stores to open in the morning or driving wildly about town looking for any supplier who's open late at night.

WEARING PROPER ATTIRE

Not every rental has them — busybodies who thrive on buttonholing the manager or owner and babbling on interminably. If you do have such tenants, however, you know they're more of a nuisance than hemorrhoidal tissues. They're usually model tenants otherwise and you hate to offend them, but you also hate to waste your precious time lending them your ears.

Take courage. You can avoid these gossipmongers by wearing overalls that are all speckled with paint when you set foot on your rental property. You may have just showered or awakened from your afternoon nap, but they won't think so. Those overalls clothe you with a certain busy-worker mystique and give you license to do what you came to do and then leave without having to make or listen to small talk.

FORMS

The thirty-four forms in this section, all of which have been introduced in the text, are included here so you may reproduce them on any copier according to your needs.* If you do plan to copy them, keep them clean and free of marks. These are your originals, remember, and any marks will show up on your copies.

Altogether, there are five forms categories in this section:

1) Tenants   3) Employees   5) Taxes
2) Notices   4) Records

A title page precedes each category and lists the forms which follow.

To assist you in finding the blank forms you seek, we put small page numbers in the upper corners. When you go to copy these forms, either white-out the page numbers, cut them off, or fold the corner of the page over so the number will not show up on your copies.

*The author hereby grants permission to the purchaser of this book to copy any or all of these forms for personal use. Reproduction of these forms for sale or distribution to others shall constitute an infringement of copyright.

Tenants

Rental Application

for (address)_____

| | Home | Work |
| | Phone | Phone |

Name_____Phone_____Phone_____

Date of _____ Social _____ Driver's _____
Birth   Security No.   License No.

Present Address_____
  How long at   Reason for
  this address?_____Rent $_____moving_____

  Owner/Manager_____Phone_____

Previous Address_____
  How long at   Reason for
  this address?_____Rent $_____moving_____

  Owner/Manager_____Phone_____

Name, relationship, and age of every person to live with you_____

_____

Any pets?_____Describe_____Waterbed?_____
Present
Occupation_____Employer_____Phone_____
  How long with
  this employer?_____Supervisor_____Phone_____
Previous
Occupation_____Employer_____Phone_____
  How long with
  this employer?_____Supervisor_____Phone_____

Current gross income per month (before deductions) $_____

Amount of alimony or child support you pay $_____ or receive $_____
Savings
Account Bank_____Branch_____Acct. No._____
Checking
Account Bank_____Branch_____Acct. No._____

Major Credit Card_____Acct. No._____
Credit   Balance
Reference_____Acct. No._____Owed_____Payment_____
Credit   Balance
Reference_____Acct. No._____Owed_____Payment_____

Have you ever filed bankruptcy?_____Have you ever been evicted?_____
Vehicle(s)--
Make(s)_____Model(s)_____Year(s)_____License(s)_____
Personal
Reference_____Address_____Phone_____
Contact
in Emergency_____Address_____Phone_____

I declare that the statements above are true and correct, and I hereby authorize
verification of references given and a credit check.

Date_____   Signed_____

Rental Agreement

Dated_____

Agreement between_____, Owners, and
_____, Tenants, for a dwelling located at
_____.
Tenants agree to rent this dwelling on a month-to-month basis for $_____
per month, payable in advance on the _____ day of every calendar month to
Owners or to their Agent,_____.
When rent is paid on or before the _____ day of the calendar month, Tenants
may take a $_____ discount.

   The first month's rent for this dwelling is $_____.

   The security/cleaning deposit on this dwelling is $_____. It is
refundable if Tenants leave the dwelling reasonably clean and undamaged.

   A deposit of $_____ for _____ keys will be refunded after the keys
have been returned.

   Tenants will give _____ days' notice in writing before they move and
will be responsible for paying rent through the end of this notice period
or until another tenant approved by the Owners has moved in, whichever
comes first.

   Owners will refund all deposits due within _____ days after Tenants
have moved out completely and returned their keys.

   Only the following persons and pets are to live in this dwelling:

_____
No other persons or pets may live there without Owners' prior written permission, and it may not be sublet.

   Use of the following is included in the rent:_____
_____

   Remarks:_____
_____
_____

   Tenants agree to the following:

1) to keep yards and garbage areas clean.
2) to keep from making loud noises and disturbances and to play music
   and broadcast programs at all times so as not to disturb other people's
   peace and quiet.
3) not to paint or alter their dwelling without first getting Owners'
   written permission.
4) to park their motor vehicle in assigned space and to keep that space
   clean of oil drippings.
5) not to repair their motor vehicle on the premises (unless it is in an
   enclosed garage) if such repairs will take longer than a single day.
6) to allow Owners to inspect the dwelling or show it to prospective
   tenants at any and all reasonable times.
7) not to keep any liquid-filled furniture in this dwelling.
8) to pay rent by check or money order made out to Owners. (Checks must
   be good when paid or Owners will not grant discount.)
9) to pay for repairs of all damage, including drain stoppages, they or
   their guests have caused.
10) to pay for any windows broken in their dwelling while they live there.

   Violation of any part of this agreement or nonpayment of rent when
due shall be cause for eviction under appropriate sections of the applicable code, and the prevailing party shall recover court costs and reasonable attorney's fees involved.

   Tenants hereby acknowledge that they have read this agreement, understand it, agree to it, and have been given a copy.

Owner_____ Tenant_____

By_____ Tenant_____

Lease

Dated_____

Agreement between_____, Owners, and
_____, Tenants, for a dwelling located
at_____. Tenants agree to lease this
dwelling for a term of _____, beginning_____
and ending_____ for $_____ per month, payable in advance
on the _____ day of every calendar month to Owners or to their Agent,
_____. When rent is paid on or before the
_____ day of the calendar month, Tenants may take a $_____ discount.
     The first month's rent for this dwelling is $_____.
     The entire sum of this lease is $_____.
     The security/cleaning deposit on this dwelling is $_____. It
is refundable if Tenants leave the dwelling reasonably clean and undamaged.
     If Tenants intend to move at the end of this lease, they agree to
give Owners notice in writing at least 30 days before the lease runs out.
Otherwise they will be regarded as automatically switching over to a month-
to-month tenancy.
     A deposit of $_____ for _____keys will be refunded after
the keys have been returned.
     Owners will refund all deposits due within_____days after Ten-
ants have moved out completely and have returned their keys.
     Only the following persons and pets are to live in this dwelling:
_____.
No other persons or pets may live there without Owners' prior written
permission and it may not be sublet.
     Use of the following is included in the rent:_____
_____
     Remarks:_____
_____
     Tenants agree to the following:
1)   to keep yards and garbage areas clean.
2)   to keep from making loud noises and disturbances and to play music
     and broadcast programs at all times so as not to disturb other people's
     peace and quiet.
3)   not to paint or alter their dwelling without first getting Owners'
     written permission.
4)   to park their motor vehicle in assigned space and to keep that space
     clean of oil drippings.
5)   not to repair their motor vehicle on the premises (unless it is in an
     enclosed garage) if such repairs will take longer than a single day.
6)   to allow Owners to inspect the dwelling or show it to prospective
     tenants at any and all reasonable times.
7)   not to keep any liquid-filled furniture in this dwelling.
8)   to pay rent by check or money order made out to Owners. (Checks must
     be good when paid or Owners will not grant discount.)
9)   to pay for repairs of all damage, including drain stoppages, they or
     their guests have caused.
10) to pay for any windows broken in their dwelling while they live there.

     Violation of any part of this agreement or nonpayment of rent when
due shall be cause for eviction under appropriate sections of the applicable code, and the prevailing party shall recover court costs and reasonable attorney's fees involved.

     Tenants hereby acknowledge that they have read this agreement, under-
stand it, agree to it, and have been given a copy.

Owner_____   Tenant_____

  By_____   Tenant_____

Condition & Inventory Checksheet Dated _____

Tenant Name _____ Address _____

Date Moved in _____ Date Notice Given _____ Date Moved Out_____

Abbreviations:

Air Conditioner, A/C	Dinette, Din	Hood, Hd	Shades, Sh
Bed, Bd	Dishwasher, Dish	Just Painted, JP	Sofa, Sfa
Broken, Brk	Disposer, Disp	Lamp, Lmp	Stove, Stv
Carpet, Cpt	Drapes, Drp	Lightbulbs, LtB	Table, Tbl
Chair, Ch	Dryer, Dry	Linoleum, Lino	Tile, Tl
Chest, Chst	Fair, F	Nightstand, Ntst	Venetian Blinds, VB
Clean, Cl	Good, G	OK, OK	Washer, Wsh
Cracked, Cr	Heater, Htr	Poor, P	Waxed, Wxt
Curtains, Ctn	Hole, H	Refrigerator, Ref	Wood, Wd

Circle applicable rooms and enter appropriate abbreviations:

	Walls, Doors cond.	chgs.	Floors cond.	chgs.	Windows, Screens, Coverings cond.	chgs.	Lt. Fixt. cond.	chgs.	Inventory: Appliances, Furniture item	cond.	chgs.
Liv. Rm.											
Kitchen											
Bath											
Dining											
BR 1											
BR 2											
BR 3											
Other											

Charges   _____   _____   _____   _____

Total Itemized Charges   _____

Other Charges Not Itemized
   (Broken Locks, Dirty Garage, etc.
    Explain on Backside)   _____   Total Deposits   _____
Deduction for Improper Notice   _____   Less Deductions & Charges   _____
Deduction for Missing Keys   _____   Deposit Refund or
Total Deductions & Charges   _____   (Amount Owed)   _____

    Tenants hereby acknowledge that they have read this Condition & Inventory Checksheet, agree that the condition and contents of the above-mentioned rental dwelling are without exception as represented herein, understand that they are liable for any damage done to this dwelling as outlined in their Lease or Rental Agreement, and have received a copy of this checksheet.

Owner _____ Tenant _____

By _____ Tenant _____

BANK INFORMATION AUTHORIZATION

BANK: This request to report your direct experience and transactions is for the purpose of establishing your customer's ability to pay rent to the landlord or landlady whose name appears below. It is understood that this report is a business courtesy and is strictly confidential. Its authorship will not be disclosed nor will your bank assume any obligation for errors, omissions, or changes in this information.

	Savings	Commercial (Checking)	Loans	
Date Opened	_____	_____	No Experience	_____
High	_____	_____	Date Opened	_____
Medium	_____	_____	Open Balance	_____
Low	_____	_____	Date Closed	_____
Date Closed	_____	_____	How Paid	_____
			Satisfactory____ Unsatisfactory____	

Remarks _____

Authorized Signature _____   Bank Stamp:

TENANT-CUSTOMER: Please complete all information in this section and forward to your bank along with a stamped envelope addressed to the landlord or landlady whose name appears below.

Last Name (Print)	Husband (First Name)	Wife (First Name)

Address _____

Bank _____   Savings Account No. _____

Address _____   Checking Account No. _____

_____   Loans _____

Tenant-Customer Signatures (His & Hers)

LANDLORD/LANDLADY: Print your name and address in the blanks provided, sign your name as acceptance of the above statement to bank, and give this form to the tenant who has applied to rent from you.

Name _____

Address _____

_____   _____
                                              Signature

Pet Agreement

Dated_____

(Addendum to Rental Agreement)

This agreement is attached to and forms a part of the Rental Agreement

dated_____between_____, Owners,

and_____, Tenants.

Tenants desire to keep a pet named_____and described

as_____in the dwelling they occupy under the

rental agreement referred to above, and because this agreement specifically

prohibits keeping pets without the Owners' permission, Tenants agree to the

following terms and conditions in exchange for this permission:

1) Tenants agree to keep their pet under control at all times.

2) Tenants agree to keep their pet restrained, but not tethered, when
   it is outside their dwelling.

3) Tenants agree not to leave their pet unattended for any unreasonable
   periods.

4) Tenants agree to dispose of their pet's droppings properly and quickly.

5) Tenants agree not to leave food or water for their pet or any other
   animal outside their dwelling.

6) Tenants agree to keep pet from causing any annoyance or discomfort to
   others and will remedy immediately any complaints made through the
   Owner or Manager.

7) Tenants agree to get rid of their pet's offspring within eight weeks
   of birth.

8) Tenants agree to pay immediately for any damage, loss, or expense
   caused by their pet, and in addition, they will add $_____ to
   their security/cleaning deposit, any of which may be used for cleaning,
   repairs, or delinquent rent when Tenants vacate. This added deposit
   or what remains of it when pet damages have been assessed, will be
   returned to Tenants within _____ days after they prove that they
   no longer keep this pet.

9) Tenants agree that Owners reserve the right to revoke permission to
   keep the pet should Tenants break this agreement.

Owner_____   Tenant_____

By_____   Tenant_____

Page_____ of _____

Waterbed Agreement

Dated_____

(Addendum to Rental Agreement)

This agreement is attached to and forms a part of the Rental Agreement dated

_____ between _____, Owners,

and_____, Tenants.

Tenants desire to keep a waterbed described as_____

_____

in the dwelling they occupy under the Rental Agreement referred to above, and because this agreement specifically prohibits keeping waterbeds without the Owners' permission, Tenants agree to the following terms and conditions in exchange for this permission:

1) Tenants agree to keep one waterbed approved by Owners for this dwelling. Waterbed shall consist of a mattress at least 20 mil thick with lap seams, a safety liner at least 8 mil, and a frame enclosure which meets the Waterbed Manufacturers' Association standards.

2) Tenants agree to consult with the Owners about the location of the waterbed. They agree to hire qualified professionals to install and dismantle the bed according to the manufacturer's specifications and further agree not to relocate it without the Owners' consent.

3) Tenants agree to allow Owners to inspect the waterbed installation at any and all reasonable times and Tenants agree to remedy any problems or potential problems immediately.

4) Tenants agree to furnish Owners with a copy of a valid liability insurance policy for at least $100,000 covering this waterbed installation and agree to renew the policy as necessary for continuous coverage.

5) Tenants agree to pay immediately for any damage caused by their waterbed, and in addition, they will add $_____ to their security/cleaning deposit, any of which may be used for cleaning, repairs, or delinquent rent when Tenants vacate. This added deposit or what remains of it when waterbed damages have been assessed, will be returned to Tenants within _____ days after they prove that they no longer keep this waterbed.

6) In consideration of the additional time, effort, costs, and risks involved in this waterbed installation, Tenants agree to pay additional rent of $_____, which /includes/does not include/ the premium for the waterbed liability insurance policy referred to in item 4.

7) Tenants agree that the Owners reserve the right to revoke this permission to keep a waterbed should the Tenants break this agreement.

Owner_____   Tenant_____

By_____   Tenant_____

Page_____ of _____

Dear

    You probably know already that the building where you live
has changed hands. Because tenants usually feel some apprehension
every time such a changeover occurs, we would like to take this
opportunity to clear the air by letting you know just what you can
expect in the future about a few things.

    DEPOSITS...One special concern you must have is your deposits.
We are concerned, too, and we want to make absolutely certain that
all of your deposits are credited to you. To avoid any misunderstandings about your deposits and other matters related to your
living here, we would like you to answer the questions on the sheet
attached. They are questions which you should be able to answer
quickly from memory or by referring to information readily available to you. Please do so as soon as possible and return your
answers to us in the envelope provided.

    PAYMENT BY CHECK OR MONEY ORDER...Since it is unwise for any-
one to keep or carry cash around in quantities, we request that
you pay your rent by check or money order (made payable to us exactly as underlined below). You will be protected and so will we.

    PROMPT PAYMENT...You are expected to pay your rent within
three days after the due date. For example, rent due on the first
must be paid by the fourth at the very latest. If you anticipate
being late beyond that for any reason whatsoever, please let us
know beforehand. If you don't, we will assume that you are deliberately avoiding payment, and we will immediately serve you with
the notice which starts eviction proceedings.

    MAINTENANCE...We expect you to pay your rent promptly, and
you can expect us to respond promptly to maintenance problems.
Sometime within the next week, we will visit you to inspect for
any building maintenance work that should be taken care of. You
can help by starting now to make a list of such work which you
notice around the house.

    RENTAL AGREEMENT...We will also stop by soon to explain to
you the standard rental agreement we use, and we will leave you
with a copy of your own.

    We are reasonable people and we will try anything within
reason to make living here enjoyable for you, but naturally we
need your cooperation. If we have it, we will get along well together and we can all take pride in this place that you call home.

                    Sincerely,

Tenant Information:

Your Name_____

Your Address_____

Your Home Phone Number_____Your Work Phone_____

Who lives with you? (Include ages of the children, please)_____

_____

What pet(s) do you have?_____ _____

Do you have a waterbed?_____

What car(s) do you have? Make(s)_____License(s)_____

Where do you work? Company name_____

Where does your co-tenant work? Company name_____

When did you move in?_____

What is your current rent per month? $_____

What date is your rent paid up to right now?_____

When is your rent due each month?_____

What refundable deposits have you paid? Keys $_____Security $_____

    Cleaning $_____ Other $_____

When you moved in, you paid your first month's rent. Did you also then pay

    your last month's rent?_____If so, how much was it? $_____

Which of the following furnishings belong to the owners of the building?
    (Please give room locations if appropriate)

    Carpets_____Drapes_____

    Shades_____Blinds_____

    Stove_____Refrigerator_____

    Other appliances? (Please list)_____

    Other furniture? (Please list)_____

Do you have a rental agreement or lease in writing?_____

    If so, what is the date of the latest one?_____

In case of an emergency, what friend or relative of yours should we contact?

    Name_____Telephone Number_____

Date_____Your Signature_____

For Your Information:

Important Numbers:

Police_____   Telephone Co._____

Fire_____   Gas Co._____

Ambulance_____   Electric Co._____

Doctor_____   Water Co._____

Manager_____

Helpful Hints:

1) A fire extinguisher is located_____.
Use short bursts aimed at the base of the fire. On grease fires, never use water; either use the extinguisher provided or throw baking soda on the fire.

2) The electrical shutoff for your dwelling is located_____.
Check there to see whether a fuse has blown (have an extra on hand) or a circuit breaker has tripped. Restore service by replacing any fuse which appears to be blown (use one with the same number on it) or by flipping the circuit breaker switch back and forth.

3) The gas shutoff for your dwelling is located_____,
but there may be an individual valve on the line supplying each appliance as well. Shut off the gas by turning the valve 90°, so it crosses (is perpendicular to) the direction of the supply line.

4) The water shutoff for your dwelling is located_____,
but you may be able to shut off the water to an individual faucet by turning off the supply valve below your sink or toilet (not your tub or shower). If hot water is leaking anywhere, shut off the valve on top of the hot water heater.

5) Whenever you defrost the refrigerator, turn it off or set the control knob to defrost. Place a pan to catch the water and empty it when necessary. Do not force the ice with any instrument; let it melt on its own or hurry it up by placing a pot of hot water in the freezing compartment. Dry the floor throughly when you have finished.

6) Whenever you use the garbage disposer, feed garbage in gradually along with lots of cold water, and let the water run for half a minute after you turn off the switch. Use the disposer only for those things which are edible; put everything else in the trash. Keep metal objects out of the sink while using the disposer and turn off the switch immediately if you hear any loud metallic noises. Do not put your hand into the disposer (use tongs to retrieve objects) and do not use any chemical drain openers.

7) Whenever water rises in the toilet bowl, do not try flushing again. The bowl can hold just one tank of water. More water from the tank will only cause the bowl to flow over. Use a plunger first, and then try flushing again.

8) Whenever you have showered or bathed, please take a moment to mop up the excess water on the bathroom floor. A dry floor is a safe floor.

9) Whenever you want to hang anything from or stick anything to, the walls or ceilings in your dwelling, please ask the manager to explain how to do it acceptably.

10) Whenever you want to remove the screens from your windows, please ask the manager how to do it properly. Some screens have to be removed from the inside and some from the outside. The manager will show you how.

Dear

Moving time is always a busy time, and you will have lots of things on your mind now that you have given notice you are moving. One of those things undoubtedly is how to get your deposits back promptly. In your case, they amount to $_____.

Contrary to what some tenants believe, we WANT to return your deposits, and we WILL return them to you so long as you leave your place "reasonably clean and undamaged." That's what your rental agreement says and that's what we will do. You're probably wondering, however, what "reasonably clean and undamaged" means, so we'd like to tell you how we interpret it and tell you also what you should do to get your deposits back.

"Reasonably clean" to us means as clean as you would leave your dwelling if you knew your best friend or favorite aunt were going to move in after you. To get it that clean, we expect you to clean the appliances, stove hood, and cabinets (under sinks, too) both inside and out; remove all non-adhesive shelf paper; use an appropriate cleanser on the showers, tubs, toilets, sinks, mirrors, and medicine cabinets (inside as well); dust the ceilings (for cobwebs), baseboards, window sills, and closet shelving; wash the kitchen and bathroom walls, and spot-clean the walls in other rooms; wash the light fixtures and windows inside and out; vacuum the floors; scrub the floor tile or linoleum; sweep the entry, patio, storage enclosure, and garage; remove all personal belongings (including clothes hangers and cleaning supplies); and dispose of all trash. PLEASE DO NOT CLEAN THE DRAPERIES, SHAMPOO THE CARPETS, OR WAX THE FLOORS. We prefer to do those cleaning chores ourselves, and you will not be charged for our doing them.

"Reasonably undamaged" to us means that items which we have supplied should not be missing (including light bulbs) or broken; that there should be no new burns, cracks, chips, or holes in the dwelling or its furnishings; and that the paint on the walls should be sufficient to last at least two years from the time they were last painted. PLEASE DO NOT REMOVE ANYTHING YOU HAVE ATTACHED TO THE WALLS OR CEILINGS WITHOUT FIRST TALKING TO US, and please try to avoid nicking the paint in the halls and doorways as you move things out.

After you have returned the keys, we would like to inspect your dwelling with you to check it for cleanliness and damage, and unless we have to get prices on special work or replacements, we will refund all deposits owed to you at that time.

We expect you to have moved out completely by _____. Because we are making arrangements for new tenants to move in soon after that, we would appreciate hearing from you immediately if your moving plans should change.

We hope your moving goes smoothly, and we wish you happiness in your new home.

                              Sincerely,

Dear

    As we do every year, we have been reviewing our in-
surance policies, and we thought that you might like to
know how you are affected by the insurance we carry.

    Basically, our policies cover only the building it-
self where you live. They do not cover any of your own
belongings against damage or disappearance, nor do they
cover you for negligence should you, for example, leave a
burner going under a pan of grease and start a fire which
damages the kitchen.

    To protect yourself against these calamities, you should
get a tenant's insurance policy. Most insurance companies
and agents will write such a policy for you, and we would
strongly urge that you inquire about getting one.

    For the peace of mind that it gives, a tenant's in-
surance policy is reasonable indeed.

        Sincerely,

Notices

NOTICE OF INTENTION TO VACATE   Date _____

TO:_____

FROM:_____

    Please be advised that on _____ we intend to
move from our residence at _____.

    We understand that our rental agreement calls for _____ days'
notice before we move and that this is _____ days' notice. We understand that we responsible for paying rent through the end of the
notice period called for in the rental agreement or until another
tenant approved by the management has moved in, whichever comes first.

    We understand that our deposits will be refunded within _____
days after we have moved out completely and returned our keys to the
management, so long as we leave our dwelling reasonably clean and undamaged.

    Reasons for leaving: _____

_____

    Forwarding address: _____

    In accordance with our rental agreement, we agree to allow the
management to show our dwelling to prospective tenants at any and all
reasonable times.

                                Tenant _____

                                Tenant _____

NOTICE TO CHANGE TERMS OF TENANCY

To _____, Tenant in Possession

_____

_____

    YOU ARE HEREBY NOTIFIED that the terms of tenancy under which you occupy the above-described premises are to be changed.

    Effective _____, 19_____, your rent will be increased by _____ per month, from _____ per month to _____ per month, payable in advance.

    Dated this _____ day of_____, 19_____.

_____
              Owner/Manager

NOTICE
to Pay Rent or Quit

TO _____, TENANT IN POSSESSION:

You are hereby notified that the rent is now due and payable on the premises now held and occupied by you, being those premises situated in the

City of _____, County of _____,

State/Province of _____, commonly known as

_____

Your account is delinquent in the amount of $_____, being the rent for the period from _____ to _____.

You are hereby required to pay said rent in full within _____ days or to remove from and deliver up possession of the above-mentioned premises, or legal proceedings will be instituted against you to recover possession of said premises, to declare the forfeiture of the Lease or Rental Agreement under which you occupy said premises and to recover rents and damages, together with court costs and attorney's fees, according to the terms of your Lease or Rental Agreement.

Dated this _____ day of _____, 19 _____.

_____
Owner/Manager

PROOF OF SERVICE

I, the undersigned, being at least 18 years of age, declare under penalty of perjury that I served the Notice to Pay Rent or Quit, of which this is a true copy, on the above-mentioned Tenant in Possession in the manner(s) indicated below:

☐ On _____, 19 _____, I handed the Notice to the tenant.
☐ I handed the Notice to a person of suitable age and discretion at the tenant's residence/business on _____, 19 _____.
☐ I posted the Notice in a conspicuous place at the tenant's residence on _____, 19 _____.
☐ I sent by certified mail a true copy of the Notice to the tenant at his place of residence on _____, 19 _____.

Executed on _____, 19 _____, at _____.

_____

NOTICE
to Perform Covenant

TO _____, TENANT IN POSSESSION:

PLEASE TAKE NOTICE that you have violated the following covenant(s) in your Lease or Rental Agreement:

_____

_____

_____

You are hereby required within _____ days to perform the aforesaid covenant(s) or to deliver up possession of the premises now held and occupied by you, being those premises situated in the
City of _____, County of _____,
State/Province of _____, commonly known as
_____.

If you fail to do so, legal proceedings will be instituted against you to recover said premises and such damages as the law allows.

This notice is intended to be a _____ day notice to perform the aforesaid covenant. It is not intended to terminate or forfeit the Lease or Rental Agreement under which you occupy said premises. If, after legal proceedings, said premises are recovered from you, the owners will try to rent said premises for the best possible rent, giving you credit for sums received and holding you liable for any deficiencies arising during the term of said Lease or Rental Agreement.

Dated this _____ day of _____, 19 _____.

_____
Owner/Manager

PROOF OF SERVICE

I, the undersigned, being at least 18 years of age, declare under penalty of perjury that I served the Notice to Perform Covenant, of which this is a true copy, on the above-mentioned Tenant in Possession in the manner(s) indicated below:

☐ On _____, 19 _____, I handed the Notice to the tenant.
☐ I handed the Notice to a person of suitable age and discretion at the tenant's residence/business on _____, 19 _____.
☐ I posted the Notice in a conspicuous place at the tenant's residence on _____, 19 _____.
☐ I sent by certified mail a true copy of the Notice to the tenant at his place of residence on _____, 19 _____.

Executed on _____, 19 _____, at _____.

_____

30-DAY NOTICE
to Terminate Tenancy

TO _____, TENANT IN POSSESSION:

PLEASE TAKE NOTICE that you are hereby required within 30 days to remove from and deliver up possession of the premises now held and occupied by you, being those premises situated in the
City of _____, County of _____,
State/Province of _____, commonly known as
_____.

This notice is intended for the purpose of terminating the Rental Agreement by which you now hold possession of the above-described premises, and should you fail to comply, legal proceedings will be instituted against you to recover possession, to declare said Rental Agreement forfeited, and to recover rents and damages for the period of the unlawful detention.

Please be advised that your rent on said premises is due and payable up to and including the date of termination of your tenancy under this notice, that being the _____ day of _____,
19 _____.

Dated this _____ day of _____, 19 _____.

_____
Owner/Manager

PROOF OF SERVICE

I, the undersigned, being at least 18 years of age, declare under penalty of perjury that I served the 30-Day Notice to Terminate Tenancy, of which this is a true copy, on the above-mentioned Tenant in Possession in the manner(s) indicated below:

☐ On _____, 19 _____, I handed the Notice to the tenant.
☐ I handed the Notice to a person of suitable age and discretion at the tenant's residence/business on _____, 19 _____.
☐ I posted the Notice in a conspicuous place at the tenant's residence on _____,
19 _____.
☐ I sent by certified mail a true copy of the Notice to the tenant at his place of residence on _____, 19 _____.

Executed on _____, 19 _____, at _____.

_____

Employees

Employment Application

Name_____ Home Phone_____ Work Phone_____

Date of Birth_____ Social Security No._____ Driver's License No._____

Own ____ How long
Rent ____ at address?_____

Present Address_____

How many years of schooling have you had?_____

Present/Last Occupation_____ Employer_____ Phone_____

Monthly Gross_____ How long with this employer?_____ Name of Supervisor_____ May we contact?____ Phone_____

Spouse's Name_____ Date of Birth_____ Social Security No._____ Driver's License No._____

How many years of schooling has your spouse had?_____

Present/Last Occupation_____ Employer_____ Phone_____

Monthly Gross_____ How long with this employer?_____ Name of Supervisor_____ May we contact?____ Phone_____

Dependents' names and ages_____

What skills do you or your spouse have related to this job?_____

What experience have you or your spouse had related to this job?_____

What physical handicaps do you or your spouse have?_____

Are you and your spouse bondable?_____ Previous bonding?_____

When are you available for this job?___ _____

Savings Account Bank Name_____ Branch_____ Account Number_____

Checking Account Bank Name_____ Branch_____ Account Number_____

Major Credit Card Name_____ Account Number_____

Credit Reference_____ Account Number_____ Balance Owed_____ Monthly Payment_____

Personal Reference_____ Address_____ Phone ( )_____

Personal Reference_____ Address_____ Phone ( )_____

Contact in Emergency_____ Address_____ Phone ( )_____

   I/we declare that the statements above are true and correct, and I/we hereby authorize verification of those statements.

Date_____ Signed_____

Management Agreement

Dated_____

Agreement between _____, Owners, and

_____, Managers, for management of property

located at _____.

Compensation for Managers shall be $_____ per month at a guaranteed minimum and shall be computed at an hourly rate of $_____. Unless Managers obtain Owners' permission in advance or, in case of emergency, unless they notify Owners within 48 hours afterwards, Managers shall spend no more than _____ hours per month on managerial responsibilities. Managers shall record working hours on time sheets provided by Owners, one time sheet for each person exercising managerial responsibilities, and shall submit those time sheets at least once a month.

Other compensation shall be as follows:_____

_____

Managers shall have days off as follows:_____;

vacation time as follows:_____;

sick leave as follows:_____.

Managers' duties and responsibilities, which will be reviewed jointly in ninety days and annually after that, shall be as follows:_____

_____

_____

_____

Managers shall receipt all monies collected on the Owners' behalf and shall deposit or transfer those monies within_____ of collection as follows:_____

_____

Managers shall spend or commit to spend no more than $_____ on the Owners' behalf without first obtaining permission.

Either Managers or Owners may cancel this agreement upon providing _____ days' written notice.

Managers hereby acknowledge that they have read this agreement, understand it, agree to it, and have been given a copy.

Owner_____   Manager_____

By_____   Manager_____

Time Sheet

_____

Employee's Name

_____

Employee's Signature

_____

Property

Pay Period_____to_____

DATE	TIMES		HOURS	DESCRIPTION OF WORK PERFORMED	CONTRACT AMOUNT

Total Hours _____

Rate _____

Hourly Gross _____

Contract _____

Total Gross _____

Total Contract _____

_____
Approved by   Date

Records

	Blank Form	Example Form
Tenant Record	239	148
Monthly Rental Income Record	240-241	149
Laundry Income	242	151
Depreciation Record	243	155
Other Receipts & Income	244-245	150
Expense and Payment Record	246-247	152-153
Expense and Payment Record — Annual Summary	248-249	157
Payroll	250	157
Summary of Business and Statement of Income	251	158
Loan & Note Record	252	159
Insurance Record	253	160

239

Tenant Record

Location _____

	Unit	Tenant	Phone	Moved In	Out	Rent Date	Deposit/Rent		Bank/Ckg. Acct. Nos.
1									
2									
3									
4									
5									
6									
7									
8									
9									
10									
11									
12									
13									
14									
15									
16									
17									
18									
19									
20									
21									
22									
23									
24									
25									
26									
27									
28									
29									
30									

MONTHLY RENTAL INCOME RECORD

Page _____

Location(s) _____

Period _____

	Unit	Jan.	Feb.	Mar.	Apr.	May	
1							1
2							2
3							3
4							4
5							5
6							6
7							7
8							8
9							9
10							10
11							11
12							12
13							13
14							14
15							15
16							16
17							17
18							18
19							19
20							20
21							21
22							22
23							23
24							24
25							25
26							26
27							27
28							28
29							29
30							30
31							31
32							32
33							33
34							34
35							35
36							36
37							37
38							38
39							39
40							40
41							41

MONTHLY RENTAL INCOME RECORD

Page _____

	Jun.	Jul.	Aug.	Sep.	Oct.	Nov.	Dec.	Year's Totals	
1									1
2									2
3									3
4									4
5									5
6									6
7									7
8									8
9									9
10									10
11									11
12									12
13									13
14									14
15									15
16									16
17									17
18									18
19									19
20									20
21									21
22									22
23									23
24									24
25									25
26									26
27									27
28									28
29									29
30									30
31									31
32									32
33									33
34									34
35									35
36									36
37									37
38									38
39									39
40									40
41									41

242

Laundry Income

location _____

period _____

Date	Washer	Dryer	Both	Cumulative Totals	Monthly Totals	
1						1
2						2
3						3
4						4
5						5
6						6
7						7
8						8
9						9
10						10
11						11
12						12
13						13
14						14
15						15
16						16
17						17
18						18
19						19
20						20
21						21
22						22
23						23
24						24
25						25
26						26
27						27
28						28
29						29
30						30
31						31
32						32
33						33
34						34
35						35
36						36
37						37
38						38
39						39
40						40
41						41

DEPRECIATION RECORD

Property or Capital Improvement Location and Description _____

_____

Date Acquired or Converted to Business _____

New or Used _____

Cost or Other Basis _____

Land Value (Not Applicable to Capital Improvements) _____

Salvage Value _____

Special 20% First Year Depreciation _____

Depreciable Basis _____

Method of Depreciation _____

Useful Life _____

Tax Year	Prior Deprec.	Deprec. Balance	% Year* Held	% Bus. Use	Deprec. This Year		Special 20%		Total First Year Deprec.
1st ____						+		=	
2nd ____									
3rd ____									
4th ____									
5th ____									
6th ____									
7th ____									
8th ____									
9th ____									
10th ____									
11th ____									
12th ____									
13th ____									
14th ____									
15th ____									
16th ____									
17th ____									
18th ____									
19th ____									
20th ____									
21st ____									
22nd ____									
23rd ____									
24th ____									
25th ____									

*Conversion: Months to % of Year

Months	%
1	8.3
2	16.7
3	25
4	33.3
5	41.7
6	50
7	58.3
8	66.7
9	75
10	83.3
11	91.7
12	100

244

OTHER RECEIPTS & INCOME

Added Appliances or Furniture,
Deposits, Interest on Deposits,
Late Charges, Laundry, Garages, etc.

Page _____

Location(s) _____

Period _____

Description of Income	Jan.	Feb.	Mar.	Apr.	May	
1						1
2						2
3						3
4						4
5						5
6						6
7						7
8						8
9						9
10						10
11						11
12						12
13						13
14						14
15						15
16						16
17						17
18						18
19						19
20						20
21						21
22						22
23						23
24						24
25						25
26						26
27						27
28						28
29						29
30						30
31						31
32						32
33						33
34						34
35						35
36						36
37						37
38						38
39						39
40						40
41 Totals						41

OTHER RECEIPTS & INCOME

Page_____

	Jun.	Jul.	Aug.	Sep.	Oct.	Nov.	Dec.	Year's Totals	
1									1
2									2
3									3
4									4
5									5
6									6
7									7
8									8
9									9
10									10
11									11
12									12
13									13
14									14
15									15
16									16
17									17
18									18
19									19
20									20
21									21
22									22
23									23
24									24
25									25
26									26
27									27
28									28
29									29
30									30
31									31
32									32
33									33
34									34
35									35
36									36
37									37
38									38
39									39
40									40
41									41

EXPENSE AND PAYMENT RECORD

Page _____

Location(s) _____

Period _____

	Date	How Paid	To Whom Paid	For	1 Total Paid Out	2 Mortgage Principal	3 Interest	4 Taxes, Licenses	
1									1
2									2
3									3
4									4
5									5
6									6
7									7
8									8
9									9
10									10
11									11
12									12
13									13
14									14
15									15
16									16
17									17
18									18
19									19
20									20
21									21
22									22
23									23
24									24
25									25
26									26
27									27
28									28
29									29
30									30
31									31
32									32
33									33
34									34
35									35
36									36
37									37
38									38
39									39
40									40
41			Totals						41

DISTRIBUTION OF EXPENSES AND PAYMENTS

Page _____

	5 Insurance	6 Utilities	7 Services, Repairs, Maint.	8 Merch., Supplies	9 Impounds	10 Payroll	11 Misc.	12 Non-deductible	
1									1
2									2
3									3
4									4
5									5
6									6
7									7
8									8
9									9
10									10
11									11
12									12
13									13
14									14
15									15
16									16
17									17
18									18
19									19
20									20
21									21
22									22
23									23
24									24
25									25
26									26
27									27
28									28
29									29
30									30
31									31
32									32
33									33
34									34
35									35
36									36
37									37
38									38
39									39
40									40
41									41

EXPENSE AND PAYMENT RECORD

Annual Summary

Location(s) _____

Year _____

	Units	1 Total Paid Out(2-12)	2 Mortgage Principal	3 Interest	4 Taxes, Licenses	5 Insurance	
1							1
2							2
3							3
4							4
5							5
6							6
7							7
8							8
9							9
10							10
11							11
12							12
13							13
14							14
15							15
16							16
17							17
18							18
19							19
20							20
21							21
22							22
23							23
24							24
25							25
26							26
27							27
28							28
29							29
30							30
31							31
32							32
33							33
34							34
35							35
36							36
37							37
38							38
39							39
40							40
41	Totals						41

DISTRIBUTION OF EXPENSES AND PAYMENTS
Annual Summary

	6 Utilities	7 Services, Repairs, Maint.	8 Merch., Supplies	9 Impounds	10 Payroll	11 Misc.	12 Non-deductible	13 Depreciation	
1									1
2									2
3									3
4									4
5									5
6									6
7									7
8									8
9									9
10									10
11									11
12									12
13									13
14									14
15									15
16									16
17									17
18									18
19									19
20									20
21									21
22									22
23									23
24									24
25									25
26									26
27									27
28									28
29									29
30									30
31									31
32									32
33									33
34									34
35									35
36									36
37									37
38									38
39									39
40									40
41									41

PAYROLL RECORD

Property _____

Employee _____

Social Security No. _____

Pay Rate _____

Exemptions _____

☐ Married
☐ Single

	Period	Gross	Federal Withholding Tax	State Disability	Employee FICA	Employer FICA	State Withhding Tax	Other	Net	Ck No.	
1											1
2											2
3											3
4											4
5											5
6											6
7											7
8											8
9											9
10											10
11											11
12											12
13											13
14											14
15											15
16											16
17											17
18											18
19											19
20											20
21	Qtr. Totals										21
22											22
23											23
24											24
25											25
26											26
27											27
28											28
29											29
30											30
31											31
32											32
33											33
34											34
35											35
36											36
37											37
38											38
39											39
40											40
41	Qtr. Totals										41

Summary of Business and Statement of Income

Location(s) _____

Year / Month _____

Totals

1				1
2				2
3	INCOME:			3
4	Rental			4
5	Other			5
6	TOTAL INCOME			6
7				7
8				8
9				9
10				10
11	EXPENSES:			11
12	Mortgage Principal			12
13	Interest			13
14	Taxes, Licenses			14
15	Insurance			15
16	Utilities			16
17	Services, Repairs, Maintenance			17
18	Merchandise, Supplies			18
19	Impounds			19
20	Payroll			20
21	Miscellaneous Expenses			21
22	Non-deductible			22
23				23
24				24
25				25
26	TOTAL EXPENSES (GROSS)			26
27	less mortgage principal and Non-deductible			27
28	TOTAL			28
29	less impounds			29
30	TOTAL EXPENSES (NET)			30
31	plus depreciation			31
32	TOTAL EXPENSES (for tax purposes)			32
33				33
34	TOTAL INCOME			34
35	LESS TOTAL EXPENSES (item 32) (for tax purposes)			35
36	NET PROFIT OR (LOSS)			36
37				37
38				38
39				39
40				40
41				41

LOAN & NOTE RECORD

Page _____

Property _____

Noteholder & Address _____

Loan Number_____ Original Loan_____

Interest _____ Payment _____ Due Date _____

	Payment Date Paid / If Changed	Principal	Interest	Impounds & (Imp. Disb.)	Impound Balance	Principal Balance	
1							1
2							2
3							3
4							4
5							5
6							6
7							7
8							8
9							9
10							10
11							11
12							12
13							13
14							14
15							15
16							16
17							17
18							18
19							19
20							20
21							21
22							22
23							23
24							24
25							25
26							26
27							27
28							28
29							29
30							30
31							31
32							32
33							33
34							34
35							35
36							36
37							37
38							38
39							39
40							40
41							41

Insurance Record

Property_____

Company / Agent	Type of Policy	Policy Number	Limits	Premium	Expiration Date

Taxes

FORM E-3	RENTAL INCOME AND EXPENSE		YEAR 19

NAME(S) OF TAXPAYERS		SOC. SEC. NUMBER		

PROPERTY LOCATION & DESCRIPTION

GROSS INCOME

PROPERTY A _____

PROPERTY B _____

PROPERTY C _____

PROPERTY D _____

PROPERTY E _____

PROPERTY F _____

PROPERTY G _____

Total Income (to Schedule E, Part II, Column B)

EXPENSES

	A	B	C	D	E	F	G	TOTALS
Interest								
Taxes, Licenses								
Insurance								
Utilities								
Service, Repairs, Maintenance								
Merchandise, Supplies								
Payroll								
Miscellaneous Expenses								
Other:								
Subtotal								
% Bus. Use								
Subtotals (to Schedule E, Part II, Column E)								
Depreciation (Form D-1)								*
Supp. Depreciation (Form SD)								*
Totals								

*Sum of depreciation and supplemental depreciation totals (to Schedule E, Part II, Column D)

| FORM D-1 | DEPRECIATION WORKSHEET | YEAR 19 |

NAME(S) OF TAXPAYERS

SOC. SEC. NUMBER

PROPERTY LOCATION & DESCRIPTION

PROPERTY A _____

PROPERTY B _____

PROPERTY C _____

PROPERTY D _____

PROPERTY E _____

PROPERTY F _____

PROPERTY G _____

	A	B	C	D	E	F	G	TOTALS
Date Acq'd or Conv. to Bus.								
New or Used								
Cost or Other Basis								
Land Value								
Salvage Value								
20% 1st Year Deprec.								
Deprec. Basis								
Prior Deprec.								
Deprec. Balance								
Method of Deprec.								
Useful Life								
Full Year Deprec.								
% Year Held								
% Bus. Use								
Deprec. This Year								

PAGE TOTAL

FORM SD	SUPPLEMENTAL DEPRECIATION	YEAR 19

NAME(S) OF TAXPAYERS	SOC. SEC. NUMBER			

CAPITAL IMPROVEMENT LOCATION & DESCRIPTION

1 _____

2 _____

3 _____

4 _____

5 _____

6 _____

7 _____

	1	2	3	4	5	6	7	TOTALS
Date Acq'd or Conv. to Bus.								
New or Used								
Cost or Other Basis								
Salvage Value								
20% 1st Year Deprec.								
Deprec. Basis								
Prior Deprec.								
Deprec. Balance								
Method of Deprec.								
Useful Life								
Full Year Deprec.								
% Year Held								
% Bus. Use								
Deprec. This Year								

PAGE TOTAL

REFERENCES

MANAGEMENT

Kelley, Edward. *Practical Apartment Management.* 430 North Michigan Avenue, Chicago, IL 60611: Institute of Real Estate Management, 1976.

This is a somewhat pedantic, but thorough, treatment of the subject, written primarily for managers of large apartment complexes.

MAINTENANCE

Ebeling, Walter. *Urban Entomology.* 1422 Harbour Way South, Richmond, CA 94804: University of California, Division of Agricultural Sciences, Publications Office, 1975.

More than a big book about city bugs, it's over six hundred pages of detailed, factual information about all kinds of cosmopolitan pests, from cockroaches to snakes. It explains where they come from, how they live, and how they die. It may save you from having to hire a professional exterminator.

How Things Work in Your Home (and What to Do When They Don't). Alexandria, VA: Time-Life Books, 1975.

In clear illustrations and tight prose, this book outlines how plumbing, electrical, heating, and cooling systems work. It explains how the various components of these systems operate, and it details ways to troubleshoot malfunctioning heaters, appliances, septic tanks, faucets and the like.

Reader's Digest Complete Do-It-Yourself Manual. Pleasantville, NY: The Reader's Digest Association, 1973.

It's a valuable book full of good illustrations and photographs. If you have a job to do, like pouring a cement walkway or repairing a decayed threshold, you can look it up in the index and then turn to practical hints for doing the job right.

Whole House Catalog. New York: Simon and Schuster, 1976.

This book resembles the famous *Whole Earth Catalog* both in size and format. Besides giving tips on do-it-yourself projects around the house, it also lists, by brand name, various materials and tools which might prove useful to complete a project.

LAWS & EVICTIONS*

Faber, Stuart. *How to Outsmart Your Landlord (If You're a Tenant) or How to Outsmart Your Tenant (If You're a Landlord).* 658 S. Bonnie Brae St., Los Angeles, CA 90057: Good Life Press, 1978.

Written from a reasonable perspective by someone who is a landlord, a tenant, and a lawyer, this is an understandable outline of landlord-tenant law.

Goddard, John. *California Landlord-Tenant Law and Procedure.* 316 W. Second St., Los Angeles, CA 90012: Legal Book Corp., 1977.

This is a law book like those ponderous tomes which sit impressively on lawyer's bookshelves. It's very dry, but very important stuff, a source of much good landlording information.

Moskovitz, Myron; Ralph Warner; and Charles Sherman. *California Tenants' Handbook.* Berkeley, CA: Nolo Press, 1979.

Some landlords and landladies might think it's the enemy's battle plan and might even regard it offensive. Some of it is. But it's primarily defensive, and it gives you a chance to consider the tenant's point of view for a change.

Robinson, Leigh. *The Eviction Book for California.* Box 1373, Richmond, CA 94802: ExPress, 1980.

It details each step of the entire legal eviction process in California and includes the forms necessary to do an eviction yourself. When you've exhausted every possible method for getting problem tenants to move without resorting to the courts, find a copy of this book and get them out by going to court.

INVESTMENTS

Greene, Bill. *Two Years for Freedom.* Box 408, Mill Valley, CA 94941: BGTC, 1978.

This earthy, uneven book will make a tycoon out of you yet, if only you will compromise, sacrifice, and adopt a few of its ideas on life-style and investing — live on no more than five percent of your gross income, avoid paying income tax, establish credibility with your banker, familiarize yourself with an area before buying properties there, etc.

Haroldsen, Mark. *How to Wake Up the Financial Genius Inside You.* 2612 South 1030 West, Salt Lake City, UT 84119: National Institute of Financial Planning, 1976

This beginner's book has inspired many a tyro to begin investing in rental property. If you

*These four books are intended for use in California.

already have a grasp of the principles of real estate investment, it may be too elementary for you, but you might want to buy a copy to give to a friend and sneak a peak at it before you give it away.

Lowry, Albert. *How You Can Become Financially Independent by Investing in Real Estate.* New York: Simon and Schuster, 1977.

This is pretty much an amplification and updating of *How I Turned $1,000 into Three Million in Real Estate in My Spare Time.* Read the Nickerson book first and decide whether you need more of the same applied to the real estate market of the late 70's.

Nickerson, William. *How I Turned $1,000 into Three Million in Real Estate in My Spare Time.* New York: Simon and Schuster, 1969.

Classic enough so that most buyers of income property know what a "Nickerson" is, it's loaded with sage advice and good information about purchasing and managing rental properties.

Realty Bluebook. Box 4187, San Rafael, CA 94903: Professional Publishing Corporation, 1979.

It's written for real estate professionals and there's some stuff you wouldn't be interested in, but it has some most useful loan tables and tax information, as well as helpful explanations of real estate contract clauses. A newly revised edition comes available every November.

Tappan, William. *Real Estate Exchange and Acquisition Techniques.* Englewood Cliffs, New Jersey: Prentice-Hall, 1978.

If you are to preserve your capital in real estate transactions, you must understand how exchanges work. This book not only explains the mechanics of exchanging, but it also provides information about the benefits of exchanging (tax benefits aren't the only possible benefits), the special techniques which help to consummate exchanges, and the legal basis for exchanging.

TAXES

Greer, Gaylon. *The Real Estate Investor and the Federal Income Tax.* New York: John Wiley & Sons, 1978.

A nontechnical treatment of income taxes as they affect real estate investors, this book includes numerous examples which help to clarify complicated tax concepts. It covers the many tax implications in acquiring, owning, and disposing of property, and it also discusses the tax traps which await the greedy and unwary.

Lasser Tax Institute. *Your Income Tax.* New York: Simon and Schuster, 1979.

The newsprint and small type used in this book make it look distinctly like a dull IRS publication, but, then, maybe federal tax rules are always dull no matter who publishes the information. It has concise explanations of tax laws and practices which you should be familiar with, even if someone else does prepare your taxes. It also has a good index and good cross references.

PERIODICALS

Creative Real Estate. Professional Publishers, Box 2446, Leucadia, CA 92024. (714) 438-2446. 12 issues a year, advertising, $27*.

Aimed primarily at real estate professionals and published by the group which presents the "largest real estate trading floor in the world" every year, this magazine generally contains twenty short articles on subjects such as financing, time management, taxes, and exchanging. Subscribe only if you're serious about your real estate investments and if you want to become even more actively involved.

Impact Reports. Impact Publishing Company, 1601 Oak Park Blvd. Pleasant Hill, CA 94523, (415) 689-5090. 10 issues a year, no advertising, $59*.

Each report (6,000–10,000) words is devoted to a single subject of interest to the small real estate investor. Subjects covered have ranged from options to foreclosures and exchanges. There is a full money-back guarantee for those who are dissatisfied after two issues. (I confess to having contributed two *Impact Reports* myself, as well as an "Update" article — an eight-page supplement included with each *Report* — on avoiding the high cost of termite repairs.)

Journal of Property Management. Institute of Real Estate Management, 430 N. Michigan Ave., Chicago, IL 60611, (312) 440-8615. 6 issues a year, advertising, $15.

This bimonthly journal is written by and for the managers of large apartment complexes. It's somewhat high falutin and includes certain articles, such as those about elevators and computer bookkeeping, which are of no practical value to the do-it-yourself landlord or landlady, but every so often it does have articles which are of practical value, such as those on painting and energy conservation. If you are thinking about acquiring large properties or if you want to learn about some of the concerns of professional property managers, you might want to read it.

Property Management Journal. Mid-Valley Publishing Co., 10933 Valley Blvd., El Monte, CA 91731, (213) 443-1753. 12 issues a year, advertising, $7.

Although it has the format of a tabloid and includes advertising directed primarily at landlords and landladies in the Los Angeles area, this publication prints news and a smattering of practical information relevant to property management around the country.

Real Estate Investing Letter. United Media International, Box 957, Farmingdale, NY 11737. (212) 888-3598. 12 issues a year, no advertising, $39*.

This ten-page publication is subtitled "A Guide to Prudent Investing," and it is just that, investment- rather than speculation-oriented. The articles run the gamut from investing in land to evaluating older houses and using a mortgage broker. There's a full refund available after three issues.

*Ask whether there's a promotion bonus available for new subscribers.

WORDS IN EDGEWISE

Yours is a thankless job, dear landlord and landlady. Just remember that landlording is a business. People are not going to commend you for your efforts, but neither are they going to stop depending on you. People who are too timid, too insolvent, too young, too feeble, too smart, too stupid, or otherwise too indisposed to own their own housing are all depending on you to provide them with housing. Do just that, and do it as best you can.

There will be times when you will feel distraught over your landlording troubles and trials, times when you will have tried your best and yet you find yourself on the short end. Don't show your anger. Keep a punching bag at home for that. But if you cannot get along with a tenant or a tenant with you, get the tenant out. You know how to do it. Run your business yourself. Don't let your tenants run it for you.

INDEX

ORDER FORMS

EXPRESS, P.O. BOX 1373, RICHMOND, CA 94802

Dear EXPRESS:

I'm not a landlord or landlady yet, but I'd like to be one someday, and I think I'd like to be one who's scrupulous. Show me how.

Please send me ____ copies of LANDLORDING @ $15 $ _____

Please send me ____ copies of THE EVICTION BOOK FOR CALIFORNIA @$10 $ _____

California residents add 6% sales tax (6½% in transit counties) $ _____

Shipping and handling $ __1.00__

Make check or money order payable to EXPRESS. TOTAL DUE $ _____

SEND TO _____

_____

_____ ZIP _____

EXPRESS, P.O. BOX 1373, RICHMOND, CA 94802

Dear EXPRESS:

I'm an unscrupulous landlord or landlady who's merciless, lowdown, and greedy, and I'll pay double the usual price for your books just to lay my hands on all that great information. It may even reform me, who knows?

Please send me ____ copies of LANDLORDING @ $30 $ _____

Please send me ____ copies of THE EVICTION BOOK FOR CALIFORNIA @$20 $ _____

California residents add 6% sales tax (6½% in transit counties) $ _____

Shipping and handling $ __1.00__

Make check or money order payable to EXPRESS. TOTAL DUE $ _____

SEND TO _____

_____

_____ ZIP _____

EXPRESS, P.O. BOX 1373, RICHMOND, CA 94802

Dear EXPRESS:

I'm a scrupulous landlord or landlady and I'd like copies of your books for my very own. Hurry up with my order. I need all the help I can get right now.

Please send me ____ copies of LANDLORDING @ $15 $ _____

Please send me ____ copies of THE EVICTION BOOK FOR CALIFORNIA @$10 $ _____

California residents add 6% sales tax (6½% in transit counties) $ _____

Shipping and handling $ __1.00__

Make check or money order payable to EXPRESS. TOTAL DUE $ _____

SEND TO _____

_____

_____ ZIP _____